Maurice
and Thérèse

MAURICE AND THÉRÈSE

The Story of a Love

~

Patrick Ahern

Doubleday

New York London Toronto Sydney Auckland

PUBLISHED BY DOUBLEDAY
a division of Bantam Doubleday Dell Publishing Group, Inc.
1540 Broadway, New York, New York 10036

DOUBLEDAY and the portrayal of an anchor with a dolphin are
trademarks of Doubleday, a division of Bantam Doubleday Dell
Publishing Group, Inc.

Book design by Susan Maksuta

Library of Congress Cataloging-in-Publication Data

Ahern, Patrick V.
Maurice and Thérèse : the story of a love / Patrick Ahern.
— 1st ed.
p.   cm.
Includes biographical references.
1. Thérèse, de Lisieux, Saint, 1873–1897—Correspondence.
2. Bellière, Maurice, b. 1874—Correspondence.   3. Christian
saints—France—Lisieux—Correspondence.   4. Seminarians—
France—Correspondence.   I. Bellière, Maurice, b. 1874.
II. Thérèse, de Lisieux, Saint, 1873–1897.   III. Title.
BX4700.T5A4   1998
282′.092′2—dc21
[B]   98-13268
CIP

ISBN 0-385-49261-8

October 1998

First Edition

7 9 10 8

In Memory of
Sister Mary Purissima Reilly, O.P.
Who Through More Than Forty Years
of Friendship
Shared with Me
Her Lifelong Love of St. Thérèse

Contents

*Follows order in which letters were received.

III. Africa

The Correspondence of Maurice Bellière to Mother Gonzague and Father André Adam

IV. The Passion and Death of Maurice Bellière

V. Epilogue

Saint Thérèse of Lisieux

Not as a prima donna in a pose
Before the swaying curtain when the play
Is clamorously ended, her bouquet
Loosed on the throng,—not even as a rose
Can I conceive of you. Let others, those
Whose lyric season is incessant May,
Cull similes to strew your "little way"
With hothouse verse and honeysuckle prose.

You are too real, too actual, Thérèse,
To live in metaphor. The girl behind
The legend, could the legend fade, would be
The girl you were, sobbing upon your knees
In lowliness and love and anguish, blind
With the beauty of a stark Gethsemane.

A Sonnet by Alfred Barrett, s.j.

Preface

My interest in St. Thérèse of Lisieux goes back to 1939 when I first read her autobiography and knew she was the saint for me. I was twenty at the time and she spoke to my deepest needs. She convinced me that someone as ordinary as I could aspire to the love of God which filled her heart to overflowing—in my own more modest measure, of course. The book has remained the companion of a lifetime and has never lost its power to sustain me.

When the complete correspondence between her and Maurice Bellière appeared a quarter of a century ago, I read it with deep interest and went back to it many times, convinced it held a story that was crying to be told. If I was the one to tell it, however, I needed to know more about Maurice, who came to public attention only with the publication of the correspondence. For seventy years following his death he remained, for the most part, a forgotten man. I had no idea who he was before his remarkable encounter with Thérèse, nor what became of him after she died.

Good fortune put me in touch with Soeur Cécile de l'Immaculée, a highly respected scholar from Thérèse's Carmel in Lisieux and a member of the team responsible for the critical edition of her writings. After *The*

General Correspondence of St. Thérèse was published in 1973, she and Père Jean Creff, a member of the White Fathers of Africa, the order to which Bellière belonged, set out to discover whatever could be learned about him. Their research resulted in four excellent articles in *Vie Thérèsienne,* written by Soeur Cécile. When I wrote to her she sent me the articles and generously shared with me the full file of their research. Without the help and encouragement of Soeur Cécile and Père Jean, this book could not have been written, and I am grateful beyond words to both of them.

The list of authors to whom my thanks are due is longer than a reader's patience might endure. There is little about St. Thérèse in these pages that has not been borrowed from others.

The English quotations from Thérèse's writings are generally in Father John Clarke's translation, but occasionally in that of Father Ronald Knox. For the most part the translation of the letters of Thérèse and Maurice is my own. I fell in love with them and felt a need to translate them myself.

Just a word about the title. Thérèse's autobiography is called *Story of a Soul.* The splendid biography by Bishop Guy Gaucher is called *The Story of a Life.*[1] I

---

[1] Guy Gaucher, *The Story of a Life,* (San Francisco: Harper San Francisco, 1993).

have chosen to name this book *Maurice and Thérèse: The Story of a Love*. Obviously it was not a romantic love, but a love between a man and a woman whose lives were given totally, in vowed celibacy, to God and to others. Such a love can be—and often in the history of the Church has been—a very beautiful human love. Sometimes the partners have both been saints. In this case one was "the greatest saint of modern times." The other was not a very great saint at all.

Introduction

When St. Thérèse lay dying in the Carmel of Lisieux, she overheard a conversation which amused her. The infirmary window was open and two nuns outside were discussing the obituary which by custom was sent to other Carmels when one of the sisters died. They were wondering what could be written in hers that might be of interest, since she had never done anything exceptional. Thérèse was amused and smiled with pleasure, for she had succeeded in keeping the low profile for which she always aimed.

Her life indeed seemed uneventful. She had never traveled beyond Alençon, where she was born in 1873, or Lisieux, where she grew up, save for one brief journey to Rome when she was fourteen. At the age of fifteen she entered the Carmelite cloister, a short walk across town from her home, and there she died nine years later. Nobody knew her but her family, a few friends and schoolmates, and two dozen nuns who shared her life in the convent.

Today she is known all over the world. She is the only western saint besides St. Francis of Assisi who was popularly revered in Russia during the heyday of communism. Not even the iron curtain could shut her out of a country avowedly atheistic. People of all races and cultures, of every religion and of none, those with little education and scholars of renown, have been fascinated by her. She has been the subject of nine hundred biographies, almost one a month on average, in the hundred years since her death.

People as diverse as the American social activist Dorothy Day and the French novelist Georges Bernanos have loved her. Day was converted from atheism to Catholicism through reading her autobiography, and in 1968 she wrote a biography called *Thérèse* which has gone through several printings. A significant portion of the dialogue in Bernanos's *The Diary of a Country Priest* is taken almost verbatim from *Her Last Conversations*. In Graham Greene's novel *Monsignor Quixote* she is the secret *dulcinea* of the hero. The influential Jewish philosopher Henri Bergson spent years admiring the works of the great St. Teresa of Ávila, but when he read the .works of Thérèse he thought she was the greater mystic. The renowned priest-scientist Teilhard de Chardin, whose lyrical vision of the world has captivated so many, testified to her profound influence on his spiritual life. Hans Urs von Balthasar, often called a Renaissance man for the breadth of his learning, compared her mission to that of St. Paul. Jean Guitton, a member of the French Academy and a leading intellectual in France, counts her as one of the handful of spiritual geniuses since the time of Christ, ranking her with St. Paul, St. Augustine, St. Francis of Assisi, St. Joan of Arc, and St. Teresa of Ávila. When Thomas Merton first encountered Thérèse, he thought she was of minor importance. Later, when he studied her mysticism in depth, he was appalled by his misjudgment. "I owe her a profound public apology," he wrote.

Mother Teresa of Calcutta, so widely acclaimed for her love of the poor, was fond of pointing out that she took her name not from the great St. Teresa of Ávila but from the Little Thérèse of Lisieux, for whom she had unbounded admiration.

Thérèse attracts unlikely people. Jack Kerouac, the "King of the Beats," was intrigued by the heroism of her holiness and the power of her prayers. Edith Piaf, who charmed the clubs of Paris with her songs, always kept Thérèse's picture on her night table. Jacques Fesch, guillotined in 1957 for killing a Paris policeman in a bank holdup, was dramatically converted during three years of solitary confinement through reading her autobiography. The depth of holiness revealed in Fesch's diaries has prompted Cardinal Jean-Marie Lustiger of Paris to propose his canonization.

Thérèse's stature keeps growing a full century after her death. Note is now taken of her remarkable influence on the Second Vatican Council. She is the most quoted woman saint in the best-selling new *Catechism of the Catholic Church*. In 1997, Pope John Paul II declared her a Doctor of the Church, making her the third woman in history to receive this prestigious title, alongside St. Teresa of Ávila and St. Catherine of Siena. More than fifty National Conferences of Bishops throughout the world, the United States Conference among them, had requested that he do so.

It is her autobiography, *Story of a Soul,* which explains the extraordinary place she occupies in today's religious world. Had she not written it, she would have passed into the obscurity she sought when she entered the cloister, as unknown to the world as are the thousands of her sisters in contemplative religious orders. She did not write it on her own initiative, but under obedience to her superior, who directed her to recount what God had accomplished in her soul. She wrote with scarcely a note to assist her memory and with only the brief snatches of time which her busy days afforded. At the end of a year she handed back her copybooks. She altered nothing as she wrote, setting down her experience in a steady stream of recollection, yet her autobiography ranks as one of the great classics of religious literature.

The book was published on September 30, 1898, exactly one year after her death. It was distributed to Carmelite convents, where it was shared with the families and friends of many sisters. The first edition, a printing of two thousand copies, sold out almost immediately and was followed by others in rapid succession. Soon translations appeared and *Story of a Soul* began its travels. Today it can be found in nearly sixty languages everywhere in the world. There is no way to estimate the number of its readers, as copies pass freely from hand to hand. A full century after its publication it remains a best-seller on the list of religious books. Thérèse captures the interest of millions of readers and starts them on a journey of spiritual discovery that continues for a lifetime. Many read and reread the autobiography because each reading takes them deeper into her doctrine, into their own souls, and into an ever-increasing intimacy with God.

Thérèse of Lisieux is the saint for our times. She died in 1897 at the age of twenty-four, but if she had lived to the same age as her sister Céline, she would have died in 1963. She belongs to the modern world, the one in which we live, a world of science and technology, a world in which great numbers do not believe in God. She lived when men like Sigmund Freud, Karl Marx, Friedrich Nietzsche, and Charles Darwin were forming the culture of the modern age. Cloister walls did not keep her from being part of that world. In the field of religion she was far ahead of her time, and students of her thought speak of the "Copernican revolution" she created.

She was no stranger to the stresses of our time. She battled with neurosis, and in the last desperate moments of a long illness she was tempted to suicide. During the dark night of her soul she stared straight into the eyes of atheism. Her astute intelligence recognized the force of its arguments, and, feeling unequipped to answer them, she simply confronted them with a fierce, unyielding faith. She wrote out the Apostles' Creed in her own blood and pinned it beneath her habit close to her heart. She experienced the pain of the atheists, saw clearly the desperation of their plight, and loved them with deep sympathy and concern. She was glad to *"sit at their table and eat their food,"* she said, for as long as God desired her to remain there, which turned out to be till the last moment of her life. For their salvation she offered the trial of faith that she endured in her final eighteen months.

That trial of faith was a darkness blacker than any of us may ever expect to experience. But the rest of her life was for the most part ordinary, the kind of life we ourselves encounter every day. She faithfully followed the routine of a cloistered Carmelite, with its many demands. She patiently tolerated the difficulties of living in close quarters with more than twenty sisters, who came from different social classes and had different levels of education and personalities that did not always mesh. She obeyed the Carmelite rule to the letter, but without drawing attention to the perfection with which she kept it. She put up with the old sister seated behind her in choir, who almost drove her crazy by scraping her false teeth with her fingernails. She carried the heavy burden of her father's mental illness, as he slowly lost his mind and had to be confined for nearly four years in a mental institution far from home.

These are no more than the ordinary trials of life which many of us endure. Pope Pius X went to the heart of her sanctity when he said it consisted in readily, generously, and constantly fulfilling her vocation "without going beyond the common order of things." Thérèse did not die at the stake like Joan of Arc. She died propped up in a clean bed, cared for by her devoted sisters. She never levitated with the power of her prayers, as St. Teresa of Ávila reputedly did. In fact, she often fell asleep trying to say them. Her mother, in one of her letters, remarked about her stubborn streak as a child. She played checkers, had a cocker spaniel named Tom whom she loved to take for walks and a favorite blue hat which she thought was ravishing. She wondered how she could love God so deeply and at the same time love that hat so much.

This is not the stuff of high adventure. It is rather the ordinary and unexciting tale of what appeared to be a common little life. But in the framework of that life she became a great saint. Therein lies the genius of her message: she teaches us to become holy in the framework of *our* lives, however ordinary they may seem to be. God is in the center of every person's present moment; therefore, no human being is ordinary.

Each is uniquely created by Him and uniquely called to love Him.

Into the life of this saint, less than two years before she died, came a young man named Maurice Bellière. They never met, but they exchanged twenty-one letters, and that correspondence opens a window on the heart of St. Thérèse which would have remained forever closed if Maurice had not written to the Carmel, asking for a Sister to pray for him. We are greatly in his debt.

Letters have a charm of their own. They are confidential conversations, overheard from the past, between two people unaware that anyone is listening. Consequently, it is in letters that people best reveal themselves. In the eleven letters of Maurice we discover a man who is like us in many ways, with human limitations which we readily recognize and which perhaps we share. In Thérèse's ten letters we see a uniquely great and very famous saint imparting her spirit and her teaching to a friend who is very dear to her. Indeed, it is in these letters that she reveals her extraordinary capacity for friendship to a degree not found elsewhere in her works. In writing to Maurice she also writes to us, and it is the hope of this book that we shall read her letters with this understanding.

The correspondence of Maurice began with a letter addressed to the Mother Prioress, whose name he did not know at the time.

I

A LEAP OF FAITH

~

The Correspondence
of Maurice Bellière
to Mother Prioress
of Lisieux

Reverend Mother Superior,

It is in the name of the great St. Teresa and on her Feast day that I come to you with a request, and I am doing it as if I were being sent by her, because the thought of writing you came to me yesterday, after I had put it off for some time.

But first, Mother, allow me to introduce myself, and from this point on please forgive my extreme simplicity, which perhaps already astonishes you. I am a seminarian of the Diocese of Bayeux, in second year at the Seminary of Sommervieu, guided into this house by the grace of God Who wants me to become a priest. Moreover, while waiting for a definitive decision I am an aspiring missionary listed on the roster of the Seminary of Rue du Bac in Paris.

But as I was about to tell you, Mother, the grace of God which impelled me toward the Sanctuary has not washed away the last traces of a thoughtless life which preceded my decision, and in spite of my efforts I have a hard time absorbing the spirit of the Church and holding myself to all the demands of the seminary rule.

But here I am now making a Retreat, and I just read of a young man who was suddenly converted and brought back to God by the prayers of his sister or his mother. All of a sudden it occurred to me that if somebody prayed for me, I too would be fully and generously converted, and I said to myself: I'm going to write to a Carmelite Community and I'll ask that a nun devote herself particularly to the salvation of my soul, and obtain for me the grace to be faithful to the vocation God has given me, that of a priest and a missionary.

So I'm asking you, Mother, to propose that task to one of your Sisters. I am rash and for that I humbly ask pardon, but I'm so much in need of help! In addition to which, if I respond to my vocation I shall save other souls, and that good nun to whom I entrust my own soul will have saved other souls as well.

In the name of St. Teresa and of those souls, are you going to turn down my request?

Perhaps, Reverend Mother, I shall obtain this favor from you, this grace, if you will take into account that within a month I'm going into the army, and I shall be subjected once again to the assaults of a world which is not entirely dead for me.

It is for myself, Mother, that I am pleading, but it is also for God and for souls—and you too have taken the salvation of souls greatly to heart. O souls!

Please, I beg you, look favorably on my request and entrust me particularly—I was about to say exclusively— to the prayers of one of your Sisters. And once more pardon my boldness. I don't know you and I don't know anyone in your Community, and yet here I am coming to you with confidence.

Please in any case, whatever you may think of my request, keep both it and my name in confidence.

In return, I promise that once I am a priest I will always have a remembrance in the memento of Mass both for the Religious who will have devoted herself to my salvation, as well as for you, Mother, and your Community. Henceforth I shall acquit myself of my debt of gratitude by entrusting it to Jesus Christ.

I don't know how to apologize to you, Mother Superior; but I ask you to accept the homage of my deep respect and my filial gratitude.

Devotedly yours in Christ
Maurice Barthélémy Bellière
Aspiring Missionary

Maurice's letter arrived at the Carmelite convent in Lisieux two days after it was written. It was received by Thérèse's older sister Pauline, whose name in the community was Mother Agnes of Jesus and who was Prioress at the time. She took the letter to the laundry where Thérèse was doing the week's wash with the other sisters and, showing it to her, asked her to be the spiritual sister of Maurice.

Thérèse was overjoyed. To have a missionary priest for a brother was the fulfillment of a family dream. She was the youngest of nine children, seven girls and two boys. Her parents had always wanted a son who would enter the priesthood and serve the Church as a missionary, but both boys and two of the girls had died in their infancy, long before Thérèse was born. They were far from forgotten. The family honored their memory and often turned to them in prayer.

It would be hard to imagine a family more religious than that of Thérèse. Both her parents had wanted to enter religious life when they were young. Louis Martin had applied for entrance to an Augustinian monastery in the Swiss Alps but was denied admission because of his inability to master Latin, a requirement in a community whose chief activity was to chant the Divine Office in the official language of the Church. Zélie Guerin had tried to become a Sister of Charity but, after long consultation with the superior, concluded that her vocation was to marry and raise a family. She was twenty-seven and Louis thirty-five when they met one morning, in a chance encounter on a bridge while on their way to work. It was a bridge of destiny, for when their eyes met they fell in love at once. They never doubted they were meant for each other, and they were married within three months.

At the time of the marriage each owned a prosperous business in Alençon, which meant that their family was well off. Louis, who had learned the watchmaker's trade in Strasbourg, had a jewelry shop in town, and Zélie operated a small lace-making company with twenty women in her employ. The famous lace of Alençon brought a good price in the better shops of Paris, and her business prospered.

Prosperity, however, did not interfere with the practice of the faith in the household of this couple. Louis and Zélie rose before dawn each morning and made their way to the five-thirty Mass in their parish church. It was the one attended by the workers of the town and they liked to pray side by side with them. The children often accompanied their parents to church. They studied their religion daily, and at night the family gathered for evening prayer. Faith and devotion were part of their family life. Eventually, one by one, the girls all became nuns, and the family's only regret was that no son survived to serve God in the priesthood, especially as a foreign missionary.

When Thérèse read Maurice's letter she at once saw him as the priest-brother she had never had. She later recorded her reaction in her autobiography: *"Not for years had I experienced this kind of happiness. It was as if someone had struck chords of music long forgotten."*

Maurice Bellière, just twenty-one at the time, was a seminarian at Sommervieu, not far away in Normandy. He wanted to give his life entirely to God and the salvation of others. From his letter we gain the impression of a young man who was open and simple, unsure of himself but filled with high ideals. He strikes us as a man to be taken seriously, yet also as one very much in need of help. In comparison with Thérèse, who was fully mature, Maurice was a callow youth, impetuous and naive.

We shall learn from a later letter that he had heard some of his fellow seminarians discussing the Carmelite cloister in Lisieux, where the Martins moved after the death of Zélie. They spoke of a remarkable family by the name of Martin who lived there and of the amazing fact that four of the five daughters had entered that Carmel. Maurice did not know that the Prioress to whom he addressed his letter was a member of this family, nor did he know that the nun she would select to pray for him was her youngest sister, Thérèse. All he knew was that he was in desperate need of the prayers of someone holy. He was about to interrupt his seminary training for a mandatory year of military service and was very much afraid that his vocation to the priesthood might not survive the test of that year.

In 1894 Maurice had entered the seminary at Sommervieu to prepare for the priesthood in the local Diocese of Bayeux-Lisieux, and in his first year he had applied to the Foreign Missionary Society of Paris (Missionaires Étrangères de Paris, or the MEP's as they were called), a fast-growing band of missionaries who went to Third World countries. They were not a religious order, but a society of secular priests similar to the Maryknoll Society in the United States. It was a time of great religious fervor in France, and although new communities of missionaries were forming, they could not keep pace with the number of applications they received.

Maurice had just made a very prayerful retreat and he was ready for a bold step. Glancing at his calendar, he noticed that it was the feast of St. Teresa of Ávila, October 15. St. Teresa, the great sixteenth-century reformer of the Carmelite order, had called her nuns to a strictly cloistered regime of penance and prayer. They had only one apostolate: prayer and sacrifice for the Church's mission in the world. They were to give everything of themselves for the world's salvation, and especially they were to pray for priests. Where better to turn for the help he needed than the nearest Carmel he could find, the one in Lisieux?

Maurice took up his pen and wrote the letter we have just read. Little did he know what a chain of events he was setting in motion.

How good God is, Reverend Mother, and in giving Him thanks how I marvel at His merciful Providence which has done such great things for me!

But after thanking Him how I thank you, Mother, for showing so much kindness to somebody who deserves it less than anyone. It's only in those who are filled with God that such kindness is found.

Now I am no longer afraid and I feel in my heart a new fervor that is going to triumph. I shall be a saint, I want to be a saint. Besides, anyone who speaks of a priest, and especially of a missionary, has to be speaking of a saint. And if I say a saint why shouldn't I say a martyr? What an ideal that is, Mother: priest, apostle and martyr! But how many graces and how much virtue and finally how much holiness must go into meriting this high privilege! And I have so little of all that! But I am going to have it, because my sister and I will storm heaven and the beloved Queen of Apostles and Martyrs will be good enough to accept me into her company of the elite. And it will be to you, Mother, that I shall owe it, to you who have so graciously listened to my desperate request. Thank you—I cannot thank you, I don't even know how. To say the least, it is with the full outpouring of my grateful heart.

On top of everything, who is it that you have given me for a sister? A saint—an angel, as you put it yourself! I

*was well aware that there were only saints among you,
but I did not dare to imagine that a saint among saints
would become my sister. Oh Mother, you treat me like a
son. Allow me to think of myself as one and to come into
your family to pour out my sorrows and my joys. Permit
me to write to you, or to come and tell you whatever
befalls me, be it happy or sad, with all the different things
happening in a life that needs to be rebuilt and is just
starting to be. Let me speak to you about the things of
God and draw strength and virtue from being near you,
with all the simplicity of a child, indeed as the saying goes,
"a spoiled child."*

*I'd be happy also to tell my sister, Thérèse of the Child
Jesus, how touched I have been by her charity, her devot-
edness, drawn from the purest well of God's Love. No
doubt the rules of your Congregation don't allow me to
write to her, so I'm going to ask you, Mother, to act as my
messenger to her, as you have already done so successfully
and happily. Tell her please, good Mother, that with much
feeling I have thanked the divine goodness for choosing
this Sister to help me in doing the work of Jesus Christ,
and that I have read with deep emotion that inspired
prayer which she made up and is saying for me every day.
I ask you to give her this Sacred Heart badge as a sign of
our association in God, which lacks only her signature
because you, Mother, and God have already given ap-
proval to it. Tell my sister also that my promise holds and
will hold forever, since in heaven for us priests there will*

be a perpetual Mass: *she will therefore always have a place in the Memento, as you will also, Mother, and your Community.*

From now on I will reserve a decade of the Rosary for her each day, and every month I will offer my Communion for her, usually on the First Friday or on the first Sunday. For this month of October I will receive that Sunday Communion on the Feast of the Holy Heart of Mary, our patronal feast at the Seminary. Ask her to be associated with me in this. It is in the Eucharist that I shall return my thanks for the prayers and sacrifices which she is offering on my behalf. But her great wish shall be realized as well: I shall be a priest, an apostle after God's own heart. I sense it, and together we shall save souls so dear to Jesus Christ. What a beautiful procession there will be when she enters Heaven for all eternity. Oh this is no illusion: whatever good I shall do I shall owe to her, in the same way that St. Francis Xavier was sure that most of the souls that he was the instrument of saving by his zeal owed their salvation to the prayers of Carmelites. I shall only be the instrument; it is you, my sister, who will do the converting. During this distressing military year may I labor for God and not come back with empty hands, without bringing some souls back to the true Light. May the things of the world not enter into my heart, and may I return to Mary as pure as the angels of Heaven, full of zeal for God's love and zeal for souls—souls, the rest is up to God!

À Dieu, my Mother, à Dieu, my Sister; forever in the Sacred Hearts. Thank you also for the golden Ave Maria.[2]

Your respectful and grateful son, and your brother forever,

M. Barthélémy-Bellière
Child of Mary and Joseph
Guard of honor of the Sacred Heart
Aspiring Missionary

---

[2] A holy picture which Pauline had sent him.

A Saint among Saints for a Sister

*P*auline wrote immediately to tell Maurice that his request was granted and to describe the sister she had chosen to be his partner in prayer. The text of that letter has been lost, but we know from his response that Pauline spoke of Thérèse as "a saint among saints."

She always enjoyed a special relationship with her youngest sister. She was Thérèse's confidante from childhood. Their mother died of breast cancer in 1877 at the age of forty-seven, leaving five daughters: Marie, seventeen years old; Pauline, sixteen; Léonie, fourteen; Céline, eight; and Thérèse, just four and a half. After the funeral, when Céline "adopted" Marie as her second mother, Thérèse threw herself into Pauline's arms, saying, *"From now on, you will be my mother."*

The two sisters became very close. Pauline presided over Thérèse's upbringing, supervising her education and acting as her chief teacher of religion. She was aware of the amazing adventure of God's love in Thérèse, whose contemplative nature was evident from earliest childhood. Thérèse once said that from the age of three and a half she was never more than five minutes without thinking about God. Sometimes she would hide herself between the wall and the curtains of her bed. When asked what she did there, she answered simply: *"I think. I think about God, about life, about ETERNITY."* A similar state of awareness is revealed in her memories of going fishing with her father when she was five or six, which she later described for Pauline in her autobiography: *"Sometimes I would try to fish with my little line, but I preferred to go alone and sit down on the grass bedecked with flowers, and then my thoughts became very profound indeed! Without knowing what it was to meditate, my soul was absorbed in real prayer."* Even the jam sandwich which Pauline packed for her lunch took on a symbolic meaning: *"The beautiful bread and jam you had prepared had changed its appearance. Instead of the vivid color it had earlier, I now saw only a light rosy tint and the bread had become old and crumbled. Earth seemed a sad place and I understood that in heaven alone joy will be without any clouds."*[3]

Thérèse had an intuitive sense not only of the Divine Presence but also of her destiny to embrace this Presence completely. She once confided to Pauline a desire *"to be like a hermit and go away with her alone to a faraway desert place."* Although she was desolate when as a child of nine she overheard Pauline say to Marie that she had decided to enter the Carmel and

[3] *Story of a Soul*, 37.

would leave home soon, she realized even then that this was exactly what she desired for herself:

> *I felt Carmel was the* desert *where God wanted me also to go and hide myself. I felt this with so much force that there wasn't the least doubt in my heart. It was not the dream of a child led astray, but the* certitude of a divine call. *I wanted to go to Carmel not for* Pauline's sake *but for* Jesus alone. *I was thinking* very much *about things which words could not express but which left a great peace in my soul.*[4]

Thérèse possessed a unique certitude about her vocation; by age fourteen she put behind her the emotions of a stormy preadolescence and made the firm decision to enter the Carmel by her fifteenth birthday. The opposition she encountered was formidable, but three months after turning fifteen she joined one of the most austere religious orders in the Catholic Church. By that time she was *"walking with the stride of a giant."* Pauline was the companion of Thérèse's remarkable journey. She became her mother a second time when she was elected Prioress, and watched her sister grow as a Carmelite.

Maurice had no idea of the dimensions of the

---

[4] *Story of a Soul,* 58.

of the woman whom Pauline had selected to pray for him. He did not know that within fifteen years a Pope would speak of her as "the greatest saint of modern times." All he knew was his own desperate spiritual need, and he would bank on the word of Pauline that the sister she gave him was "a saint among saints." She was just the one he needed to stand by him as he set off for his year in the army.

The camp to which he was headed was in Caen, where he arrived on November 12, 1895. When he stepped from the train in the station, he dropped a postcard in the mailbox:

> L'Abbé M. Barthélémy-Bellière
> (Langrune)

comes to greet his mother in the Carmel and his sister Thérèse before entering the barracks today at two o'clock. He recommends to you the seminarian-soldiers and their saddened families. Always in union of prayers and graces, that we may do good and that the kingdom of God may come.

Caen, Tuesday night
July 21, 1896

Reverend Mother Superior,

It's been a very long time since I've had the pleasure of chatting with you, but if I am doing so today it is once again for the purpose of begging.

I am a soldier, Mother, and the time spent as one has been of no help to the seminarian. I have had many falls and committed unheard-of blunders in the atmosphere of this world which recaptured me. I have just committed the worst blunder of all, but it is so outrageous that it will be my last because it teaches me a lesson. I have gotten into a deplorable predicament. My sister Thérèse of the Child Jesus must at all costs get me out of it. She has to storm heaven, which will let itself be moved by her prayers and her penance. Mother, she has to do this or I am lost—so much the more because this will be for a greater good. Tell her that she has to do it. Pardon me for my insistence, and pray for me yourself, good Mother. Get your Community to pray for me, because my needs are great and urgent.[5]

Pardon me, plead for me, and help me, I beg you in the name of the Virgin of Carmel and St. Joseph.

Reverend Mother, I dare once more to call myself your very humble son.

---

[5] The emphasis is Bellière's.

You remember me, the one who wrote you last November, asking you to appoint one of your Religious to be my Sister. You were so kind then. Now be more so if that is possible. If you could only know how much I need God's help!

Ever yours, Mother, in Jesus Christ,

Maurice Bellière
Seminarian
Soldier, 5th Line
4th Company
Caen

The Worst Blunder of All

In his first letter to the Carmel, Maurice had deplored his misspent past which he was trying to put behind him in the sequestered atmosphere of the seminary. In the army he had a rude awakening, for his past came back to haunt him. His military service, to which he went off with high hopes, proved disastrous. "During this distressing military year," he had written to the Carmel with pious naiveté, "may I labor for God and not come back with empty hands, without bringing some souls back to the true Light. May the things of the world not enter into my heart, and may I return to Mary as pure as the angels of Heaven, full of zeal for God's love and for souls." He came back with neither spiritual victories nor even a single stripe on the sleeve of his jacket to indicate any military accomplishment. Instead of leading others, he had let others lead him, in ways that he very much regretted. Thoroughly chastened, he now begged for mercy and for prayers.

What happened that so painfully afflicted his conscience? In particular, what was "the worst blunder of all"? Since he does not say, we are left to conjecture.

The General Correspondence of St. Thérèse of Lisieux

suggests in a footnote[6] that it may have been a decision Bellière nearly made to abandon his vocation to the priesthood in favor of an army career. The reader is referred to a letter he wrote in April 1897,[7] in which he listed for Thérèse a number of important events in his life that took place in the month of June, pointing out that in that month he made the important decision to give up the thought of a military career to pursue the priesthood.

The speculation is not plausible. First, in this letter of July 21, 1896, Maurice agonized over a blunder which he *committed* and deeply regretted, not one which he *almost* committed but happily avoided. Second, in his letter of April 1897 he did not say that he made this decision while he was in the army. The decision was in all likelihood made earlier in his life, when we know that he had dreamed of a military career.

We must therefore seek another explanation for "the worst blunder of all." It is hard to imagine what it may have been unless it was the sort of blunder sometimes made by young men set free from the restraints of home and thrown in with others in a situation where they are suddenly responsible to no one.

---

[6] *The General Correspondence of St. Thérèse of Lisieux,* trans. by John Clarke, O.C.D., 11:972, n. 3 (Washington, D.C.: ICS Publishing Co., 1988).

[7] *General Correspondence,* 11:1083, n. 7.

His blunder may have been in the area of drinking and carousing, and perhaps was a regrettable sexual encounter. Such a thing would sear the conscience of a young man fresh from the seminary, with its demands of chastity.

Whatever the incident was, it so deeply concerned Maurice that his first letter to the Carmel after a significant silence of nine months clearly revealed his state of panic. It began casually enough—"It's been a very long time since I've had the pleasure of chatting with you"—but it quickly turned into a cry of desperation. He needed help, and he needed it badly enough to plead for it: "I have gotten into a deplorable predicament. My sister Thérèse . . . must at all costs get me out of it. She has to storm heaven . . . or I am lost. . . . Tell her that she has to do it."

This letter gives a strong impression of instability in young Maurice. A look at his background may help us to understand him. He had signed his first letter to the Carmel with the name Maurice Barthélémy Bellière. The signature on the letter of July 1896 is simply Maurice Bellière. There is a story behind the two names.

He was born in Caen on June 10, 1874, the son of Alphonse and Marie Bellière. His mother died a week after his birth, and his father brought him to Langrune, where his mother's sister Antoinette, who was also his godmother, was married to Louis Barthélémy. The couple were childless, and when Alphonse asked them to take his son into their home and raise him, they were delighted.

His father left Maurice in Langrune and dropped out of his life completely. He was not legally adopted and he was allowed to grow up believing that he was the son of the Barthélémys. No doubt this was thought to be in his best interest, to avoid confusing him until he was old enough to understand his situation. When he was nearly eleven years old, Maurice was told the truth. We may imagine the shock this was for a boy on the threshold of adolescence. At that critical moment in his life he had to face the question of his identity. To whom did he really belong? Who *was* his mother, and what was she like? And why did his father never come to see him? These questions would agitate him and leave him emotionally shaken. While Maurice seems to have handled this disclosure reasonably well, it left its mark on his personality, and it will be helpful to keep it in mind as we read his letters and follow his career.

The letter of July 1896 to the Prioress was received by Mother Gonzague, who had succeeded Mother Agnes in office. We do not possess her reply, but she responded quickly, eager to allay his anxiety. She succeeded in doing so, as we can see from his next letter.

Reverend Mother,

When dear Mother Agnes of Jesus handed over her Office to you, she also gave you her heart, for I find her heart in yours. I thank you, Mother, for the help you gave me in a moment of distress. The storm has passed, calm has returned, and the poor soldier has become again the seminarian that he used to be.

And praise be to God, Mother, because struggle strengthens a man and gives him light. So today I'm happy, with the joy that comes from God—thanks to you and thanks to my dear little Sister, Thérèse of the Child Jesus. I don't know her, but I want to tell her that I will see her in heaven one day, and I will walk up to her bringing with me the souls whom she will have helped me save.

Right at this moment the question of my vocation is being decided for me: am I to be a priest in ordinary ministry, or am I to be a missionary priest? My Director has given me permission to be put on the list of Aspirants by the Superior of the Foreign Missionaries. I'm hoping that the good Lord will tip the scales in my favor. As soon as this good news is certain I will pass it on to you, Mother, as well as to my Sister Thérèse. May she pray for me and rejoice with me, and save souls with me—poor instrument that I am.

And you yourself, Mother, if you have a prayer to spare please remember to say it for the poor soldier whom you have strengthened and for the seminarian who wants to work for the glory of God.

I remain, Reverend Mother, very respectfully your humble and devoted son,

M. Barthélémy-Bellière
Student at the Major Seminary of Sommervieu

[He enclosed with his letter a card for Thérèse:]

Abbé M. Barthélémy-Bellière
Sommervieu

Glory to St. Teresa.

It will be a year ago tomorrow that the Lord united me in Charity to my Sister Thérèse. Tomorrow is the feast day of the one who is your holy patroness,[8] and if nothing serious prevents me I shall offer Holy Communion in her honor for you and for your Community. United in prayer.

---

[8] St. Teresa of Ávila.

Uncertain Future

Nearly three months had gone by since Maurice had last written to the Carmel and by now he had regained his peace of mind: "The storm has passed, calm has returned."

At this point he was still awaiting a decision on the application he had made to the Foreign Missionary Society of Paris (MEPs). With so many candidates for the priesthood choosing congregations which sent missionaries abroad, the MEPs led the field with an amazing three hundred and thirty young men entering its ranks in 1896. The Board of Admissions needed to be selective and it closely observed Maurice's progress at Sommervieu before coming to a judgment on his suitability for the missions. What he did not know was that reports had been sent to the MEPs by some of his professors, who expressed misgivings about his qualifications.

Compared with a diocesan priest in France, a missionary in a foreign land faced extreme hardships. A parish priest at home would be well provided for, with a housekeeper to maintain the rectory and prepare his meals. The ordinary comforts of life were assured, and by and large his parishioners would accept and honor him. In places like China and Africa, a missionary would be confronted with a society which did not understand him. He would be a stranger preaching a strange God, a Savior who died on a cross. There would be no physical comforts and the climate would often be unbearable for a European. Life would be hard, and Maurice was a man who enjoyed his comforts and relied heavily upon friends.

There may also have been reservations about his academic ability. Father Destombes, a member of the MEPs who has written a great deal about St. Thérèse, has studied the life of Maurice and written three articles about him in *Vie Thérèsienne*.[9] He points out that whereas Maurice did well in French literature, showed a bent for dramatics, and excelled in the study of English, he had no special gifts in philosophy and theology, obviously two very important subjects in a priest's preparation.

If he did not impress some, however, Maurice had the support of others. When he came to public attention in the mid-1970s with the publication of his correspondence with Thérèse, one person who had known him was still living—Father Isidore Delaunay. Although younger than Maurice and not a classmate, he nevertheless knew him in the seminary and was very friendly with him. Delaunay died in 1978 at the age of ninety-eight and remained in excellent health to the end, with a remarkable memory. He had often visited

---

[9] *Vie Thérèsienne,* October 1963, January 1964, and April 1964.

Maurice's home on summer holidays and remembered his mother well. He described the young seminarian as energetic, joyous, full of imagination, very interested in dramatics, and gifted in staging and acting in plays which were put on by the students. When asked to sum up his recollection of the Maurice he had known more than seventy years before, the old priest did so in a single word: "Marvelous!"

Maurice also favorably impressed a Sulpician priest, Father Charles DeBarry. He was important because he was the rector of the seminary and was highly regarded for the quality of his scholarship and the depth of his holiness. Maurice was attracted to this man as soon as he entered the seminary and chose him as his spiritual director. Father DeBarry clearly admired Maurice's high ideals and ready generosity. He saw in him what Thérèse was quick to observe, *"a soul full of energy,"* a quality she greatly prized.

Maurice also had another friend in Mother Gonzague. She has not always been treated well by her critics, but her importance in the lives of Thérèse and Maurice deserves acknowledgment. Her shortcomings have received their share of attention: her sometimes haughty manner, which was perhaps a result of her aristocratic background (she was one of two nuns in the Carmel who came from the aristocracy), her changing of rules and directives with the changing of her moods, her well-known preoccupation with the convent cat, who was very much a favorite—above all, the harshness with which she sometimes treated Thérèse during her first days in the Carmel. Whatever faults she may have had, she had a profound appreciation of Thérèse and truly loved her. If she was severe with her in the beginning, it was because she feared that Thérèse's youth would tempt the others to spoil her and make her the pet of the community. Moreover, we know that she saw in Thérèse the makings of a future Prioress, and she did not want anything to interfere with her development. We must keep in mind what it would have been like for a group of older nuns to be suddenly confronted with a fifteen-year-old girl in their company.

Mother Gonzague deserves credit especially for the generosity with which she encouraged Thérèse to correspond with Maurice. When the letter of October 21, 1896, arrived, Mother Gonzague was ill and asked Thérèse to answer it. Thereafter she allowed her to continue writing to him. Inclined by temperament to be jealous, Mother Gonzague showed no jealousy at all in this regard. In the 1890s it would have been considered inappropriate and even dangerous for a cloistered nun to correspond with a young man. Mother Gonzague was remarkably broad-minded in the matter. It was the custom of the time for religious superiors to read the incoming and outgoing letters of the sisters. She read every letter Thérèse sent and received, yet she never criticized anything she wrote to Maurice, never suggested that she tone down the affection she expressed for him. The extent to which Mother Gonzague trusted Thérèse and gave her a free hand was remarkable, and she deserves great credit for her common sense. Without her encouragement we should never possess this rich correspondence. Moreover, if Thérèse had been limited to praying and sacrificing for Maurice and had not been permitted to correspond with him, there would not have developed the special relationship which grew between them.

II
Souls Made to Understand Each Other

~

The Correspondence between Maurice Bellière and Thérèse of Lisieux

Monsieur l'Abbé,

Our Reverend Mother has given me the task of answering your letter because she's not well. I'm sorry that you're deprived of the holy words this good Mother would have written you, but I'm happy to be her emissary and to let you know of her joy in learning about the work Our Lord has just accomplished in your soul. She will continue to pray that He will bring His work of grace in you to fulfillment.

I don't think I have to tell you, Monsieur l'Abbé, how much I share our Mother's happiness. Your letter in July distressed me very much, because I blamed my lack of fervor for the struggles you went through. I haven't stopped begging the maternal help of the beloved Queen of Apostles for you. Also, I have been much consoled to receive as a feast day present[10] the assurance that my poor prayers had been answered.

Now that the storm has passed, I thank the good God for making you go through it, for we read these beautiful words in our Bible: "Happy the man who has suffered temptation,"[11] and again: "He who has not been tempted,

---

[10] October 15, the day she received his letter, was the feast day of St. Teresa of Ávila. Since Thérèse was named after her both in Baptism and in religious life, it was her personal feast day on two scores.

[11] See James 1:2.

what does he know?"[12] *In fact, when Jesus calls a person to lead a great number of others to salvation, it is very necessary that He make him experience the trials and temptations of life. Since He has given you the grace to come out of the stuggle victorious, Monsieur l'Abbé, I hope that our kind Jesus will fulfill your great desires. I ask Him that you may become not only a good missionary but a* saint, *all on fire with the love of God and of souls. I beg you to obtain this same love for me, so that I may be able to help you in your apostolic work. You must know that a Carmelite who did not want to be an Apostle would be walking away from the purpose of her vocation, and would cease to be a daughter of the seraphic St. Teresa, who would give her life a thousand times to save a single soul.*

Monsieur l'Abbé, I am sure that you will earnestly want to join your prayers to my own that Our Lord will make our Venerated Mother well.

In the sacred Hearts of Jesus and Mary I shall always be happy to call myself

> *Your unworthy little sister*
> *Thérèse of the Child Jesus*
> *and of the Holy Face*
> *rel. carm. ind.*[13]

---

[12] See Sirach 34:10.

[13] Unworthy Carmelite religious.

Night of Nothingness

As we take up Thérèse's first letter to Maurice, it is important to mark the point she had reached in her life. She was not quite twenty-four years old and would die in less than a year. Six months earlier she had become aware that she had contracted tuberculosis, for which there was then no cure. Although she was still able to carry on with her daily routines, the disease would take its toll increasingly over the next eleven months.

Simultaneously a terrible darkness had fallen on her spirit. The intimacy which she had always felt with God, her lively faith that gave her strength and brought her consolation, suddenly vanished. She was experiencing what St. John of the Cross called the "dark night of the soul," a stage which he said often occurs in people of great holiness before they reach the moment of total union with God. She was close to the summit of her spiritual journey, and she was in great anguish.

The child who had hidden behind the curtains of her bed *"to think about God"* and who was reminded of Him by the faded jam sandwich in her picnic basket had entered the Carmel at the age of fifteen *"to love Him as He had never been loved before."* On the day of her entry, she wore the customary white gown of a bride and was said to be radiantly beautiful. She believed that to be a Carmelite was to become the bride of Christ. Later, on the day of her profession, she would compose a wedding invitation, announcing her marriage to Him.

The concept of being God's bride, so startling at first to our modern sensibilities, is an authentic biblical image with which Thérèse was very familiar. It is found in the Psalms, in the writings of the Prophets, in the Song of Songs (often called the Canticle of Canticles), and in the New Testament, where Jesus is the Bridegroom and His Church is the Bride.

A line in the Canticle held her attention: "Draw me, and we shall run." Noting that the *me* becomes *we,* she read the line as her call to action. If He drew *her* to His love, she in turn would inevitably draw others in her wake. She would not only love Him herself, she would lead others to love Him. Thérèse believed that Jesus came to save everyone and that all must be drawn to His love. She knew that God is no distant deity who looks down on the world from afar. God is a Lover. His love is as personal and intimate as love is able to be, and like all lovers He longs for the love of those He loves. When Thérèse said she wanted to love Him as He had never been loved before, she used no exaggeration. She could never settle for less than her full human destiny: to love God in the way He deserves to be loved.

This love of Thérèse would mature in the Carmel,

where we might say the honeymoon ended and the marriage began. Life was far from idyllic in this religious community, often trying her patience in ways she never experienced at home. Even her prayer life, which was always inspired, no longer gave her emotional satisfaction—*arid* was the word she used to describe it. None of this surprised her, nor did it shake her confidence. For her, loving God had little to do with what some think of as "religious experience," often confusing it with *emotional* experience. She accepted her responsibility to join with Christ in the hard work of saving the world. He died on the Cross, crying out to His Father: "My God, why have You forsaken me!" She was consumed with pity for Him. Her prayer was for *His* consolation and not for her own. It did not matter to her that she fell asleep during Thanksgiving after Holy Communion. What difference did that make? she asked. Did not doctors put patients to sleep to operate on them? What mattered was for one's heart to be in the right place, to love Jesus and to want to help Him. As for the other trials of the cloister, the austerity of the life, the freezing cold of the Norman winter, the severe correction of the Prioress, the petty annoyances from some of the nuns—all of this was simply part of the Cross to be shared with her Lord. She had gone to Carmel in search of the desert and the desert is what she found.

Two years after she entered, during her private ten-day retreat in preparation for her profession, she sent Pauline a letter describing what was going on in her soul and the path she believed Christ had chosen for her. She was seventeen at the time, and her letter reveals her prodigious spiritual development and the mystic she had already become.

Jesus took me by the hand, and He made me enter a subterranean passage where it is neither cold nor hot, where the sun does not shine, and which the rain or the wind does not visit, a subterranean passage where I see nothing but a half-veiled light, the light which was diffused by the lowered eyes of my Fiancé's Face!

My Fiancé says nothing to me, and I say nothing to Him either, except that I love Him more than myself, and I feel at the bottom of my heart that it is true, for I am more His than my own! I don't see that we are advancing toward the summit of the mountain since our journey is being made underground, but it seems to me that we are approaching it without knowing how. The route on which I am has no consolation for me, and nevertheless it brings me all consolations since Jesus is the One Who chose it, and I want to console Him alone, alone!

Now, five years since that retreat, at the time she wrote this first letter to Maurice she was far closer to the final stage of her mysticism. She had recorded her major insights. Only one month earlier, she had written her famous Manuscript B. A year and a half before, she had composed and formally pronounced her Act of Oblation to the Merciful Love of God, a decisive event on her spiritual journey. She had long been searching to trace out exactly what she called her Little Way, and by the end of 1895 it had become clear to her and she was ready to propose it to others. She was at last sure of her footing on the path she was taking. But the more she advanced, the more God seemed to withdraw. As she wrote this letter to Maurice, she was enduring the last of her purifications, her Dark Night of Faith. The half-veiled light that she lived under since joining the Carmel was now a pitch-black darkness. *"The veil of faith is no longer a veil for me but a wall that rises up to the heavens,"* she wrote.

Her Dark Night had begun on Good Friday six months earlier, when her first hemorrhage from tuberculosis occurred. Her initial reaction was one of joy. Heaven, she said, was the sum of all her happiness. Soon she would be united in heaven with her Beloved. But two days later, on Easter Sunday, she began to experience a void in her faith which she desolately described as her Night of Nothingness. She was suddenly seized by the possibility that there was no heaven and that instead of eternal light she would find eternal darkness. That which had always given her joy became a source of torture. In her autobiography she has left us a graphic description of what happened to her:

> [Jesus] allowed my soul to be overrun by an impenetrable darkness, which made the thought of heaven, hitherto so welcome, a subject of nothing but conflict and torment. . . .
>
> I try to refresh my jaded spirits with the thoughts of that bright country where my hopes lie; and what happens? It is worse torment than ever; the darkness itself seems to borrow from the sinners who live in it the gift of speech. I hear its mocking accents: "It's all a dream, this talk of heaven bathed in light, and of a God who made it all, who is to be your possession in eternity! You really believe, do you, that the mist which hangs about you will clear away later on? All right, go on longing for death. But death will make nonsense of your hopes; it will only mean a night darker than ever, the night of mere nonexistence."

In 1896 a wave of atheism was sweeping across France and much of Europe. Although Thérèse was sequestered in the Carmel, she was not immune to the forces at work in her world. As a child she had been fascinated by science and thrilled by the early advances of technology. Now, however, she did not want to duel with those in science who denied God's existence. At first, she tried to counter their arguments, but felt unequal to the task. *"I don't suppose I've made as many acts of faith in all the rest of my life as I have during this past year. Every time the conflict is renewed, at each challenge from the enemy, I give a good account of myself—by meeting him face to face? Oh no, only a coward accepts the challenge to a duel. No, I turn my back in contempt, and take refuge in Jesus, telling him that I'm ready to defend the doctrine of heaven with the last drop of my blood. What does it matter, that I should catch no glimpse of its beauties, here on earth, if that will help poor sinners to see them in eternity."*

Thérèse turned her pitch-black night to advantage. She identified with atheists, calling them her brothers and casting her lot with them. *"By way of asking pardon for these brothers of mine, I am ready to live on a starvation diet as long as You will have it so—not for me to rise from this unappetizing meal I share with poor sinners until the appointed time comes. Meanwhile, I can only pray in my own name, and in the name of these brothers of mine: 'Lord, have mercy on us, we are sinners! Send us home restored to your favor. May all those who have no torch of faith to guide them catch sight, at least, of its rays.' "*

The Night of Nothingness went on without remission for eleven more months, until the moment of her death. The importance of this final trial cannot be sufficiently stressed. God was stripping from her every vestige of selfishness and pride, fashioning her into a masterpiece of grace that was unique.

In her letter to Maurice there was no mention of the

cruel suffering she was enduring. It opened routinely with a formal explanation of why it was she and not Mother Gonzague who was answering him, and went at once to her distress over *his* suffering from the bitterness of the defeat he had experienced during his time in the army. She placed the blame for it not upon him but upon herself and rejoiced that *"the storm has passed."* She told him that he needed to go through that experience to learn how weak he was, that the humiliation was good for him and would help him become a better priest. *"He who has not been tempted, what does he know?"* she quoted from the Book of Sirach.

In one brief paragraph she disposed of his "worst blunder of all" and turned it into a grace which would help him, once he realized his dream of serving God in the missions. It did not seem to cross her mind to caution him that, if he was guilty of a serious lapse at this stage of his seminary training, perhaps he should give up the idea of going on for the priesthood. She would not allow him to be discouraged, but rallied his spirit to get up and go on from where he was. This was the task which she set for herself throughout her entire correspondence with Maurice, one of spiritual counseling and unfailing sisterly support.

She ended with the encouraging words *"I shall always be happy to call myself your unworthy little sister."*

My good little Sister,

The Lord is sending me a hard trial—as He does with those He loves—and I am very weak. Within a few days He will undoubtedly send me to the Seminary of the African Missions. My desire will at last be realized, but I still have to struggle with a lot. I have to break myself away from a number of cherished and strong attachments, as well as from some soft and expensive habits of easy living, from a whole pleasant and happy past which still strongly appeals to me. I need strength, my very dear Sister. Ask God to give me, with the clear light I need, the courage of a strong and a noble self-surrender—as well as zeal for His glory, with the humility that is the foundation of holiness. The missionary has to be a saint, and a saint I am not.

I've left the Major Seminary. Maybe I'll go back there for six more months, or maybe I shall leave within a few days. I'm waiting for a final decision.

Dear Sister, since you are my good angel, I entrust myself to your prayers again, always. The trial must be decisive, and I need all kinds of grace from God. As soon as the way opens up I shall let you know. Just now I'm taking a rest and staying with my family in Langrune in Calvados.

Sister, your letter last month encouraged me and was

good for me. If your kindness prompts you to write me again, this will be a great consolation and a further support for me.

My very dear sister, in the Heart of Jesus let us stay united in charity, in the apostolate, and in suffering.

Your miserable, very grateful and very devoted brother,

Maurice Barthélémy-Bellière
Aspiring Missionary

P.S. Pray also for my poor mother.
P.S. Your Mother Prioress, has she gotten back her health?

A Saint I Am Not

I n this first of his letters to Thérèse, Maurice was
candid about himself. He was eager for her to
know that she was committed to pray for a man
who could make no claims to greatness. Straight off in
the opening paragraph he stated his position clearly:
"A saint I am not." He wanted this new person in his
life, who he was sure was very holy, to know that he
was far from holy, that if he was ever to become a
missionary he would have to make a lot of changes,
and that she would have to pray very earnestly for
him.

While he was frank about his need for prayers, once
again Maurice was not totally forthcoming about recent events. He did not mention that the MEPs had
definitively rejected him, nor that they had done so
because his tonsure had been deferred by the seminary
in Sommervieu. In those days tonsure, the first step to
the clerical state, made one eligible for the minor and
major orders, which led to the priesthood. A seminarian could be deferred anywhere along his way through
the seminary. Deferment of orders was a warning to
the candidate that he was not, in the opinion of the
faculty, measuring up to expectations and would not
reach the priesthood unless he improved. For Maurice
the deferment of his tonsure ended his chances with

the MEPs, whose standards for acceptance were very high. The tone of this letter indicates that the rejection had cooled his confidence in himself, but he avoided details which troubled him. His reticence about facts in certain matters is interesting. On the one hand, he was very straightforward about his faults. He signed his letter "your miserable . . . brother," and it would not be the last time he would use the phrase. On the other hand, he concealed facts which reflected poorly on him. Later we shall notice an omission of something about which he was extremely sensitive. The omission will be understandable, but it will show that even with Thérèse he could not bring himself to tell all.

Thérèse, for her part, had her own areas of privacy in writing to Maurice, but her motive for not revealing certain things had nothing to do with protecting her self-esteem. She did not tell him the grim details of the sickness which was consuming her, and she never revealed to him the terrifying night of faith she was enduring. Sharing these things with him would do him no good and quite conceivably his own faith might have been disturbed if she had revealed her struggle over the reality of eternal life. She would tell him only what would help him, support him with her love, and encourage him along his path in the service of God.

Probably with the support of Father DeBarry, Maurice applied to another missionary community, the Society of the African Missions, then popularly known as the White Fathers because of the white robes they wore. While he was awaiting a reply from them, he went home to Langrune for a visit with his mother.

This rest period at home, away from the structured atmosphere of the seminary, was an anxious time for him. Thérèse had no difficulty in understanding his concerns, and she would make every effort to bolster his courage. At this time, she was functioning as the assistant Novice Mistress of the community, counseling young Sisters, helping them sort through their doubts and giving them a clear vision of what it meant to belong to one of the most austere religious orders in the Church. We know from the testimony of some of her novices how perceptive and realistic Thérèse was. One or two even thought she possessed the power to read their very souls, so accurate was the evaluation she sometimes gave them—a power she laughingly denied possessing.

We may be sure that as she read Maurice's letters she also read Maurice, gauged his qualities accurately, and observed his inconsistencies and anxieties with an objective eye. Like Father DeBarry, however, she never lost her confidence in him, and she was never shaken in her conviction that he had an authentic vocation both to the priesthood and to the missions.

Deeply concerned for his welfare, she wanted to respond at once to his letter, but Advent intervened and she was prevented from writing by the Carmelite rule forbidding correpondence during the penitential season. As soon as Christmas came, she let no more time go by before replying to him. She wrote on the very next day.

Jesus+
Monsieur l'Abbé,

I would have liked it if I could have answered you sooner, but the rule of Carmel doesn't allow us either to write or to receive letters during Advent.[14] However, by way of exception, our Reverend Mother let me read your letter, because she knew that you needed to be specially sustained by prayer.

I assure you, Monsieur l'Abbé, *that I am doing the very best I can to get you the graces you need. These graces will certainly be given you, because Our Lord never asks us for sacrifices that are beyond our strength. It is true that sometimes this divine Savior makes us taste all the bitterness of the chalice which He presents to our soul. When He asks the sacrifice of all that is most dear in this world it is impossible, apart from a very special grace, not to cry out as He did Himself in the Garden of His agony: "Father, let this chalice pass from me . . . nevertheless, not my will but Yours be done."*

It is most consoling to remember that Jesus, the Strong God, experienced our weakness, that He trembled at the sight of His Own bitter chalice, the very one which He had once so ardently desired to drink.[15]

---

[14] Four weeks of reflection and penance in preparation for the feast of Christmas.

[15] Luke 22:42.

Monsieur l'Abbé, *your lot is truly beautiful, since Our Lord chose it for Himself and first put His own lips to the cup which He now holds up to yours.*

A Saint has said: "The greatest honor that God can pay to anyone is not to give him much but to ask much from him!"[16] *Jesus, then, is treating you in a privileged way. He wants you to* begin your *mission already and to save souls through suffering. Isn't it by suffering and dying that He Himself redeemed the world?*

I know that you aspire to the joy of laying down your life for the divine Master, but martyrdom of the heart is no less fruitful than that of bloodshed, and from now on this martyrdom is yours; so I have good reason to say that your lot is a beautiful one and that it is worthy of an apostle of Christ.

Monsieur l'Abbé, *you come seeking consolation from the one whom Jesus has given you for a sister, and you have every right to do so. Since our Reverend Mother al-*

---

[16] Thérèse is referring to Père Almire Pichon, a friend of the Martin family and spiritual director of the Martin sisters. He left for Canada to preach parish missions and retreats for a number of years. Thérèse wrote approximately one hundred letters to him, all of which he destroyed. She remarked that her whole soul was in one particular letter.

She is generous in calling Pichon a saint. She also said of him once that he treated her too much like a child, from which we might gather that her admiration for him must not have been unqualified. Thérèse could be quite objective in estimating character, even that of a very good friend, which Père Pichon certainly was.

lows me to write you, I would like to carry out the pleasant mission she has given me, but I feel that the surest means of achieving my purpose is through prayer and suffering.

Let us work together for the salvation of souls. We have only the one day of this life to save them and thus to give Our Lord some proof of our love. The tomorrow of this day will be eternity, when Jesus will reward you with the hundredfold of those sweet and lawful joys which you are giving up for Him. He recognizes the extent of your sacrifice. He knows that the suffering of those who are dear to you adds to your own suffering. But He too suffered this martyrdom. To save souls He too left His Mother; and He looked down at the Immaculate Virgin standing at the foot of the Cross, with a sword of sorrow piercing her heart.

I also hope that our Divine Savior will console your dear Mother, and I urgently ask Him to do so. Ah! If the divine Master were to let those you are leaving for love of Him know the glory He has in store for you, and the host of souls who will form your cortege in heaven, they would already be rewarded for the great sacrifice your going away is going to cause them.

Our Mother is still not well. However for some days now she is a bit better. I hope that the divine Child Jesus will give her the strength to carry on for His glory. This beloved Mother sends you a picture of St. Francis of Assisi, who will teach you how to find joy in the midst of life's trials and struggles.

I hope, Monsieur l'Abbé, *that you will continue to pray for me, who am no angel as you seem to think, but a poor little Carmelite who is very imperfect—yet who in spite of her poverty wants, like yourself, to work for the glory of God.*

Let us stay united in prayer and suffering, close to the crib of Jesus.

Your unworthy little sister
Thérèse of the Child Jesus
and of the Holy Face
rel. carm. ind.

The Christmas Miracle

hérèse left no doubt in this second letter to Maurice that she was pleased to correspond with him. She replied at the first opportunity, explaining that she would have done so sooner if she could have. The task of writing him was a *"pleasant mission,"* and she spoke of his right to seek consolation from her letters.

At the same time it was clear to her that the prayer and suffering which she offered to God for his welfare were much more useful to him than the letters she might write. Her conviction on the point was crystal clear. She was a Carmelite, devoting her life to prayer and sacrifice for others, especially for priests and the conversion of sinners. She remembered the saying of Archimedes: "Give me a fulcrum and I will lift the world." Prayer was her fulcrum, she said, and she would use it to lift up the world.

As for suffering, she was convinced of its immense power to win God's grace for others. The mystery of the Cross stands at the center of the Catholic faith, which holds that we are saved not so much by the preaching of Jesus nor by the goodness of His life, but precisely by His suffering and death on the Cross. Thérèse believed this without compromise, and she wanted personally to participate in the mystery of the

Cross—to live it. She would not leave the One she loved with all her heart alone in His agony. When she entered religious life she was named Sister Thérèse of the Child Jesus. Afterward she added: "And of the Holy Face," a reference to Jesus whose face was bruised and bloodied and whose head was crowned with thorns. Of the two titles, she much preferred the second. To share His Passion she welcomed all the pain that came to her—not out of love for suffering but out of love for Him. For Thérèse there was no such thing as "cheap grace." Grace was bought at a high price and she wanted to pay her share.

Suffering had come to her when she was very young. In the opening of her autobiography she spoke of three stages in her life. The first lasted until she was four and a half and was marked by great happiness. *"Everything on this earth smiled on me,"* she wrote, recalling the love of her adoring parents and sisters and their joyful times together. The death of her mother was the beginning of the second stage, which Thérèse said was *"the most painful of the three"* and which lasted until she was fourteen years old. Most of her pain during this time was psychological. A happy and cheerful child until then, she changed into one who was deeply serious, shy in the presence of strangers, extremely sensitive, and given to frequent tears. This phase reached a crisis when she was ten in what might be called a complete nervous breakdown. It was provoked by the sudden departure of Pauline, who had been her second mother for six years and who, almost with no warning, joined the Carmelites, leaving Thérèse without her much-needed support. For two months after Pauline left, Thérèse went through an episode which no doctor at the time could diagnose and which psychologists have since examined without an exact conclusion. She had terrifying hallucinations, thrashed about in her bed, even banged her head against its wooden posts. Fearing for her life, her family prayed one day in desperation before a statue of the Blessed Virgin in her room. Suddenly she was cured. The cure was instantaneous and permanent, and they always considered it miraculous.

But her excessive sensitivity continued to plague her and peaked again at the age of twelve with an attack of scrupulosity which lasted for a year and a half. Scrupulosity is an anxiety neurosis which torments its victims with painful feelings of guilt over thoughts or actions that, in fact, are not sinful at all. It can, for instance, focus on sexual images which obsess the imagination against one's will. They become obsessive for the very reason that they are the last thing about which the person actually wishes to be imagining. This was almost certainly the form of scruples experienced by Thérèse. Today the malady is treated, and usually cured, by psychotherapy. The only "therapist" available to her was her oldest sister, Marie, who took the place of Pauline as her mother when Pauline entered the Carmel. Marie was a rock of common sense who counseled her adolescent sister with patience and firmness and kept her fears under control, but she was not a trained psychotherapist and the malady persisted. Then Marie suddenly decided, like Pauline, to become a Carmelite. The news took everyone by surprise, for Marie never gave the impression of being especially pious. Papa's nickname for her was "the Bohemian," because of her nonchalance about things in general, including matters of religious practice.

Once again Thérèse was deprived of a "mother" in the midst of a painful personal crisis. When Marie departed for the cloister, Thérèse felt alone and trapped in her neurosis. Left with no alternative, she turned in prayer to the four brothers and sisters who had died in infancy and who the family believed were in heaven. Thérèse pleaded with them in her apparently hopeless situation. After all, she reasoned with them, she was their youngest sister and they had to help her. Her prayers were answered. To her great relief, she soon was set free from the psychological tyranny of scruples.

But her extreme sensitivity which plagued her while growing up did not go away with the scruples. It remained a pronounced flaw in her character, about which she spoke with remarkable candor in her autobiography: *"I was truly impossible because of my oversensitivity. If it should happen that involuntarily I had caused some slight to a person whom I loved, instead of rising above it and not bewailing it (which only made my original offense greater) I would weep like a Magdalen. Then, when I had begun to be reconciled to the fact itself, I would weep for having wept! All endeavors to reach a reasonable attitude in this matter were unavailing, and I was unable to correct this nasty fault."*

On Christmas 1886 this fault was dramatically corrected. At long last she emerged from her troubled adolescence through an experience she never forgot. When she and Céline returned with Papa from midnight Mass and entered their living room, under the chimney were her slippers, filled with presents, a custom Céline had continued ever since Thérèse was a little girl. She was delighted as usual, but Papa, thinking his youngest should have outgrown this custom, was clearly annoyed. As she went upstairs to take off her hat, she heard him say to Céline: "Fortunately, this will be the last year!" He didn't intend that she hear the remark but Céline saw that she did and knew the effect it would have on her. She went to caution her sister to get hold of herself, but Thérèse, forcing back tears, walked rapidly down the stairs. In her autobiography she recalled the pounding of her heart. She picked up the slippers and brought them to her father. With unfeigned gaiety she tore the wrappings from her presents and thanked him for them one by one. Forgetting his displeasure, he was soon laughing with her and enjoying the little ritual as much as he ever did. From that day until the end of her life, she never cried over trifles again.

For most of us such an experience would pass and be forgotten. For Thérèse it was a "miracle" and was stamped upon her memory as the greatest grace of her life. For ten years she had battled her childish immaturity and simply could not overcome it. What she was not able to do in all that time for herself, God accomplished in a single moment. *"It was the grace of my complete conversion,"* she wrote emphatically in her autobiography, and we shall see how much turned upon it. In such ordinary ways her graces always came to her, without fanfare, in the routine of daily life.

The Christmas miracle inaugurated the final and *"most beautiful"* period of her life, a time she recalled as being filled with grace. *"I felt God's love enter my soul, the need to forget myself and please others. I felt a great desire to work for the conversion of sinners which I had never felt so intensely before."*

The desire was put to work at once. Just at that time, the papers were filled with the trial of a notorious criminal named Pranzini. He was finally convicted for the murder of two women and a young girl. Nobody in France was more widely despised, but Thérèse was filled with concern for him and, dismayed by his obstinate refusal to be reconciled to God, she prayed ardently for his conversion. On the day following his execution she eagerly read the account in the newspaper. To her delight, at the last moment as he mounted the scaffold to the guillotine, he seized the crucifix from the chaplain's hand and devoutly kissed the wounds of Christ. She had asked God for some sign of his repentance and she took that final dramatic gesture as God's answer. She always looked upon Pranzini as her first convert, and from then on she prayed with unlimited confidence for the salvation of others, especially if they were in particular need of prayers. Significantly, in recounting the story she added that even if no sign had been given, she would still have believed in Pranzini's salvation. But, of course, she was delighted with the sign, which she took as further encouragement to trust implicitly in God's readiness to answer her prayers.

While the Christmas miracle brought an end to her tears, it did not bring an end to her suffering. But she who for years had cried over trifles, now greeted even the most intense suffering with a smile—not a smile forced onto her face with an effort, but one which welled up from the reserves of peace and joy in the deep interior of her soul.

Writing to Maurice on the day after Christmas, Thérèse endeavored to initiate him into the mystery and the meaning of suffering. *"Our Lord never asks us for sacrifices that are beyond our strength. . . . When he asks the sacrifice of all that is most dear in this world it is impossible . . . not to cry out as He did Himself in the Garden of His agony: 'Father, let this chalice pass from me . . . nevertheless, not my will but Yours be done.' It is most consoling to remember that Jesus, the Strong God, experienced our weakness. . . . Monsieur l'Abbé, your lot is truly beautiful, since Our Lord . . . first put His Own lips to the cup which He now holds up to yours."* If he was to be a missionary, he had to be ready to suffer in union with Christ.

But he should not worry that he was not yet a saint. Neither was she, she assured him. "Monsieur l'Abbé, *. . . pray for me, who am no angel as you seem to think, but a poor little Carmelite who is very imperfect—yet who in spite of her poverty wants, like yourself, to work for the glory of God."*

She still had a way to go on her journey, though she was close by now to its end. Maurice had a much longer road to travel on his, but she never doubted that he would reach the journey's goal, nor that she would be able to help him along his way.

R.A.[17]

My very dear Sister in Our Lord,

The goodness God shows me is very touching, and that goodness which He has imparted to you is working in the depths of my soul. I am greatly cheered up by the care your kindness bestows on me. I feel myself becoming better each time a bit of the holiness lived at Carmel comes my way. I wish I could love Jesus as all of you do there.

Sister, when you were composing that canticle of love which you were good enough to have sent me, you had Him in your heart. One breathes in from it a divine inspiration which makes one pure and strong. On the evening of the day when I had the joy of receiving the poem, it was the object of a long and delightful meditation in the company of my Director, who is so happy to know that my soul and my work are entrusted to your care. Since then I have used it the day before yesterday and today as my prayer of thanksgiving. I'm going to learn it by heart and use it as an ejaculatory prayer during the day, and at night when I wake up. I have put it in my New Testament and since that holy book never leaves me, this canticle of love will always accompany me, even to the end of the world.

I would like to be able to write poetry like you, dear

---

[17] *Regina Apostolorum,* Queen of Apostles.

Sister, so that I could tell Jesus the feelings which your own inspire in me. But He, Who is goodness itself, sees fit to grant me only my rough and ready prose. His Heart is so kind that He pays little attention to form, and His Grace is always coming down upon us.

When I baptize my first little native baby, I shall ask your Reverend Mother to let you be the godmother, for he will belong to you. You more than I shall have brought him to God. À Dieu, my very dear Sister, pray always for my conversion, that the Master may produce some progress in me. I pray to Him for you often and very earnestly.

Forever in His holy Heart, your miserable brother,

M. Barthélémy-Bellière

a.m.

I ask your prayers especially for the examinations which begin tomorrow, Monday, and end on the 14th.

"To Live by Love"

It is evident that in this second letter Maurice began to open up with Thérèse, as he was drawn more closely into the orbit of her inspired thought. What caused him to react so strongly was the poem which Mother Gonzague had sent him, *"Vivre d'Amour"* ("To Live by Love"). Deeply impressed, he showed it to his spiritual director, Father DeBarry, who evidently was as fascinated by it as he. Together they made it the subject of their meditation.

"To Live by Love" is a lengthy poem of fifteen stanzas, each containing eight lines. The way it was conceived is noteworthy. Thérèse composed it in the chapel during the Forty Hours Eucharistic Devotion, without writing it down. When she went back to her cell, she wrote word for word what had come to her spontaneously during her time of prayer. Her memory was prodigious and her power of concentration extraordinary. Far more astonishing than the way she composed it, however, is the richness of its content, which probes the mystery of love to its depth. Many consider "To Live by Love" the finest of her sixty-two poems, and it is a tribute to the perceptiveness of Mother Gonzague that it was the first of Thérèse's poems that she sent to Maurice. He saw the poem's worth at once. His letter spoke of almost nothing but his reaction to it.

Love, the theme of the poem, was the central reality of Thérèse's life: God's love for her and her love for God, fused into one with her love for everyone she encountered. It was the intensity of this love that set the missionary spirit on fire in her heart. Two years earlier, it had been suggested that she might be assigned to the new Carmel in Hanoi, Vietnam, and she desperately longed to go there. She was prevented from doing so by the bad turn in her health. But she was already a missionary in her heart and this helps to explain her strong attachment to Maurice. The two would work together to increase the ranks of those in the world who would give Him the love for which He longed. *"To love Him and to make Him loved"* was the purpose for which she lived, to which she added characteristically, *"and to give pleasure to others."*

The key word in the title of the poem is *live*. Loving became her very life, the meaning of her existence. Eventually she *became* love. In her autobiography, she discussed the day she first fully realized this. It was the sixth anniversary of taking her vows and she was in her cell, writing her reflections on the past several weeks. She knew she was skirting an issue. She had wanted to become a cloistered Sister ever since she was young, but as she came closer to God, she was no longer satisfied with this vocation. Something else was beckoning her, something which she knew by a deep intuition was to be her unique destiny. What was *this* vocation? She longed to be a priest and carry her Lord in her hands, but she admired St. Francis of Assisi, who out of humility elected to remain a deacon. She wanted to travel the world, preaching the word of God, but she also aspired to be like the Doctors of the Church, enlightening souls with their understanding of the Gospel. And she dreamed of dying a martyr's death, but which death would she choose, since she would gladly endure all martyrdoms?

While she knew the folly of such desires, Thérèse did not take them lightly. She believed that God did not inspire desires in her without wanting to fulfill them. She picked up the New Testament in search of an answer and opened to St. Paul's letter to the Corinthians. She read his words: "The Church is composed of different members just as the body is—the eye cannot be the hand at one and the same time. To each his own." Unsatisfied, she pressed on until she came to his passage on the importance of love: "I point out to you a more excellent way." Its familiar words were like a streak of lightning in a dark sky. "If I have all the eloquence of men or of angels, but speak without love, I am simply a gong booming or a cymbal clashing." She leaped at the passage, discovering that for which she was searching. *"I finally had rest,"* she wrote. *"Con-*

sidering the mystical body of the Church, I had not recognized myself in any of the members described by St. Paul, or rather I desired to see myself in all of them. Love gave me the key to my vocation. . . . I understood it was Love alone that made the Church's members act. I HAVE FOUND MY PLACE IN THE CHURCH. In the heart of the Church, my Mother, I shall be Love. . . . Thus I shall be everything, and thus my dream will be realized."

A scholar might say she took liberties with the text of Paul, but she found her vocation in reading his words and was glad to give him credit. The capital letters printed in her manuscript and the exultation of her prose reveal the excitement of her great discovery. Thérèse pushed love to the limits of its meaning and anchored it in its foundation, which is God. She aspired to *be* love, even as God himself is Love. No other saint we know of ever entertained such an aspiration.

Each of the fifteen stanzas of *"Vivre d'Amour"* spells out the reality of love in the various ways in which Thérèse conceived and experienced it, so that the poem may be said to contain her whole theology of love. The boldness of her vision is astonishing. It became clear the night she knelt in the chapel adoring the Blessed Sacrament, and she expressed it beautifully in the poem she composed while she tried to pray. *"Vivre d'Amour"* is not a poem readily understood. One has to dig deep in its verses for the treasure they contain, as Maurice and Father DeBarry did during their long hours of meditation on it. Maurice carried it with him wherever he went and often returned to it for the inspiration it always gave him.

Thursday night
February 24, 1897

Jesus+
Monsieur l'Abbé,

   *Before we enter into the silence of the holy forty days,[18]
I want to add a little word to our Beloved Mother's letter,
to thank you for the one you sent me last month.*

   *If you find consolation in knowing that in Carmel a
Sister prays without ceasing for you, my gratitude is no less
than yours to Our Lord Who has given me a little brother
whom He is choosing to become His Priest and Apostle.
Truly, only in heaven will you know how dear you are to
me. I feel our souls are made to understand each other.
Your prose, which you call "rough and ready," reveals to
me that Jesus has put desires into your heart that He gives
only to those called to the highest holiness. Since He Himself has chosen me to be your sister, I hope that he will not
take notice of my weakness, or rather that He will use that
very weakness to do His work; for the Strong God likes to
show His power by making use of nothing.[19] United in
Him, our souls will be able to save many others, for this
kindly Jesus has said: "If two among you agree together on
something which they ask from my Father, it will be given*

---

[18] The forty penitential days of Lent were to begin on March 3. Normally in a
Carmelite cloister no letters would be written or received during that time.

[19] 1 Corinthians 1:27–29.

to them."[20] *Ah! What we ask of Him is to work for His glory, to love Him and make Him loved. How should our union and our prayers not be blessed?*

Monsieur l'Abbé, since the canticle on love has given you pleasure, our good Mother has told me to copy for you a number of my other poems, but it will be some weeks before you receive them because I have little free time, even on Sunday, on account of my sacristan's work. These poor poems will reveal to you not what I am but what I would like to be and ought to be. In composing them I have paid attention more to substance than to form. Also, the rules of versification aren't always honored. My aim was to convey my feeling (or rather those of a Carmelite) in answer to my Sister's requests. These verses are more suitable for a religious woman than for a seminarian, but I hope they will give you some pleasure. Is not your soul the fiancée of the divine Lamb and will it not soon become His spouse on the happy day of your ordination to Subdiaconate?[21]

Thank you, Monsieur l'Abbé, *for choosing me as god-*

---

[20] Matthew 18:19.

[21] In those days, before the liturgical reforms of the Second Vatican Council, the commitment of celibacy was made at subdiaconate. The order of subdiaconate has been eliminated and the commitment of celibacy is now made when a candidate is ordained a deacon. Thérèse pointed to the profound meaning of celibacy. It is not so much a promise to give up marriage as it is a choice of another kind of marriage. Instead of being bonded to another human being, a celibate is bonded in a spiritual marriage to Christ and, through this sacred bond, is committed until death to the service of His Mystical Body, the Church.

mother for the first child you will have the joy of baptiz-ing. *It is, then, for me to choose the names of my future godchild. I wish to give him as his protectors the Holy Virgin, St. Joseph, and St. Maurice, the patron of my little brother. Granted that this child exists as yet only in the mind of God, nevertheless I am praying for him already and doing my duty as a godmother in advance. I pray also for all the souls who will be confided to your care, and above all I beg Jesus to embellish your own soul with every virtue, and especially with His love. You tell me that you pray very often for your sister. Since you have the goodness to do this, I would be very happy if you will agree to say this prayer for her every day. It sums up all her desires: "Merciful Father, in the name of our lovable Jesus, of the Virgin Mary and of the Saints, I ask You to set my sister on fire with Your Spirit of Love, and to grant her the grace of making You deeply loved."*

You have promised to pray for me for the rest of your life. *No doubt your life will be longer than mine, so you cannot sing as I do: "I hope that my exile will be brief.*[22] *But you're not allowed ever to forget your promise. If the Lord takes me to Himself soon, I ask you to continue saying the same little prayer every day, because in heaven I shall want the same thing that I want on earth: to love Jesus and to make Him loved.*

Monsieur l'Abbé, *you must find me very strange.*

---

[22] A line from her poem *"Vivre d'Amour."*

Maybe you regret having a sister who seems to want to go to enjoy eternal rest and leave you to labor on alone. But let me assure you, the only thing I desire is God's Will, and I want you to know that if in heaven I would no longer be able to work for His glory, then I would far prefer the exile to the homeland.

I don't know the future, but if Jesus makes my premonition come true, I promise to remain your little sister in heaven. Far from being broken, our union will become a closer one, for then there will be no more cloister and no more grills, and my soul will be free to fly with you to the missions far away. Our roles will still be the same. Yours will be apostolic labor, and mine will be prayer and love.

Monsieur l'Abbé, *I notice I'm forgetting myself. It is late and the bell is going to ring in a few minutes for the Divine Office. But I have one last thing to ask you. I would very much like you to send me the memorable dates of your life, so that I can be united with you in a very special way, to thank our Beloved Savior for the graces He has given you.*

In the Sacred Heart of Jesus in the Blessed Sacrament, which will soon be exposed for our adoration, I am happy to call myself forever:

> *Your very little and unworthy sister*
> *Thérèse of the Child Jesus*
> *and of the Holy Face*
> *rel. carm. ind.*

An Author, but Not by Choice

With the approach of Lent, Thérèse was eager to send Maurice a letter which would carry him through forty days of silence. If he was grateful for their relationship, so was she, and she was very straightforward in saying so. *"Truly, only in heaven will you know how dear you are to me,"* she told him. *"I feel our souls are made to understand each other."* This was a very open declaration of friendship, which must have touched him deeply. *"How dear you are to me"* are not words spoken lightly. This was only Thérèse's third letter to him, and already their relationship was very close, and one in which she did not hesitate to take the initiative.

She referred again to her own imperfections, with which she had to contend. In many of her letters to him she will come back to the point. They were equal partners and he must not idealize her, thinking that because she was a cloistered nun she must be perfect. She saw herself as far from perfect, having constantly to seek God's forgiveness for her shortcomings. She too was human. Thérèse never separated herself from the company of sinners, never thought of herself as anything but a sinner, and so she asked for his prayers and composed one for him to say for her every day: *"Merciful Father, in the name of our lovable Jesus, of the*

Virgin Mary and of the Saints, I ask You to set my sister on fire with Your Spirit of Love, and to grant her the grace of making You deeply loved." It is a simple prayer of only one sentence, but it captures the essence of Thérèse. The Father is addressed as the *Merciful Father;* she prayed in the name of Jesus first, but then in union with the Virgin Mary and all the saints, and she asked for only one thing, that He would send into her heart the Spirit of *His* Love and use her as an instrument to win for Him the love of others. She stressed that Maurice must say the prayer for the rest of his life.

This is the first letter in which she made direct reference to her impending death. No doubt he had not missed the reference in her poem to the fact that her exile would be brief, and here again she raised the possibility that she would die before he did. It was now almost a full year since her lungs had begun to hemorrhage. The disease was claiming victims throughout France by the hundreds of thousands, and almost every week someone—usually a young person—died from it in Lisieux. It was clear what the future held for her, and she wanted her brother to be warned.

Thérèse would not let Maurice criticize his prose as "rough and ready." She did not find it so. She was just in the process of copying several more poems for him as Mother Gonzague had suggested. In these poems, she told him, she paid attention *"more to substance than to form."* She did not write for effect nor cultivate style. In fact, she was an author not by personal choice but out of obedience to her superiors, who commanded her to write. On the cover of each notebook in which her manuscripts of the autobiography are found, she wrote the words *"Notebook of Obedience."* Unlike *"Vivre d'Amour,"* almost all of her sixty-two poems were written on request or to celebrate the feast day of one of the sisters, and her eight short plays were written as "pious recreations" for the entertainment of the community.

The first part of her autobiography, Manuscript A, was written at the command of Pauline when she was Prioress. One winter night the Martin sisters—Marie, Pauline, Céline, and Thérèse—were warming themselves at the fireplace in the recreation room, the only heated area in the convent. Thérèse, a gifted storyteller and mimic, was regaling her sisters with recollections of their years in Les Buissonnets, the home in Lisieux to which they moved after their mother died. Marie suggested that she put these recollections in writing. Thérèse thought she was joking and laughed aloud. Realizing that Thérèse did not take her seriously and would never write them unless her superior commanded her to do so, Marie asked Pauline as the Prioress to place her under obedience, which she did.

It was Marie who also prompted the writing of

Manuscript B, just a few months earlier during Thérèse's annual retreat. Marie asked her to clarify what she meant by the Little Way. Thérèse responded with a letter to Marie, which has been incorporated into the autobiography as Manuscript B. It is considered the best of her writing and contains the core of her revolutionary thought.

Manuscript C which was not yet written at this time, would be requested by Mother Gonzague at the prompting of Pauline. She would ask Thérèse to finish her memoirs by recounting the story of her experience as a Carmelite. Thérèse began to write Manuscript C in the beginning of June 1897, four months before she died, and finished it in a month.

Her writings are extensive. She wrote more prose than St. John of the Cross, the great Spanish Doctor of the Church in the sixteenth century, and three times more poetry than he—which is astonishing in light of the fact that he lived to age forty-nine and she died at twenty-four. She was a prodigy. If the bell sounded, she put down her pen at once, and the next day was able to continue where she had left off, without apparent difficulty. When asked how she could write with such facility, she smiled and replied: *"I write whatever comes out of my pen."* Sometimes she would interrupt her thought to drop in a witty aside, as when she remarked: *"I'm running out of ink and just had to spit in the inkwell."*

Nobody has ever acclaimed St. Thérèse as a great stylist, but her prose is candid and clear. Her words convey what she wants them to say. They carry great depths of meaning, yet one seldom has a hard search to find it. Simplicity reigns in every line. And occasionally, especially when she is describing nature, passages soar to surprising heights of eloquence. As with all true art, her writings can be revisited often, and with every reading their meaning deepens. They are alive, like the great paintings which hang in museums, waiting for viewers to come back to admire them once more.

The ten letters she wrote to Maurice are among the longest she wrote to anyone, and they are especially rich because they were written at the high point of her life. For a long time they belonged to him alone. When he died in 1907, the executor of his will gave them back to the Carmel. During his lifetime, we know that he read them over and over. We may be sure that he especially loved this third letter, and often went back to dwell on the great promise which she made him and which she repeated a number of times in later letters: *"Monsieur l'Abbé, you must find me very strange. Maybe you regret having a sister who seems to want to go to enjoy eternal rest and leave you to labor on alone. But let me assure you, the only thing I desire is God's Will. . . . I don't know the future, but if Jesus makes my premonition come true, I promise to remain your little sister in heaven. Far from being broken, our union will become a closer one, for then there will be no more cloister and no more grills, and my soul will be free to fly with you to the missions far away. Our roles will still be the same. Yours will be apostolic labor, and mine will be prayer and love."*

How many nights he must have read those words by the light of his kerosene lamp, and as he drifted into slumber how they must have brought peace at the close of a day.

Alleluia!

My good and very dear little Sister,

Today Our Lord lets us pitch our tent on Tabor,[23] which only yesterday was set up at the foot of the Cross on Calvary—yesterday tears and mourning, today the joyous Alleluia. And how better to rejoice and sing than in a family? So I come to join my sister and my Mother in blessing Jesus for the joy He gives us after accepting our penance of Lent; and I lose no time in telling you all the pleasure you gave me with those poems you had the kindness to copy out for me. This must have taken a good piece of your recreation time, and I would almost ask your pardon for having caused you all this work—except that I don't want to insist on that too much, because they have really given me so much pleasure.

Sister, you're not expecting me to give you a critique of them. I wouldn't dream of doing that, knowing perfectly well that I'd not be up to the task. Just be sure that I've been very taken and happy with them. This is no empty compliment I'm giving you, but the expression of what I truly feel.

---

[23] Tabor is traditionally the mountain on which Jesus was seen by Peter, James and John as transfigured in glory and speaking to Moses and Elijah.

You were writing for Carmelite Sisters, but the Angels must have been singing with you, and men, inelegant like myself though they be, will find genuine pleasure in reading and singing this poetry of the heart. I was pleased with all of them, but especially perhaps with: My Song of Today, To Théophane Vénard *(and with good reason),*[24] Remember, To My Guardian Angel, *etc.—forgive me, it looks like I'm going to mention all of them! Yes, every one of them pleased and delighted me. Simply but sincerely I thank you for your kindness.*

You know how to manage all the nuances: gentleness with the Sacristans of Carmel right alongside the masculine accents of the warrior in My Weapons. *I love to hear you speak of the lance, the helmet, the breastplate, the athlete, and I smiled at the thought of seeing you armed in this way. However, Joan of Arc—whom you love and whom I myself pray to* every single day *under the title which I am glad to see at the end of the poem* SAINT JOAN OF FRANCE[25]—*she actually wore them; and she also carried those arms you sing about, which doubtless are her finest adornment.*

Sister, I will be faithful to the little prayer you sent me, and that is a solemn promise. I will say it always, even if

---

[24] Father Théophane Vénard was a missionary who had recently been martyred in China. He went to his death gallantly and was popularly honored in France. He has since been canonized.

[25] Joan of Arc had not yet been canonized.

your exile proves short. I had not missed what you were telling me, Sister; I had underlined that phrase in your Canticle of Love: *"I have the hope that my exile will be brief," and that other one: "I sense it, my exile is about to end." I understand your desires, your impatience. Little Sister, you're ready to go to Heaven and your Spouse Jesus can at any moment reach out His hand and lead you to the throne of glory. Like the Bride in the Canticle you are impatient: "Draw me to Yourself," she says, languishing at the feet of her Beloved, swooning in the flame which consumes her.*

While analyzing and reflecting upon this Canticle of Canticles, I was applying it to the Carmelite and her Jesus, and it's doubtless for that reason that I've written quite naturally in this vein, and that here and there some verses of To Live by Love *and other poems came to range themselves side by side with the Canticle.*

And you're correct when you say that I can't sing like you! No, in all truth. I have first to make God forget my sinful past by hard work and repentance, and after that do something for Him, work in His vineyard.[26] Before being in a place of honor Joan of Arc had to suffer, and I more than anyone else have reparation to make. And if I ever get there I will say to you then: Sister, beg God that I may be subjected to suffering. Ask him—why not?—

---

[26] Matthew 20:1.

that I may die a martyr! *This was my dream all my life. In the past I wanted to die for France, today I want to die for God. And you know: "If to die for one's country is a glorious thing, when one dies for God, how great such a death will be!"*[27]

I still have much to reply to in your letter, but I'm running out of time so I'll bring this to a close. . . . But excuse me, you asked for some dates. Thank you for that kind thought. I celebrate my birth and baptism on the 10th of June. (The date of the latter is listed as June 25th, but the nun who took care of me at birth felt I should be baptized.)[28] *My first Communion day is June 7th. My admission to the Confraternity of St. Joseph took place on September 21st, to that of the Blessed Virgin and St. Aloysius Gonzaga on the 8th of December, and on that same day, December 8th, my reception of the cassock took place and my acceptance as an Aspiring Missionary. October 15th was the day of your kindness to me and of the promise I made to remember you in the memento of Mass and offer other good works for you for all my days until eternity. Whatever has happened to me, be it joyous or sad, has almost always happened in June. This is the month*

---

[27] A line from a play by Corneille.

[28] He was thought to be in danger of dying and was baptized in the hospital. Two weeks later, on June 25, the solemn ritual known as the "supplying of the Ceremonies" was performed in church by a priest and the Church register shows that as the date of his baptism.

when I gave up the idea of Military School, which I was getting ready to enter, in order to turn toward Jesus Who was calling me to other conquests.

And you yourself, my very dear Sister, celebrate dates to remember. Will you let me associate myself with them? Next January, at least, I shall celebrate the Silver Anniversary of your birth; and that will be from Africa, I hope.

I thank you also for the names you sent for your godchild, but don't you want to bestow names in memory of yourself on some little Bedouin, in case the first should be a girl? I beg you to be so kind.

Since your exile still continues, my sister, please continue to give me the delightful consolation of sharing with me your beautiful and holy thoughts. You will never know the good they do me. The breeze that blows from the Carmel to refresh my feverish and tired head makes me a better person by renewing my fervor.

My very dear and very good little sister, in the Heart of Jesus Who is the Mediator between our souls I assure you once again of prayers and of the deeply respectful devotion of your miserable brother,

M. Barthélémy-Bellière

Leo Taxil

he long seven weeks of Lent were over and
Maurice lost no time in answering Thérèse's
letter of February 24. This was his third letter
to her and it gives indications that their relationship
continued to grow. He was more confident in compli-
menting her, and she must have been consoled to read
what he had to say at a time in her life that was extremely difficult. He was anxious to tell her how much
pleasure he had gotten from reading the poems which
Mother Gonzague had sent him. Thérèse was mistaken, he said, in thinking that since they were written
for Carmelite Sisters they would not appeal to men.
For his part, they appealed to him strongly and he was
enthusiastic in his praise of them.

He gladly complied with her request for the significant dates in his life. Celebrating important dates was
a custom with which she had grown up, and he was
honored that she wanted to know his. It was a first
step in making her new brother a member of the family.

Their friendship was further cemented by the
prayer she had composed for him to say for the rest of
his life, even after she died. He promised that he
would always be faithful to it, even if her "exile" did
prove to be short. He had taken note of her reference

to that possibility in her last letter, and indeed had not overlooked her mention of the nearness of death in her poem. He was beginning to fear that she would not be with him long, but he would not come to grips with the fact of her imminent death until later, when she was in the final stages of her tuberculosis.

Thérèse must have taken special comfort from his enthusiastic reaction to her poem on Joan of Arc. His letter arrived the day after an event took place which caused a sensation in the press and which, by a strange turn of events, brought her unexpectedly to public notice and profoundly humiliated her. It happened as a consequence of a play she had written about the famous heroine of France.

At the time, a battle was raging in France between the Catholic Church and Freemasonry, a secular movement with religious overtones which was openly hostile to the Church. At the center of the struggle for more than two years was an American woman named Diana Vaughan. She came to the attention of the public through the newspaper articles of a certain Leo Taxil,[29] who described her activities in behalf of Freemasonry in the United States. His description was sensational. He said that she was in

---

[29] Leo Taxil was a pen name for Gabriel Jogand-Pages. An anticleric and a journalist of sorts, he was born in Marseilles in 1854 and died in 1907.

league with the devil, who endowed her with dia-
bolic cunning to undermine the Church. Taxil's articles attracted great attention.

In the midst of her career as an anti-Catholic, Diana
was spectacularly converted and, eager to make
amends for the harm she had caused the Church, she
wanted to become a religious and spend her life in
penance and prayer. She attributed her conversion to
the influence and prayer of Joan of Arc, who had not
yet been canonized but was widely venerated by
French Catholics. Naturally the conversion of Diana
through the influence of Joan created a sensation. Thérèse, an ardent devotee of Joan, had written her first
play about her, which was staged by the community in
the Carmel. Her sister Céline acted in the play, and
Thérèse herself took the part of Joan. A photograph
was taken of the two in costume. Pauline suggested
that Thérèse write to Diana and send her a copy of the
photograph. Diana sent a courteous letter of thanks in
return.

Meanwhile, in spite of all the attention given to Diana Vaughan, she had never appeared in public. When
Leo Taxil was questioned about this, he replied that
she could not come out in the open for fear of the
revenge which the Freemasons would take for the
damage her conversion had done to their order. However, when he was pursued on the matter, he called a
press conference to be held in Paris, at which both he

and Diana were to speak. Scheduled for April 19, 1897, the conference received enormous attention, and a large number of French reporters were present for it. A hall was chosen for it, and one of the props on display was an enlarged photograph of Thérèse in the garb of Joan of Arc.

At the appointed hour Leo Taxil appeared, but he did not bring Diana Vaughan. The reason, he explained triumphantly, was that no such person existed. He gleefully announced that she was a creature of his imagination, invented to expose the gullibility of the Catholic Church. Almost all Catholics, even Pope Leo XIII, had been duped by the deception. If they could be made to believe such a ridiculous invention of his imagination, then what could be said of the teachings of the Church which they swallowed without a question?

It was Leo Taxil and not "Diana Vaughan" to whom Thérèse had written, and the letter from "Diana" which she still had in her cell was the work of a cruel impostor. It was he, too, who had arranged the display of her photograph at the press conference for all the world to see.[30]

---

[30] Taxil concocted this hoax in the Paris attic where he did his work. The name Diana Vaughan was not entirely an invention; it was the name of a woman who had been his secretary and did much of his typing. No doubt his use of her name added to his amusement, and presumably to hers. In 1904 he wrote a

To be the victim of so preposterous a hoax was personally humiliating, but that was not what troubled Thérèse deeply. She was an expert at handling humiliation and knew the benefit it could be to her soul. What tried her to the breaking point was the assault which the episode made on her faith, already under a heavy barrage of doubt at the time. To the inner voice which tantalized her with the threat of nonexistence after death was added the mocking voice of Leo Taxil. If, after all, he could succeed in perpetrating such a fraud, had he not unmasked the gullibility of her faith in eternal life?

The darkness overshadowing her mind grew darker still, but the darker it became, the more fiercely she clung to the faith which never wavered in her heart, a faith which was blind and offered not an ounce of consolation. "Here is a person," the well-known theologian Father Karl Rahner has said of Thérèse, "who died in the mortal temptation to empty unbelief, right down to the roots of her being, and who *in* that condition believed. She believed as she was smothering with consumption."

To the best of our knowledge Thérèse never mentioned Leo Taxil again, save in the prayers she offered

---

tract entitled *The Art of Buying,* a guide for purchasers to guard them against the fraudulent claims of advertising!

for him with love. She carried her pain in a silence that was eloquent. In silence she walked to a pile of refuse behind the convent, tore up the hateful letter from "Diana Vaughan," and left the pieces to be burned.

My dear little Brother,

My pen, or rather my heart, refuses to call you "Monsieur l'Abbé," and our good Mother has told me that from now on, in writing you I may use the name I always use when I speak of you to Jesus. It seems to me that this Divine Savior has wanted to unite our souls so that we might work for the salvation of sinners, as He once united those of the Venerable Father de la Colombière and Blessed Margaret Mary. Recently I read in the Life of that Saint: "One day when I was approaching Our Savior to receive Him in Holy Communion, He showed me His Sacred Heart as a burning furnace and two other hearts (her own and that of Père Colombière) which were about to be united and plunged into it, and He said to me: 'It is in this way that My pure love unites these three hearts forever.' He made me understand again that this union was entirely for His glory, and that for that reason He wanted us to be like brother and sister, equally sharing in spiritual benefits. When I pointed out to Our Lord my poverty and the inequality that existed between a priest of such great virtue and a poor sinner like me, He said to me: 'The infinite riches of my Heart will make up for everything and make you completely equal.' "

Perhaps, my Brother, the comparison doesn't seem right to you? It is true that as yet you are no Father de la Colombière, but I don't doubt that like him you will one day be a real apostle of Christ. For me, the thought doesn't even enter my head to compare myself to Blessed Margaret Mary. I'm only saying that Jesus has chosen me to be the sister of one of His apostles, and the words which this holy lover of His Heart spoke to Him out of humility, I repeat to Him about myself in all truth. Moreover, I'm hoping that His infinite riches will supply for everything I lack in order to achieve the work He has entrusted to me.

I am happy if the Good God makes use of my poor verses to do you a little good. I would have been embarrassed to send them to you if I had not recalled that a sister should hide nothing from her brother. It is surely with a brother's heart that you have welcomed and judged them. No doubt you were surprised to receive "Vivre d'Amour" again. I had no intention of sending it to you twice. I had started to copy it when I remembered that you already had it and it was too late to stop.

My dear little Brother, I must tell you that there was one thing in your letter which saddened me. It is that you don't know me as I am in reality. It is true that to find great souls one must come to Carmel. Just as in virgin forests flowers grow which have a fragrance and beauty unknown to the world, so Jesus in His mercy has willed that among these flowers there should grow smaller ones. I can never be grateful enough to Him, for it is thanks to that condescension that I find myself, a poor flower without distinction, on the same level as the roses who are my sisters. O my Brother! I beg you to believe me that the *good God has given you as your sister not a great soul, but one who is very little and very imperfect.*

Don't think that this is humility which prevents me from recognizing the gifts of the good God. I know that He has done great things in me and every day I sing to Him with joy for doing so. I remember that the one who has had much forgiven is obliged to love more.[31] Moreover, I try to make my life an act of love and I no longer worry about being a little soul. On the contrary I rejoice in this. That is why I dare to hope "my exile will be brief," but this is not because I am ready. I feel that I shall never be ready unless the Lord Himself sees fit to transform me. He can do it in an instant. After all the graces with which he has filled me, I still await that of His infinite mercy.

You tell me, my Brother, to request the grace of martyrdom for you. I have often asked that grace for myself, but I am not worthy of it, and one can truly say with St. Paul: "It is not the accomplishment of the one who wills nor of the one who runs, but of God Who has mercy."[32]

Since the Lord seems to want to give me only the martyrdom of love, I hope He will allow me through you to gain the other palm which we both desire. I notice with pleasure that the good God has given us the same attractions, the same desires. I have made you smile, my dear

---

[31] Luke 7:47.
[32] Romans 9:16.

little Brother, by writing a poem called "My Arms." All right! I'm going to make you smile again by telling you that in my childhood I dreamed of fighting on battlefields. When I was starting to learn the history of France, the story of Joan of Arc's exploits delighted me. I used to feel in my heart the desire and the courage to imitate her. It seemed to me that the Lord destined me too for great things. I was not mistaken. But instead of voices from Heaven calling me to combat, I heard in the depths of my soul a voice that was gentler and stronger still: the voice of the Spouse of virgins was calling me to other exploits and more glorious conquests, and in the solitude of Carmel I understood my mission was not to crown a mortal king but to make the King of Heaven loved, to conquer for Him the kingdom of hearts.

It is time for me to stop, but first I must thank you once more for the dates you sent me. I would be very happy if you would add also the years, since I don't know your age. So that you will excuse my simplicity, I am sending you the dates of my own life. It is in this way that we may be specially united through prayer and thanksgiving on these happy days.

If the good God gives me a little goddaughter, I shall be very happy to comply with your request in giving her as patrons the Holy Virgin, St. Joseph, and my own Patroness.[33]

---

[33] St. Teresa of Ávila.

Finally, my dear little Brother, I finish by asking you to excuse my lengthy scribbling and the disconnectedness of my letter.

In the Sacred Heart of Jesus I am for eternity,

>Your unworthy little sister
>Thérèse of the Child Jesus and of
>the Holy Face
>rel. carm. ind.

P.S. (It is clearly understood, is it not, that our relationship shall remain secret? No one except your Director must know of the union which has formed between our souls.)

The Little Way

hérèse lost no time in answering Maurice's letter of April 17, and her lengthy reply marked a new stage in her relationship with him. It was in this letter that she dropped the formal address of *"Monsieur l'Abbé"* to replace it with *"My dear little brother,"* the affectionate phrase she used when she prayed for him. It seemed perfectly natural to express the sisterly fondness she felt growing in her. At the same time, she was aware that the change was significant and she asked Mother Gonzague's permission for it.

She knew that her love for Maurice was grounded in her love for God. She compared it to the love, in the seventeenth century, between Margaret Mary and her confessor, Father Claude de la Colombière. The former had visions of the love which burned in the Heart of Christ for all humanity and felt herself called to establish in the Church a devotion to the Sacred Heart. Her claims were regarded with suspicion by Church authorities, but her confessor recognized their validity and staunchly defended her. Eventually she prevailed and the devotion was approved and became popular in Catholic piety. Margaret Mary was declared a saint by Rome in 1920, and Claude was canonized as a saint by Pope John Paul II on May 31, 1992.

Thérèse did not presume that she and Maurice were their equals, but saw a parallel in their God-centered relationship. Referring to Maurice in her autobiography, she wrote: *"When it pleases Jesus to join two souls for His glory, He permits them to communicate their thoughts from time to time in order to incite each other to love God more."* Her love for him was both holy and deeply human, and she expressed it freely for the comfort she knew it gave him. She would express it more and more as their correspondence continued.

It bothered her, however, that Maurice did not seem to know her as she was. He idealized her, and she was at pains to correct him. He must not think of her as someone great, she said. *"I beg you to believe me that the good God has given you as your sister not a* great *soul but one who is* very little *and very imperfect."* This was an important point which he needed to understand. It was at the heart of the spiritual discovery she had made which she called her "Little Way." The Little Way is a rich and original teaching, and it is Thérèse's great contribution to Christian spirituality. It is what people are referring to when they speak of the Copernican revolution she created in our traditional approach to God. It is hard to describe briefly because Thérèse never defined things, never put them in formulas. Rather, she *lived* them.

She was delighted that Maurice shared her enthusiasm for Joan of Arc. She began his introduction to the

Little Way by recalling that Joan's exploits as God's emissary had fired her own imagination as a young child. She even dreamed of following her example and carving out a similar destiny of greatness. This dream changed, however, as she realized that God was not calling her to glory and to fame, but to a life of love lived in the silence of a cloister. Here, unnoticed, she could *"love Jesus as He had never been loved before."* And because she never thought of her love for Jesus as something private, an exclusive relationship between Him and her, she would share this love with the whole world, with that *"vast army of little souls"* which she felt God gave her the mission to lead.

Because littleness is no obstacle to love, no greatness was required for this mission. Neither her human imperfection nor her shortcomings would keep her from God's love, for she knew that His love is by nature *merciful*. She did not come by this insight easily. She struggled for most of her brief lifetime before she saw clearly that, in approaching God, weakness is not a *liability*. It is in fact an *asset*. By September 17, 1896, she was able to express this clearly in a letter to her oldest sister, Marie.

On September 7 that year, she had begun the ten-day private retreat which would prove to be her last. Sometime earlier the two had been having discussions in which Thérèse had tried to explain the confidence she had in God's love for her, and the joy and lasting peace it gave her. Her sister found her explanation hard to understand and asked her to clarify in writing what Marie called her "little doctrine," the essence of her spirituality. Thérèse responded on September 8 with a letter which has become Manuscript B of her autobiography. Only a dozen pages long, Manuscript B is ranked among the great masterpieces of Christian literature. Actually it is made up of two documents, her answer to Marie and a "letter" which she had written to Jesus at the beginning of the retreat. The two are reversed in the autobiography, the soliloquy to Jesus placed second instead of first.

Manuscript B soars to lyrical heights in expressing Thérèse's love for God. It is here that she described the desires burning inside of her which seemed like madness: the desire to proclaim the Gospel in the four corners of the world until the end of time, to be an apostle, a priest, a missionary, a Doctor of the Church, and a martyr who would suffer all the martyrdoms of history to prove her love for God. Her desires lit fires in her heart and she felt called by God to all vocations.

What then *was* her vocation, this mysterious destiny of which she felt certain? In Manuscript B she described her relentless search to find it. She did not mean her vocation as a Carmelite but the special destiny to which she knew God was insistently calling her, *"to be love in the heart of the Church."* This is what would enable her to be everything she wanted to be because the love she envisioned embraced all vocations and reached out to the whole world.

It is in Manuscript B also that we have the memorable story of the little bird, in which she saw a symbol of herself in the terrible darkness of her night of faith. The little bird has the aspirations of an eagle but cannot soar as the eagle can to the lofty heights of *"the Divine Sun."* Unworried by its weakness, it remains steadfast in its trust that beyond the clouds the Sun goes on shining. *"Nothing will frighten it, neither wind nor rain, and if the dark clouds come and hide the Star of Love, the little bird will not change its place because it knows that beyond the clouds its bright Sun still shines on."*

Continuing the metaphor, she homed in on her human failings, which she never allowed to discourage her. *"Being unable to soar like the eagles, the poor little bird is taken up with the trifles of earth. It chases a worm, gets its feathers wet in a muddy pool, becomes preoccupied with a flower."* But instead of worrying, it never loses heart.

For all its lyrical loftiness, Marie failed to understand the point Thérèse was making in her letter. Rather than inspiring her, Thérèse's reply only heightened Marie's sense of her own inadequacy. "I have read your pages burning with love for Jesus. But a certain feeling of sadness came over me in view of your extraordinary desires for martyrdom. They are proof of *your* love. Yes, you possess love, but I myself! No." To answer her objection, Thérèse wrote a final letter on September 17, the last day of her retreat. It is regrettable that this letter is not included in Manuscript B of the autobiography because Marie is not alone in her reaction. It was in this last letter that Thérèse laid her questioning to rest with a clear statement of what she meant. Her words are revolutionary: *"Let me tell you, Marie, that my desires for martyrdom are* nothing. *It is not they which give me the unlimited confidence which I feel in my heart. . . . What pleases God in my little soul* is that He sees me loving my littleness and my poverty: it is the blind hope that I have in His mercy. [The emphasis is Thérèse's.] *That is my only treasure. Why can it not be yours? . . . To love Jesus, the more one is weak, without desires and without virtues, the more one is suitable for the operations of (God's) consuming and transforming love. It is confidence and nothing but confidence that must lead us to love."*

That passage in her letter of September 17 is the clearest expression of the Little Way that Thérèse has left us. It puts an end to all the objections which Marie or Maurice or anyone at all might make about his or her human failure. How can someone as mediocre as I, we say, presume to love God? Thérèse's answer is bold: *"The more one is weak, without desires and without virtues, the more one is suited for the operations of God's consuming and transforming love."* Discouragement is simply not allowed in the spirituality of Thérèse. We may approach Him no matter how poor we are; in fact, the poorer the better, for the more we may then rely upon God. No matter in what situation we find ourselves, the only requirement is that we put our trust in His merciful love.

The Little Way is a whole new way of life, a way of holiness that is open to all because it requires nothing from anyone but the ordinary, day-to-day experience of which every life is made. Steeped in her mission of love, Thérèse saw no reason to take upon herself great penances, which were common in the Carmel of her day. She soon gave them up, content to offer God the small sacrifices which came in the routine of community life, the little occasions to be kind to others, the apostolate of the smile when smiling at another was the last thing she felt like doing. Such opportunities to demonstrate love for God by showing it to others abound in everyone's daily life.

The Little Way finds joy in the present moment, in being pleased to be the person you are, whoever you are. It is a school of self-acceptance, which goes beyond *accepting* who you are to *wanting* to be who you are. It is a way of coming to terms with life not as it might be but as it is.

The last thing it should be seen as is mere self-help psychology, a method for calming anxiety. It is very helpful in this regard, of course, and it does result in peace of mind, but that is not its aim. The Little Way is a *theology,* one that is lived and which rests on the rock foundation of a central divine truth: that God is *"nothing but Mercy and Love"* and can be counted on for His boundless benevolence.

The Little Way is a wide-open invitation to *all* to love the God of the present moment, the only God Who exists and Who asks nothing from us but that we believe in His love. Thérèse *knew* God, she was sure of Him, and was a reliable witness to His love for each and every person. She spoke to every human being who would listen, to Marie who was disturbed by her own apparent mediocrity, to Maurice Bellière who worried greatly over his past sins, to all those who worry that they are not better than they are. It is a waste of time to regret that one is not better than one is. Thérèse made short work of regretting.

The Little Way is the joy of the Gospel from which she took it, whose Lord said that the *littlest* in the Kingdom of God is to be reckoned the greatest.

My good and very dear Sister,

I have never sung the first stanza of the Canticle of Love[34] with more spirit than I sang it yesterday. I don't think that it was ever more apropos than it was yesterday.[35] In fact, it was of the very substance of the day, because it found its place in the Pentecost Gospel.[36]

But, my very dear Sister, it held an added grace for me because yesterday, at the very hour when the Holy Spirit came down upon the Apostles with His Light and His Strength, I received His orders from the mouth of my Director. In other words, I was given an almost definitive decision on my vocation, and this is what I was told: "You have a genuine vocation in which I firmly believe, and in which God is showing His providence in a singular way. With a thousand chances of losing your soul He is giving you ten thousand more of saving it. Furthermore, He wants you to be a missionary. The road is open—go." Dear little Sister, I am about to leave. I'll spend this vacation with my family, and on the first of October I shall

---

[34] Her poem "To Live by Love."

[35] The day before he wrote this letter was Pentecost Sunday.

[36] The liturgy of Pentecost Sunday in those days used John's Gospel 14:23–30. Thérèse quotes John 14:23 in the first stanza of "To Live by Love."

arrive in Algiers to begin my novitiate with the White Fathers in Maison-Carrée. The only obstacle I can foresee might come from the Bishop. I have to have his authorization, and he sometimes creates difficulties; all the more because this year many requests have been made of him by various Congregations. I've had the joy of influencing the choice of the White Fathers' African Missions by one of my confreres, whom I shall be bringing with me.

I'm content and at peace with the decision given me, for my Director assured me that even if I had not shown a desire for the Missions he would have sent me there anyway. And so if later on I should experience failures or discouragement—which in the beginning is almost bound to happen—I can be joyful like Paul in the midst of his trials, because I'll be convinced that what I'm doing is God's Will, and because I will know that you, my sister, are near me with your sisterly love—and that will be not the least of the supports my poor soul will have. You have promised me that even after your exile you will be there, and I'm not afraid.

Let us adore God, Sister. Thank Him with me. Less than anyone else—and I ask you to believe this—am I worthy of this honor, which I can't think of without trembling. This love of God for me almost scares me. Nonetheless I hope that confidence will win out and make me give myself completely. This above all is asked of me. My spiritual Father has said to me: "You must give yourself completely to God, Who asks that you give

Him everything. You cannot serve Him by halves. You will either be a good priest or you will never amount to anything." That is my own feeling, and I want to give without counting the cost, being very sure that "when somebody loves he does not calculate," so that when I set foot on the soil of Africa I'll be able to continue with the words: "I have given all. I run with a light heart. I have nothing anymore except my only riches, namely, To Live by Love."

That will be one more link to my little sister. You said to me recently: "I feel our souls were made to understand each other." I feel the same myself. And since I'm a little superstitious when it comes to Providence, I can't help seeing these connections between us. (But how many differences I see too!) Let me share with you, in all simplicity, a few of the connections: the very same desires, namely souls, the apostolate. Before everything else you're an apostle, it seems to me. You need to be devoted to a holy cause. You love the cause of God and the Church, but also that of France and of the Pope, am I right? And if you had been called to bear the sword for one or the other, you would have done it. I must admit that I myself first thought of serving in the armed forces. This desire was overcome in me only by Christ (after a struggle with blessings and graces) to Whom I surrendered, all the while keeping in my heart an ardent love for these causes which were dear to me. And let me say this: if a war broke out to which the Pope called supporters, I think I would be among the first to sign up. One of my joys overseas will also be to work for France, insofar as I shall be able and it will be my duty.

Dear little Sister, you were deprived of maternal caresses when you were very young. Imagine, I never even saw my own mother. More than that, she died on account of me! Until I was ten or eleven I had no idea of this misfortune, accepting an aunt's devotion and kisses as those of a mother—so tender and loving were they. Thus I grew up calling by the name of "mother" this sister of my mother. And my heart will suffer just as much as it would have if I were leaving my own mother for the apostolate far away. I recommend her to you, good little sister. Each day I think of your own father and mother who are dead. My father too is dead. The only family I have is now entirely spiritual—but I believe I'm not less attached to it on that account.

It wouldn't surprise me if we also had the same devotions. It is the Sacred Heart Who converted me—after how many follies and falls. The beautiful years, the ones for which Jesus has a special love—I squandered them. I sacrificed the "talents" God gave me to the world and its foolishness. But the Holy Virgin, Notre Dame de Délivrande,[37] whose shrine you surely know, has also been a great help to me. St. Joseph, he received me into his guard

---

[37] A famous shrine to Our Lady in Normandy.

of Honor. And I depend a lot on the friendship of Sts. Paul, Augustine, Maurice, Aloysius Gonzaga, and Francis Xavier, as well as Sts. Joan of Arc, Cecilia, Agnes—you have sung of them all in your poems; Geneviève—there was a brave one!—and she comes in between your birth and your Baptism (January 3); Teresa, especially since I know that she is the holy patroness of my dear little sister; Mary Magdalene, the sinner so loved by Jesus. And then there are those dear apostles or martyrs like Blessed Perboyre, Vénard, de Brétenières, Chapdelaine, etc. Surely you know all these citizens of Heaven.[38]

And now, dear sister in God, I say thanks to you for sending me the dates which are sacred to you, and I am glad that this letter will reach you on the anniversary of a date that is memorable.[39]

Pardon me for having saddened you in my last letter— do excuse me. I am so rude and abrupt. Do not condemn my goodwill, my heart.

Thank you too for the names of your future goddaughter. They are the very ones I would have chosen myself.

I accept with the same simplicity as you do the comparison of Father de la Colombière and Blessed Margaret Mary—with some reservations, because I would have

---

[38] There were biographies of these outstanding missionaries in the library at Carmel.

[39] June 7, the second anniversary of Thérèse's Act of Oblation to God's Merciful Love.

liked to switch the roles if I were not afraid of further displeasing you! It is delightful and holy, this outpouring of the Heart of Jesus and His friends.

How I must bore you and distract you, my brave and dear little sister, with all this talking on, in which I'm afraid I speak too much about myself. Do pardon me. I assure you in all truth that I am a miserable fellow, and you will have to be there, for God to love me once again. I trust that He will reward you, and I earnestly ask Him to do so.

Very dear and very good Sister, I am forever your grateful but unworthy brother.

M. Barthélémy-Bellière

Don't worry, Sister, I am much too jealous of the grace God is giving me and the benefit of your letters to let any outsider in on our secret.

The Road Is Open—Go!

The goodness of Maurice Bellière shines through this long letter, the fourth he wrote to Thérèse. Perhaps his patriotism seems naive to us, who have lived through too many wars and been disillusioned with their outcome. We may hesitate to be easily convinced of "the rightness of our cause" in a world that is far from simple. But his was another day, when the imagination of the young could be fired by dreams of heroic service. Maurice was a romantic, who would gladly lay down his life for France.

Now a new dream took hold of him. What could be more glorious than to lay down his life to spread the Good News announced to the world by Christ, even if it meant martyrdom should God will it? Maurice was overjoyed to be accepted in the ranks of the White Fathers and could not wait to share the news with his sister, Thérèse. No words could be more welcome than those of his spiritual director: "The road is open—go!" Coming from a man whose judgment he valued, they were for him the guarantee that he was doing the Will of God, and he knew that someday they would bolster his courage if he experienced "failures or discouragement" as a missionary.

The White Fathers were founded in 1868 by Cardinal Charles Lavigerie, the first Archbishop of Algiers in North Africa. His community started with two young seminarians from his diocese. It was a time of terrible distress in Africa, a famine having devastated the country from 1869 to 1871. In its wake, a wave of cholera claimed sixty thousand lives and left thousands of children orphans.

Cardinal Lavigerie's intention was to create a band of missionaries who would carry the Gospel to the pagans and Muslims who populated the nations of Africa. They were only to blaze the trail. In 1874 he wrote to his small group of seventeen: "The missionaries must be the initiators, but the lasting work will have to be accomplished by the Africans themselves, once they become Christians and Apostles."

The White Fathers[40] were a society of secular priests and brothers bound to a common life and apostolate, not by solemn vows but simply by personal commitment. Their rule stressed a routine of daily prayer as an antidote to what was called "the heresy of action." If their work did not rest upon a solid spiritual base, it would never last.

All that could hold Maurice back from joining this group now was the refusal of the Bishop's permission. This was the same Bishop Hugonin who at first with-

---

[40] The community's name was later changed to Missionaries of Africa because of the racial overtone of "White Fathers."

held his permission for Thérèse to enter Carmel at the age of fifteen. She had gone with Papa to see him in Bayeux, with her hair in an upsweep and dressed in a manner to make her appear more mature. She made her plea with eloquence, and her father argued strongly in her favor, but the Bishop declined permission. He would have to consult with others and consider the matter further. She remembered her tears of disappointment, and never forgot the rain that fell in torrents as they emerged from the Bishop's residence. She knew from hard experience how painful it was to watch a door close on a cherished dream.

She fought valiantly for her vocation. Just after the failed visit with the Bishop, Papa brought her and Céline on the diocesan pilgrimage to Rome to celebrate Pope Leo XIII's Golden Jubilee of ordination. She took her cause directly to the Holy Father. In the general audience, the pilgrims were to be presented to him individually but were told they must not speak because the delay might tire the aging Pope. When Thérèse's turn came to kneel before him, she took his two hands in hers and made her plea. The Pope turned to the Bishop's Vicar General to be sure of what she was asking. The Vicar General, annoyed that she had broken the rule of silence, explained that the superiors were considering the matter. "Then do what the Superiors decide," the Pope said. *"Oh Holy Father,"* she urged, *"if you say yes, everyone else will too."* The Holy

Father gently placed his finger on her lips and blessed her. "If God wills it, you will enter, my child," he said. Thérèse was carried off in tears by two Roman guards.

She pursued her goal relentlessly and succeeded in forcing the door of the Carmel three months after her fifteenth birthday. Now she would plead with God that Bishop Hugonin would say yes to Maurice.

In this letter, Maurice recalled words she had written him some time ago which touched him deeply: *"I feel our souls were made to understand each other."* With such a declaration Thérèse led the dance of friendship, and he now responded by pointing to a number of similarities in their lives. He was ready to share one similarity—the loss of their mothers: "Dear little Sister, you were deprived of maternal caresses when you were very young. Imagine, I never even saw my own mother. More than that, she died on account of me!" He had come, however, to love his maternal aunt with the affection he would have bestowed on the mother he never knew, and it tore out his heart to grieve her by leaving France for the missions. He knew he was all she had and he knew how much she loved him.

Maurice, however, was still not totally forthcoming with all the details of his family. "My father too is dead," he wrote, referring to his foster father and significantly making no mention of the fact that his biological father was alive and living in a second marriage in Paris. Not only was Maurice aware of the fact, but he actually visited his father and newfound stepmother during the time that he was corresponding with Thérèse; but he never mentioned this in any of his letters to her. Given the closeness between Thérèse and Maurice, the omission is surprising. We can only surmise that his father's abandonment of him right after his birth was so sensitive a matter, and perhaps his resentment was so strong, that he could not bring himself to mention it.

Thérèse could identify with Maurice's tragedy. In fact, she suffered maternal loss not once but four times in childhood. During the first year of her life her frail health forced her parents to send her to a farm six miles from Alençon to stay with a wet nurse named Rose Taillé. Rose carried her around the farm as she performed her daily chores and was as kind as any mother could be to this lively and lovable child. Thérèse, of course, fell in love with her, and when her own family came to take her home, hale and hearty and suntanned, she wailed disconsolately. For many months after her return, if she happened to be at the window when Rose passed by, wheeling a cart of produce to the market in Alençon, Thérèse would cry at the sight of her. Then, when she was four, she lost her own mother and, after that, she was parted from two surrogate mothers when Pauline and Marie joined the Carmel.

In contrast to Maurice, who was estranged from his

father, Thérèse was very close to hers. It was he who brought her up after his wife died. He adored her and called her his Queen. He supported her entrance to Carmel at an age when almost everyone else opposed it, even though it saddened him to see her leave home.

At the time of her entry to Carmel, Papa was in excellent health. At sixty-four he was charming, with a deep baritone voice and a talent for spinning tales and doing imitations. But three months after her entry, he suddenly began to age. Arteriosclerosis of the brain caused memory loss, sudden changes in mood, and an urge to run away. To the dismay of his family, he wandered off several times, leaving no trace of where he was going. His daughters could only wait until, coming suddenly to his senses, he would wire Lisieux from a distant city. Eventually he had to be confined in a mental institution in Caen called Bon Sauveur. He remained there for nearly four years. Then, after being out for a few months, he died in the arms of Céline. It was a most distressful time for everyone and especially for Thérèse, his youngest and favorite child. She was not unaware of the local gossip which blamed his sickness on her entry into Carmel at so young an age. The townspeople were saying that she broke her father's heart with her headstrong desire to be a Carmelite.

No stranger to the pain of parental loss, Thérèse could sympathize with Maurice. Her understanding and sisterly affection for him compensated for what life had taken away, and no doubt this contributed to the warmth of their friendship.

Maurice was scheduled to enter the seminary of the White Fathers in October, in a place called Maison-Carrée in Algiers. For the remaining time at home he lived in prayerful anticipation of the life that lay before him. No doubt, he often thought of the words of Father DeBarry: "Put this down at the outset and don't forget it. God has fashioned you in such a way that you cannot half belong to Him. Either you will be good or you will be bad. But with a thousand chances of being lost, you have ten thousand of being saved."

June 9, 1897

My dear little brother, I received your letter this morning and I'm taking advantage of a moment when the infirmarian is absent to write you a last little word of farewell. When you receive it I shall have left this land of exile. Forever your little sister will be united to her Jesus. It is then that she will be able to obtain graces for you and to fly off with you to the missions far away.

Oh my dear little brother, how happy I am to die! Yes I am happy, not because I shall be set free from the sufferings of this life (suffering, on the contrary, is the only thing that seems desirable in this valley of tears) but because I really feel that this is the Will of God.

Our kind Mother would like to keep me on earth. At this very moment a novena of Masses is being offered for me at Our Lady of Victories. She once cured me in my childhood, but I believe the only miracle she will work now will be that of consoling the Mother who loves me so tenderly.

Dear little brother, at this moment when I'm just about to appear before God, I understand more than ever that

---

[41] Jesus, Mary, Joseph, and Teresa (of Ávila). Sometimes a Carmelite nun might place these initials at the head of a letter.

only one thing is necessary, and that is to work solely *for* Him *and to do nothing for ourselves or for creatures.*

Jesus wants to possess your heart completely. He wants you to be a great saint. For that you will have to suffer very much, but then what joy will flood your soul when you reach the happy moment of your entrance into Eternal Life! My brother, I shall go soon to offer your love to all your friends in heaven and beg them to protect you. Dear little Brother, I would like to tell you a thousand things which I understand as I stand at the door of Eternity. But I am not dying, I am entering into life, and all that I cannot say to you while I am still here below I shall make you understand from the heights of Heaven.

À Dieu *little Brother, pray for your little sister who says to you:* Good-bye *until we meet in Heaven!*

*Thérèse of the Child Jesus
and of the Holy Face
rel. carm. ind.*

The Letter Never Sent

Thérèse thought this would be her last letter to Maurice. Her tuberculosis had taken a sudden turn for the worse and had begun advancing rapidly. On June 6 Thérèse's aunt Mme. Guérin had written, in a letter to her daughter Jeanne, the wife of Dr. La Néele: "The sickness is progressing rapidly. She is hardly eating and is excessively weak; moreover she has sharp pains in her side. She has changed a great deal this week; she has fits of coughing, sometimes vomits her meals, and eats almost nothing." Thérèse herself was clearly aware of her condition. On June 27 she would tell Pauline: *"Since June 9 [the day of this letter to Maurice] I have been sure that I shall die soon."* She opened this brief letter to Maurice: *"I received your letter this morning and I'm taking advantage of a moment when the infirmarian is absent to write you a last little word of farewell. When you receive it I shall have left this land of exile."*

Before picking up her pen she waited for the infirmarian to leave. She needed privacy to write this letter of farewell to her *"dear little brother."* Perhaps the sister might think it excessive that she would answer his letter the very day it arrived. One of the difficulties of life in a religious community is the surrender of privacy. Her letter is evidence of a deep love and concern for Maurice, and love is something which two people keep mostly to themselves, avoiding the expression of it in the presence of third parties. Had she not cautioned him to tell no one but his spiritual director of their relationship?

When she suddenly regained her strength the following day, Mother Gonzague decided it was best not to put this letter in the mail, so that Maurice would not be alarmed prematurely.

It should be noted that Thérèse's correspondence with Maurice accounts for sixty percent of all the letters she wrote in the last four months of her life. She would write him three times—on June 9, June 21, and July 13—without receiving a reply from him. Her letter of July 13 (see page 152) would take up many of the thoughts expressed in this one of July 9; therefore, no further comment will be made on this letter which was never sent.

Often her letters to others—and they were many— were mere notes of five or six lines. Her letters to Maurice were long, sometimes extremely long, and it cost her a great deal to write them in her weak condition. But she wrote him to the last. He was much on her mind in the days of her dying.

Jesus+
My dear little Brother,
Carmel of Lisieux

I have joined you in thanking Our Lord for the great gift He graciously gave you on the feast of Pentecost. It was on that same beautiful Feast ten years ago that I received permission, not from my Director, but from my father, to become an apostle in Carmel.[42] This is still one more link between our souls.

Oh dear little brother, I beg you, never think you "bore or distract" me by speaking a lot about yourself. Would it be possible for a sister not to be interested in everything that affects her brother? As for what might distract me, you have nothing to fear. On the contrary, your letters unite me more closely to God by making me reflect deeply upon the marvels of His mercy and love.

Sometimes Jesus likes "to reveal His secrets to the littlest ones,"[43] and the proof of this is that after reading your first letter of October 15, 1895, I had the very same thought as your Director: you cannot be half a saint, you must be one completely or not at all. I felt that you must have a soul full of energy, and this was the reason I was happy to become your sister.

---

[42] It was on May 29, 1887, in a very moving scene in the garden outside their house, that Papa gave his full support to her desire to become a Carmelite.
[43] Matthew 11:25.

Don't think you frighten me by speaking of "your best years wasted." As far as I'm concerned, I thank Jesus who has looked at you with a look of love as once He looked at the young man in the Gospel.[44] More fortunate than he, you have faithfully responded to the Master's call. You have left everything to follow Him, and you have done so at the most beautiful age of your life, at eighteen. Ah, my brother, you can sing as I do of the mercies of the Lord. They shine in you in all their splendor. You love St. Augustine and St. Mary Magdalene, those two for whom "many sins were forgiven because they loved much." Me, too; I love them. I love their repentance, and especially their loving boldness. When I see Magdalene coming forward before all those guests, washing with her tears the feet of the Master she adored, Whom she was touching for the first time, I sense that her heart *understood the depths of love and mercy in the* Heart of Jesus. *And sinner though she was, this loving Heart was ready not only to forgive her, but still more to lavish upon her the blessings of His divine intimacy and lift her to the heights of contemplation.*

Ah! dear little brother, since it has been given to me too

---

[44] Mark 10:21. Thérèse referred to the man who asked Jesus what he must do to gain eternal life. "Jesus looked at him with love and told him: 'There is one thing more you must do. Go and sell what you have and give to the poor. Then come and follow me.' At these words the man's face fell. He went away sad, for he had many possessions."

to understand the love in the Heart of Jesus, I assure you that it has banished all fear from my own heart. The memory of my faults humiliates me and prompts me never to rely on my own strength, which is nothing but weakness, but this memory speaks to me even more of mercy and love.

When we cast our faults into the devouring fire of Love with total childlike trust, how would they not be consumed, so that nothing is left of them?

I know there are saints who spent their lives doing astonishing penances to make up for their sins, but what of it? "There are many mansions in the House of my Heavenly Father."[45] Jesus said that, and that's why I follow the way He is tracing out for me. I try not to worry about myself at all anymore. I leave it to Him to do in my soul whatever He wants. I did not choose a hard life to make up for my own faults. I chose it to make up for the faults of others.

I have just reread this brief word that I've written you and I wonder if you're going to understand me, because I've explained myself very poorly. Don't think I'm disparaging the repentance you feel for your faults, or your desire to make up for them. Oh no, far from it! But you understand: now that we are two *the work will go more quickly* (and I, with my way, will get more work done

---

[45] John 14:2.

than you)—and that's why I hope that someday Jesus will make you walk by the same way as me.

Forgive me, dear little brother, I don't know what's the matter with me today, for I am not saying what I would really like to say.

I don't have any more room to answer your letter. I'll do that another time. Thank you for your dates. I have already celebrated your twenty-third birthday.[46] I'm praying for your dear parents whom God has taken from this world, and I'm not forgetting the mother[47] whom you love.

Your unworthy little Sister
Thérèse of the Child Jesus and
of the Holy Face
rel. carm. ind.

---

[46] June 10.

[47] His aunt Mme. Barthélémy.

Merciful Love

Thérèse's close call with death made her hasten to finish Maurice's education in the Little Way. The memory of past sins still haunted him, and she knew that fear of God would undermine his confidence in Him, and that she must not allow this to happen.

An exaggerated fear of God still permeated the religious atmosphere of the time. Jansenism was to blame. It had its roots in the sixteenth-century teaching of Cornelius Jansen, a Dutch bishop and theologian, whose image of God was somber and severe. In his view, God kept a strict tally on human behavior, weighed people's merits on the merciless scales of justice, and was at best reluctant to forgive them when they sinned. The bishop went so far as to teach that few were saved and the vast majority of human beings were damned forever.

The Catholic Church lost no time in declaring this teaching to be heresy, but the spirit of Jansenism lingered in Europe. It was particularly strong in France even in the nineteenth century, to the immense harm of many good and earnest souls, among whom Maurice Bellière could be counted. Thérèse herself did not entirely escape its influence in early childhood. Her sister Pauline gave her a string of beads on which to count the sacrifices she made each day and the prayers she offered. The implication was that the higher the number, the closer she would be to God, a spirituality not unrelated to Jansenism. Thérèse's own scrupulosity and extreme sensitivity were doubtless due in part to the Jansenist spirit which crept into the fire-and-brimstone sermons she sometimes heard.

In general, however, the Martin family was spared the heresy's harmful fallout, thanks to the benevolent influence of Thérèse's maternal aunt Sister Dosithée. She and Thérèse's mother were always the best of friends, and even after she entered religious life she maintained close ties with the Martin family, taking a strong hand in the education of the daughters. She belonged to the Visitation order, founded by St. Francis de Sales. Having suffered painfully from scrupulosity in early life, Francis had emerged from his spiritual crisis as a great apostle of God's mercy. His gentle manner and fervent preaching of God's love for everyone made thousands of converts. As a Visitandine, Sister Dosithée inherited his spirit and introduced it to the Martin household.

By this point in her life, Thérèse had come to her own deep conviction that *"God is nothing but Mercy and Love,"* and it became the foundation of her Little Way, her definition of God. In the Old Testament He is YAHWEH, which means "I am Who am." In the New Testament John the Evangelist makes the bold statement "God is Love." Thérèse placed a nuance on his statement by saying He is *Merciful* Love. It was her most profound intuition: that the very *nature* of God's Love is to be merciful. The furthest thing from Him is the desire to punish anyone, to cause suffering. Thérèse once said that when we suffer He shields His eyes so as not to look. He is all tenderness and compassion.

Furthermore, for Thérèse, it was the nature of God's Love that His Mercy cannot be purchased. He must give it *freely*. All love is in fact freely given if it is truly love. God loves us with a sovereign freedom, out of sheer benevolence. He loves us for our sake, and He wants us to love Him for His sake, in a relationship that is pure and devoid of calculation. Thérèse explored this truth to extraordinary depths. She knew for certain that no amount of good works, no matter how heroic, could ever purchase God's love, *because He wants to and must give it freely*. She even said that our good works are all blemished and make us displeasing to Him *if* we rely on them. He does not love us because we *deserve* to be loved but because we *need* to be loved. The closest comparison in human terms is the love of mother and father for their newborn child. The baby has done nothing to deserve their love. His needs are all he has to give them. He caused his mother pain in being born, he cries in the middle of the night and gives his parents no end of work and inconvenience, robbing them of their independence and turning them into slaves. But they are *willing* slaves, glad to be at his beck and call. A good father or mother will say of the child in the cradle: "He just *pulls* the love right out of my heart!"

Thérèse understood that this is the way God loves us. We pull the love right out of His Heart. He bends low over our weakness with a love that is full of tenderness, as parents bend over their child in the cradle. He does not hate us for our sins. It is the sins He hates for the harm they do to us and to others. They deface the beauty in us, and He longs to destroy them in the fire of mercy that burns in His Heart. Thérèse was sure of this. She knew it by an intuition which left no room for doubt. With a single blow she broke the chains of Jansenism. Hers was the love that casts out fear. *"How can I fear a God,"* she kept asking, *"Who is nothing but Mercy and Love?"* The only "payment" God asks from us is that we seek His merciful love with confidence. *"Confiance, rien que la confiance"* was her battle cry—confidence, nothing but confidence, leading us to love.

In taking the stress off good works and moving it to confidence in God's love, Thérèse did not deny the *necessity* of our good works. They remain absolutely necessary, but not as bargaining chips to buy salvation. They are necessary because they are an expression of our love for God and inevitably flow from it. They make us beautiful in the eyes of God. When we fail to

perform them, however—and there will often be failure, for we are weak and our nature is skewed—our
reaction should not be a craven fear of God's punishment but a confidence which leads us to depend on
His mercy and starts us off again in the good life we
desire.

This is Thérèse's "theology," which she was at pains
for Maurice to learn. The foundation on which the
Little Way is built is the merciful love of God. Only
when she was convinced of His limitless mercy could
she walk on this joyful "Way of Confidence and
Love." This is what would free Maurice from the guilt
which plagued him and it would make him the missionary he must become, a preacher of the Good News
of God's love to those who have never heard of it.

In this letter, Thérèse was concerned to bolster
Maurice's morale, pointing to all the good that was in
him. Had he not, she asked, forsaken everything to
follow Jesus, and at the age of eighteen when life beck-
oned with so much promise? She was remembering
her own seventeenth and eighteenth years, when with
wide-eyed wonder she read the mystical works of St.
John of the Cross and found in them the confirmation
of her own insights. They were years of prodigious
growth for her. Now Maurice must grow.

She agreed with his director that God was calling
him to be a saint and that he could not be one by
halves. From the beginning, she said, *"I felt that you*

must have a soul full of energy, and this was the reason I was happy to become your sister." The words must have made him glow with pride. She applauded his hope for martyrdom, never doubting its sincerity. She contrasted him with the young man in the Gospel who, unlike Maurice, counted the cost of discipleship. *He* would not count the cost. Yet in all her letters to him she never placed burdens on his shoulders which he might not be able to bear. If her expectations were high, they were no higher than his own. All she really demanded was that he grow in his confidence in God.

As for his sins, they were to be forgotten, save for the humility they could teach him. She spoke of her own sins. *"The memory of my faults humiliates me and prompts me never to rely on my own strength, which is nothing but weakness, but this memory speaks to me even more of mercy and love. . . . My brother, you can sing as I do of the mercies of the Lord."* As I do. She never stood over him, never lectured him. It is characteristic of Thérèse that she counted herself a sinner, not from false humility but simply because she recognized the fact that she was one. If her sins were not serious, she understood that this was due to God's mercy, not to her own virtue. It was His mercy that spared her from committing grave sins. For Thérèse, sins forgiven and sins avoided seemed virtually the same. "There but for the grace of God go I," people often say. Thérèse *meant* it.

As she came to the end of her letter, she had second thoughts about its clarity: *"I have just reread this brief word that I've written you and I wonder if you're going to understand me, because I've explained myself very poorly. . . . Forgive me, dear little brother, I don't know what's the matter with me today, for I am not saying what I would really like to say."* She was within three months of dying and growing weaker by the day. It was during this month that she had also been writing Manuscript C at the direction of Mother Gonzague, the final section of her autobiography. It is a vitally important work in which she recorded the experience of her trial of faith. Thérèse can be excused if she did not have her thoughts in order as well as she might like. But reading her letter all these years later, we may rightly feel they were in better order than she thought.

She closed with the assurance of prayers for Maurice's parents—still unaware that his father was alive in Paris.

To my Sister Thérèse
My very good and very dear Sister,

It's already almost a month since I received one of your dear letters. If I had not been so caught up since I went on vacation, I would have come before now to ask for a few kind words from you, encouraging and comforting words. You understand that the atmosphere of vacation is more suitable for making a soul that is weak grow cold, and for shaking it up, than for doing it the good that is so desirable and necessary, especially on the eve of an immense grace.[49] This is by way of telling you, dear Sister, that the outpouring of your religious soul into mine becomes more necessary when I am on vacation. Come quickly, then, to talk to me of good things.

Do you realize that you open up new horizons to me? Especially in your last letter I find insights on the mercy of Jesus, on the familiarity which He encourages, and on that simplicity in the soul's relationships with the great God, which until now had hardly occurred to me—doubtless because I was never introduced to them with the same simplicity and persuasion of which your heart is full. I

---

[48] The letters of July 15 and July 13 (see page 152) are reprinted here in the order in which they were received.

[49] His approaching entrance into the White Fathers.

have come to think the way you do, except that I possess only imperfectly that delightful simplicity which I find astonishing, because I am a sad and conceited man, and I rely too much on created things.

No, dear little Sister, you haven't explained yourself badly. You're quite clear and I have understood what you're saying. As you put it so well and plainly, since we are two doing the work, I am to rely fully on the Lord and on you. This is the surest way. I look upon everything you tell me as coming from Jesus Himself. I have full confidence in you and I am guided by your way, which I would like to make my own.

My Sister, tomorrow I shall be very closely united with you and your community,[50] especially in the Holy Communion which I shall receive for this intention. One of my friends,[51] a newly ordained priest and a companion of mine for some years, will sing your Solemn Mass. He shall be very blessed. I too have asked our good Mother for permission to come some years from now, on the eve of my own departure for Central Africa, to consecrate on the altar of Carmel the Body of Our Lord, Whom I would then rejoice to place upon your tongue. At that time I'll be coming back to spend a few days in France.

Today I asked Mother for a favor with which I hope

---

[50] For the feast of Our Lady of Mount Carmel, July 16.

[51] Abbé Troude, a nephew of one of the sisters in the Carmel.

you'll agree, for I have done it myself reciprocally.[52] *As always it is to your heart that I make my appeal.*

Allow me again to recommend to your prayer some temporal concerns which are troubling my mother.

Dear, very dear little Sister, I leave you in the Heart of Jesus where I often find you, and where I shall make a rendezvous with you forever.

I am your devoted and grateful brother forever.

Maurice Barthélémy-Bellière

a.m.

A letter soon, no? I beg one from you.

---

[52] Mother Gonzague had asked him for his photo. In his reply he had promised to send one and at the same time he asked for a photo of her and one of Thérèse. Mother Gonzague declined his request for her photo, but she would send him one of Thérèse.

Talk to Me of Good Things

This is Maurice's fifth letter to Thérèse. Hers of July 13 had not yet reached him, so he was unaware of its grave message.

He would have written sooner, he said, if he had not gotten caught up in his vacation. With candor he confessed his need of contact with her "religious soul" and, ignoring the fact that she had been more faithful than he in keeping up their correspondence, he asked her for another letter. "Come quickly . . . to talk to me of good things." The touching request moved her to respond promptly.

He assured her that she had not explained herself poorly, as she thought. Her words were very clear and they opened new horizons to him. Three times in a brief paragraph he mentioned her *simplicity*. It is true of Thérèse that what she wrote was always simple. Readers would agree with Maurice that there is no difficulty in understanding this Doctor of the Church. People with little education are as drawn to her autobiography as are the learned and sophisticated. While she was an incomparably great mystic, a child can understand her. There are no flights of lofty rhetoric and no exaggerations in her writing. She had neither visions nor ecstasies. Unlike Joan of Arc, she heard no "heavenly voices" giving her directives. Thérèse's mysticism was rooted quite simply in love, the love of God for her and her love for Him which consumed her. Hers was a living faith. All that she learned about God came from the common experiences which are the currency of ordinary life. She saw Him in the beauty of all she beheld. She experienced *Him* in experiencing life, in a natural manner devoid of frills. Even as a child, the fading of the jam's bright color on a piece of bread spoke to her of God, as did the thunder and lightning in a storm that did not frighten her, and the sunlight shining on a meadow full of flowers. The God of Love was everywhere in His creation and she had eyes which saw Him there.

There was utter simplicity in her prayer. Asked one time what she said to Jesus when she prayed, she answered that often she didn't say anything. *"I just love Him,"* she said. Asked for a definition of prayer, she gave a very simple one: *"For me, it is an aspiration of the heart, it is a simple glance directed to heaven, it is a cry of gratitude and love in the midst of trial as well as in joy; finally, it is something great, supernatural, which expands my soul and unites me to Jesus."* Most of her prayer in the Carmel was offered in darkness and dryness of spirit, but this made no difference to her. The single-mindedness of her love for God remained undiminished, whether she felt it or not; she once gave the advice that we should tell God that we love Him, whether or not we feel that we mean what we say.

Her simple genius worked by intuition. During the last years of her life, complicated spiritual books bored her and she quickly closed them, turning more and more to the Scriptures, which she had no difficulty interpreting because she knew they spoke to *her.* It has been said that she understood the Bible because she believed it. In the end she abandoned almost all other reading. *"In the Sacred Scriptures I find nourishment that is solid and pure,"* she wrote in her autobiography. *"But it is above all the Gospel which speaks to me during my prayers. There I find everything that is necessary for my poor little soul. I always find new lights in it, meanings that are hidden and mysterious."*[53] She carried the four Gospels in a pocket inside her habit and took them out to read so often that she knew them almost by heart. In speaking or writing to others she could call up passages of Scripture at will. She seemed never to have been drawn to texts which might instill fear, but found and savored those which were consoling. She loved the saying attributed to St. Gertrude that the most beautiful relics Jesus left us were His words of comfort preserved in the Bible.

Thérèse did not possess a complete Bible. Much of her knowledge of it came from its reading in the lit-

---

[53] Manuscript A, 83:211.

urgy of the Divine Office and the Mass. A study made of her biblical references shows that of the seventy-two books of the Bible Thérèse referred to fifty-two, quoting some of them extensively. Hans von Balthasar speaks of "her astounding mastery of texts, not only in the New Testament but in the Old as well." She loved especially the Psalms, the Book of Proverbs and the Song of Songs, and made good use of them in fashioning her concept of God. When Céline entered the community she brought with her not only her treasured camera but also a notebook into which she had copied Isaiah's Songs of the Suffering Servant,[54] which describe the sufferings which the Messiah would undergo. Thérèse was enthralled by that text. She read it over and over, and saw that it was virtually an account of the Passion of Jesus. *"Those words of Isaiah: 'There is no beauty in him, no comeliness,' have been the whole foundation of my devotion to the Holy Face, or to express it better, the foundation of all my piety. I, too, have desired to be without beauty, treading the wine press alone, unknown to everyone."*

She reveled in the Song of Songs, God's love song for His people—so much that she wanted to write a full commentary on it. She wished for the chance to study Greek and Hebrew so that she might read the

---

[54] Isaiah 52–53.

Sacred Books in the languages in which they had been written and thus understand them better.

Simplicity is the key to Thérèse in everything. She made all things new and understandable by removing the complication that grows up around truths which should be simple, and she spoke to the underlying simplicity that is in all of us. Maurice Bellière was a simple man, a person of goodwill, and he responded to her spontaneously: "You're quite clear and I have understood what you're saying. . . . I look upon everything you tell me as coming from Jesus Himself. I have full confidence in you and I am guided by your way, which I would like to make my own."

He was one of her first readers, and he delighted in the feast of solid truth she set before him. He could never have enough of it and begged for more. "Talk to me of good things," he pleaded. His reaction was the same as that of countless others who have read Thérèse during the century since her death.

J.M.J.T.

Jesus!
My dear little Brother,

Maybe when you read this little word I shall no longer be on earth but in the land of eternal happiness! I don't know the future, but I can tell you with assurance that the Spouse is at the door. It would take a miracle to keep me in this land of exile, and I don't think Jesus is about to work this useless miracle.

O my dear little brother, how happy I am to die! Yes, I am happy, not to be delivered from the sufferings of here below (quite the opposite, suffering joined to love is the only thing that seems to me desirable in this valley of tears). I'm happy to die because I feel that it's God's Will, and because I shall be much more useful than I am now to souls who are dear to me, to yours very specially.

In your last letter to our Mother you asked that I write you often during your vacation.[55] *If the Lord still wants to prolong my pilgrimage for a few weeks, and if our good*

---

[55] On June 7 he had written to Mother Gonzague: "If you only knew how much good the letters of your dear daughter do for me! They make me good, strong, more religious, more humble, more detached. May I ask for more of them on vacation? I'm going to have to fight harder against myself first of all, and against some cherished attachments which will be hard for me to break."

Mother gives permission, I shall still be able to scribble you a few little notes like this one, but what's more likely is that I shall be doing more than writing to my dear little brother, more indeed than speaking to him in the tedious language of earth: I shall be very near *to him, I shall see everything he needs, and I shall give God no rest until He grants me everything I want! . . . When my dear little brother leaves for Africa, I shall follow him not only in thought and in prayer; my soul will be with him forever, and his faith will know very well how to discover the presence of a little sister whom Jesus gave him, to be a support to him, not for a mere two years but* until the last day of his life.[56]

All these promises, my brother, seem a little fanciful to you perhaps, but you have to start realizing that the good God has always treated me like a spoiled child. It is true that His Cross has followed me from the cradle, but Jesus made me love that Cross with a passion. He has always made me desire whatever He wanted to give me. Will He begin, then, to fulfill those desires no longer once I am in heaven? I just can't believe that, and I say to you: "Soon, little brother, I shall be near you."

Ah! I earnestly beg you to pray hard for me. I need

---

[56] Thérèse underlined these words. She was very given to underlining in her writing when she wished to stress certain words or phrases. Here she meant literally what she said. It was a solemn promise and she had no doubt at all that she would be empowered by God to fulfill it.

prayers so much right now. But above all pray for our Mother. *She would love to keep me here below for a good while yet, and to obtain that, this kind Mother has had a novena of Masses offered for me to Our Lady of Victories, who once cured me in my childhood. But feeling that the miracle wasn't going to happen, I have asked and obtained from the Holy Virgin that she console my Mother's heart, or rather that she make her agree that Jesus should carry me off to Heaven.*

À Dieu *little brother* until we meet *in Heaven soon.*

Th. de l'Enf. de la S.F.
rel. carm.
[Thérèse of the Infant and of the Holy Face
Carmelite Religious]

À Dieu, but Not Farewell

By the beginning of July, a sharp decline in Thérèse's health was obvious to everyone. Her right lung had collapsed, and for almost the entire month she coughed up blood day and night. She became so weak that the Prioress transferred her to the infirmary on July 6. It was at this time that she abandoned her pen. The shaky handwriting of her last notes and letters was in pencil. In those days medical science had little to offer her—no oxygen to ease her breathing, no medication to alleviate the terrible pain which racked her body. Her doctor ordered a diet of condensed milk. She who had always detested milk drank it valiantly but could not keep it down.

Aware that her letter of June 9 was never mailed, she wanted to be sure that Maurice was not left without a proper good-bye. The indications of death were by now undeniable: *"I can tell you with assurance that the Spouse is at the door."*

Thérèse's words in this letter need to be weighed thoughtfully for the doctrine they contain. Her concept of heaven is new and radical. Conventionally it was seen as eternal rest, a reward for a life well lived. She did not accept that idea at all. The whole purpose of her earthly life was to love God and make Him loved. That would not change after she died, as long as there were souls still to be saved. Death would free her from the boundaries of space and time, and her mission to travel the world as the messenger of God's love would begin. With unheard-of boldness she flatly stated: *"I will spend my Heaven doing good on earth,"*[57] And when Thérèse was dying, Mother Agnes asked her "You will watch over us from heaven, won't you?" Thérèse replied, "No, I shall come down!"[58] Only after she died would those desires which seemed like follies make sense: *"One mission alone would not be enough for me. I would want to preach the Gospel on all the five continents simultaneously, even to the remotest isles. I would be a missionary, not for a few years only but from the beginning of creation until the consummation of the ages."*[59]

Heaven, she saw clearly, is not eternal rest but eternal life, a life that is utterly full, without end and without beginning, for it is the very Life of God, the Life into which Jesus will draw all in His Resurrection. She believed that she would share that Life completely, and just as Jesus has transcended the limits of time and space and remains active in this present world, she would do the same. "I shall come back to take you with me, that where I am you also may be," He had said.[60] Her desires were not follies but would be ful-

---

[57] Yellow Notebook of Mother Agnes, July 17, 1897.

[58] Yellow Notebook, July 13, 1897.

[59] *Story of a Soul,* 193.

[60] John 14:3.

filled only after she died. Then her mission would begin, to love Him as He had never been loved before and to make others love Him as she did. It was all for His sake and not for her own. There was in Thérèse's love not a drop of selfishness. She was a completely converted Christian who held back nothing for herself.

We may speak of this as a new theology if we wish, but more accurately it is a new mysticism, a new vision of the Christian life through the eyes of a saint whose intuition gazed deeply into the mystery of God and was not afraid to draw conclusions from what she saw. *"He gives me everything that is His,"* she said.[61] She did not feel she was taking liberties when she placed His words in her own mouth: "It is best for you that I go. You are in sorrow now, but I will come back to you and your hearts will rejoice, and your joy no one will take away from you."[62] She did not think she was going too far in believing that Jesus would share His risen Life with her completely. His mission was to the whole human race, from the beginning of time to its end. He would allow her to share that mission with no restrictions. She would love every human being in the way He loved each one.

She took seriously the statement of St. Paul in his letter to the Galatians: "I have been crucified with

---

[61] See letter of July 18, 1897. See page 166 here.
[62] John 16:22.

Christ, and the life I live now is not my own; Christ is living in me."[63] Paul too was *completely converted* by his experience of the risen Jesus on the road to Damascus. It is said that afterwards he went into the desert for fourteen years to absorb in solitary contemplation the enormity of what happened to him when He encountered the risen Lord. Only then did his mission really begin. He was by that time nearly fifty and had but ten years of his life left. In that brief time he traveled incredible distances, crisscrossing the Roman Empire three times to proclaim the Gospel to the Gentiles.

The comparison of Thérèse to Paul is often made by scholars. While she had no single spectacular encounter with Jesus as he did, she encountered Him day by day in the depth and darkness of her contemplation. Her conversion, slow but steady, was complete, as Paul's was. She spoke of her union with Jesus as a *"fusion,"* which made the two one. Like Paul, she received a mission from Jesus, to proclaim to the whole world the message of God's merciful love. Her mission would really begin when she left the silence of her cloister and entered eternal life.

By the time Thérèse wrote this letter to Maurice, she had reached the summit of her mysticism. From the mountaintop she saw the landscape as a whole and was sure of what she said to him. This time, with a

---

[63] Galatians 2:19–20.

clarity which left no doubt, she solemnized her promise to him, knowing that it was no empty wish but something which God would bring to fulfillment. She was very specific, so that he might not misunderstand her: *"I'm happy to die because I feel that it's God's Will, and because I shall be much more useful than I am now to souls who are dear to me, to yours very specially. . . . I shall be doing more than writing to my dear little brother, more indeed than speaking to him in the tedious language of earth: I shall be* very near *to him, I shall see everything he needs, and I shall give God no rest until He grants me everything I want! . . . When my dear little brother leaves for Africa, I shall follow him not only in thought and in prayer; my soul will be with him forever, and his faith will know very well how to discover the presence of a little sister whom Jesus gave him, to be a support to him not for a mere two years, but until the last day of his life. . . . 'Soon, little brother, I shall be near you.'"*

This was her promise in what she thought would be her last letter to Maurice. In precisely the way the promise was made, it would be fulfilled.

Meanwhile, however, what she had begun to endure was almost more than she could bear: *"I earnestly beg you to pray hard for me. I need prayers so much right now."* The saint whose blinded faith saw the other world so clearly was still an ordinary mortal in great pain. She did not spell out to Maurice the details of her spiritual and physical agony. She simply asked him to pray hard for her.

Oh my poor little Sister, what a blow for my poor heart! It was so unprepared. Don't ask from it that joy which you feel at the approach of bliss. It remains attached to its heavy chain, it is nailed fast to its cross. You are about to go away, dear little Sister, and my heart will be alone once more. More than with mother or family it became focused on its sister's love. It found a lovely home in her holy friendship. My heart was happy (oh how happy!) to feel near it this friendly hand which consoled and strengthened and ennobled it. It was advancing on the way of the cross with a smile, because it no longer felt alone. It was happy and waiting impatiently to cast itself into the desert, because it was confident of being sustained. It was about to break away from its only consolation on this earth, counting for compensation on the one whom Jesus had sent it as an angel on earth. And now Jesus is taking this gift away, just when it seems most desirable.

Oh how hard it is, how painful for a soul not deeply rooted in God! Nevertheless, His Will be done. Let it be done! *. . . since you're going to be happy forever, my sister. Yes, it's a fact, right? . . . I am an egoist.*

Go, little Sister; don't make Jesus wait any longer. It is as if He is impatient to gather you up. Leave me to fight on, to carry the cross, to fall beneath it and die in pain. You will be there for me all the same. You promised me that, and I count on it. It is my last hope both for now and for the future. You shall be with me, close to me. Your soul will guide mine, speak to it and console it—unless Jesus, annoyed by my complaining, does not will it. But you, little Sister, His spoiled child, having now become His spouse and reigning with Him, you will win my cause and draw me to Him on the last day. You know by what road, the quickest: martyrdom if He wills it. I am thanking the Master just the same. He is teaching me by means of a new lesson to be detached from everything that passes and to look toward Him Alone.

Depart, then, dear little Sister of God, and my little sister too. Tell Jesus that I would like to love Him very much—with all my heart. Teach me to love Him the way you do. Tell Mary that I love her with my whole soul. Give my love to my saints whom you know. And you who will become my favorite Saint, you my very own sister, bless me and save me. And please leave me something of yourself, your crucifix if you will.

À Dieu, *dear Sister*—à Dieu *until we meet again soon. No matter how long the exile may be, it will be short compared to eternity.*

Au revoir until Heaven!
Your brother forever.
Maurice Barthélémy-Bellière
À Dieu!

A Lovely Home in
Your Holy Friendship

In no other letter is the person of Maurice Bellière reflected so clearly as in this one. He was thunderstruck by the news Thérèse gave him. Although he had known that her illness was very serious, there still remained a slender hope of a turn for the better. Now she left no doubt that her remaining days were few and it was time to say good-bye. *"The Spouse is at the door,"* she wrote. All her understanding of death, even in the darkest night of her faith, was in that beautiful phrase: not death, but the Spouse was at the door, her beloved Jesus, about to take her into His own glorious Resurrection, in the final embrace of the Bridegroom and His Bride. Dying was as simple as that. She would see His Face at last. But for Maurice the loss was overwhelming and he was numb with grief. His whole soul was in this letter.

It might be the last he would ever write her. Indeed, even as he wrote she might be already gone. He wanted her to know all that she meant to him. This man, abandoned by his father, had found in Thérèse "a lovely home in her holy friendship." Holy indeed that friendship was, fully in line with the sacred vocations to which God called them both. Their love was holy because she was God's own gift, a surprise which lit up his life, banished the fear which dogged him, and turned him into a strong and confident man. She was the sister he never had, and he was the "little brother" of whom death had deprived her before she was born. She would work at his side in the missions as she would have worked for her own brother. She would sustain him by constant prayer. He would never be far from her thoughts. She would always watch over him, *"until the last day."*

How could he have been so lucky, to become the brother of this remarkable young woman who wrote him astonishing letters and shared his noblest dreams? She understood perfectly even his secret wish for martyrdom, so bashfully confessed. She did not hide from him her own dream of heroism in the days of her adolescence and how God had changed that dream. *"It is clear to me,"* she wrote, *"that our souls were made to understand each other."* He was emboldened now to express his sense of loss without reserve.

But no sooner had he done so than he felt how selfish it was to be thinking of himself. "Oh how hard it is, how painful for a soul not deeply rooted in God! Nevertheless, His Will be done. Let it be done! . . . since you're going to be happy forever, my sister. Yes, it's a fact, right? . . . I am an egoist."

He made plain to her that he was ready for God's decision and fully accepted it. Maurice Bellière was a man of ardent faith, who never doubted for a moment that Thérèse was entering eternal life. Heaven was as real to him as it was to her, and so were those to whom he sent His love, Mary the Mother of Jesus, and the saints who had befriended him in prayer.

Toward the end of his letter he wrote prophetic words: "You who will become my favorite Saint, you my very own sister." Those words make Maurice the first to "canonize" Thérèse, even before her death. And if she is a saint, she must leave him a relic. "Please leave me something of yourself, your crucifix if you will." Mother Gonzague would honor his request by sending him the little crucifix Thérèse had venerated for years. He would cherish that beloved crucifix to the end of his days.

The close of his letter is touching. Three times he said good-bye. So that it might be his final word to her he scrawled it one last time beneath his signature: "*À Dieu.*"

My poor and dear little Brother,

Your sorrow touches me deeply—but see how good Jesus is! He lets me be able to write you again so that I can try to console you, and doubtless this will not be the last time. This lovable Savior hears your crying and your prayers, and that is why He lets me still remain on earth. Don't think that I feel bad about this. Oh no, my dear little brother, on the contrary, for I see how much Jesus loves you in what He is doing!

No doubt I explained myself very badly in my last little word to you, my very dear little brother, since you tell me "not to ask of you the joy that I feel at the approach of happiness." *Ah! if you could only look into my soul for a few moments, how surprised you would be! The thought of heavenly happiness not only doesn't cause me one bit of joy, I even wonder sometimes how it will be possible to be happy without suffering. No doubt Jesus will change my nature, otherwise I would regret leaving suffering and this valley of tears behind me. Never have I asked God to let me die young; that would have seemed cowardice. But from my childhood He chose to give me the deep intuition that my course here below would be short. So it is only the thought of doing God's Will that fills me with joy.*

O my little brother, how I would love to be able to pour the balm of consolation into your heart! I can only borrow the words of Jesus at the Last Supper—He cannot take offense at this since I am His little bride and therefore whatever is His belongs to me. I speak to you, therefore, as He spoke to His friends: "I am going to the Father; but because I have spoken to you in this way your hearts are filled with sadness. But I tell you the truth: it is best for you that I go. You are in sorrow now, but I will come back to you and your hearts will rejoice, and your joy no one will take away from you."[64] Yes, I'm certain of it, after my entrance into life the sadness of my dear little brother will change into a peaceful joy which no creature will be able to rob from him. I sense that we have to go to heaven by the same route, that of suffering joined to love.[65] When I shall have come into port I shall teach you, dear little brother of my soul, how you must sail the stormy sea of the world, with the abandon and love of a child who knows that his Father cherishes him, and would never think of leaving him alone in the hour of danger. Ah! How I would love to make you understand the tenderness of the Heart of Jesus, and what it is that He is asking from you. In your letter of the 14th[66] you made my heart tremble with joy. I understand better than ever how much your soul is the sister of my own, since it is called to lift itself up to God by the ELEVATOR of love and not to

---

[64] In the last days of her life Thérèse fell to reflecting a great deal on the Gospel of St. John. This quotation is from John 16:5–7, 22.

[65] This is very prophetic, as we shall see.

[66] Actually his letter was written on the 17th.

climb the hard stairway *of fear. I am not in the least astonished that the practice of familiarity with Jesus comes a bit hard to you. We don't get to this in a single day. But I am sure that I shall greatly help you to walk more surely by this delightful way once I have been delivered from my mortal envelope; and soon you will say like St. Augustine: "Love is the weight that pulls me forward."*

I'd like to try to make you understand, by a very simple example, how much Jesus loves even very imperfect souls, who trust in Him:

I'm thinking of a father who has two children who are mischievous and disobedient, and when he comes to punish them he sees one who trembles and draws away from him in fright, knowing in the bottom of his heart that he deserves to be punished. His brother, on the contrary, throws himself into his father's arms, protesting that he is sorry for hurting him, that he loves him, and that to prove it he will be good from now on. Then if this child asks his father to punish him with a kiss, I doubt that the heart of the happy father will be able to resist the childlike confidence of his son, of whose sincerity he is sure. He's well aware that the child will often fall back into these same faults, but he's always ready to forgive him, provided the boy always grasps him by the heart. I say nothing about the first child, dear little brother. Surely you know yourself whether his father can love him as much as the other and treat him with the same indulgence.

But why speak to you of the life of confidence and love?

I explain myself so poorly that I shall have to wait for heaven in order to converse with you about that happy life. What I want to do today is console you. Oh how happy I would be if you would welcome my death as Mother Agnes of Jesus welcomes it. Doubtless you're not aware that she is my sister twice over, and that it is she who was a mother to me in my childhood. Our good Mother[67] *was terribly afraid that her sensitive nature and her great affection for me would make my departure a very bitter experience for Mother Agnes. The opposite has happened. She speaks of my death as if it were a celebration, and this is a great consolation for me. I beseech you, my dear little brother, try to be convinced the way she is that instead of losing me you* will find *me, and that I shall never leave you again. Ask for the same grace for the Mother[68] whom you love, and whom I love even more than you do because she is my visible Jesus.[69]*

I would joyfully give you what you ask if I had not made a vow of poverty, but because of it I can't give away so much as a holy picture. It is only our Mother who can grant what you ask and I know that she will. Precisely in view of my approaching death a sister has taken my photograph for our Mother's feast day. When the novices saw

---

[67] Mother Gonzague.

[68] Mother Gonzague.

[69] She meant that she looked upon Mother Gonzague, her religious superior, as the representative of Jesus.

the picture they exclaimed that I had put on my grand look. It seems that I'm usually more smiling. But be sure, my little brother, that if my photograph does not smile at you, my soul *will not stop* smiling at you *when it will be near you.* À Dieu, my dear and much loved brother; *believe that I shall be your* true little *sister for all eternity.*

Th. de l'Enf. Jesus, r.c.i.

The Parable

Maurice's anguished letter of July 17 reached Carmel the next day. Thérèse answered him at once with the longest letter she had sent him until then—even though she had written him only five days previously. Considering the condition of her health, this must have tested her strength to the limit, but she would not leave him in his anxiety without an immediate reply. *"My poor and dear little brother,"* she began. *"Your sorrow* touches me deeply." He needed to hear that without delay.

The time had come when each letter could be her last. With this one and those that followed, she freely expressed her deep love and concern for him. Moreover, she tried to correct any false impressions he had formed from reading her letters. One was that he thought she desired to go to heaven to enjoy perfect union with Jesus, for whom she longed. Quite the opposite was true. She would gladly remain in this world until the end of time if this were the only way she could continue to work for the salvation of others. It was not for Jesus to console *her;* it was for her to console *Him,* to love Him for His own sake and to persuade as many others as possible to offer Him the love for which He yearns.

Thérèse understood that this was the reason He descended into this world, to recapture the love that was lost through sin. For her, salvation was a warfare to restore God's love in the hearts of all. To leave the battlefield before the battle ended would have been cowardice.

Once more she came back to her "theology of suffering," to her desire to go on suffering as long as this was God's Will for her. His Will was the only motive governing her life. She had always thought from childhood that she would die young, but she had never asked for this as a favor and she did not ask for it now, even though life brought her nothing but physical pain and spiritual desolation.

Yet while she sought no consolation for herself, she longed for Maurice to have it to the full. *"How I would love to be able to pour the balm of consolation into your heart."* Daringly she appropriated the words Christ spoke to His Apostles: *"I am going to the Father; but because I have spoken to you in this way your hearts are filled with sadness. But I tell you the truth: it is best for you that I go. You are in sorrow now, but I will come back to you and your hearts will rejoice, and your joy no one will take away from you."* Death, for Thérèse, would complete this identification with Him, and everything that is His would be hers. Having passed through His Passion and Death and come into the glory of His Resurrection, He was able to come back and be with His friends. Once she entered eternal life *she* would be able to do the same. She would come back to be with Maurice—and indeed with all those whose salvation she so passionately desired. *"I will spend my heaven doing good on earth,"* she boldly predicted.[70]

In spite of her many reassurances, concern over his past sins would die hard in Maurice Bellière, and Thérèse would have to return to the subject again in her letters. In this one, superb teacher that she was, she treated the matter in a parable, the story of the two brothers who incur the displeasure of their father and who each in a different way handles his predicament. The first, terrified of his father's anger and knowing he deserves to be punished, runs from him. The second throws himself into his father's arms, tells him that he loves him, is sorry for what he has done, and promises never to do it again. Although the father is perfectly aware that this son has made the same promise before and broken it, and no doubt will break it again, he cannot resist the child's trust and affection and readily forgives him. This son *"grasps* [his father] *by the heart,"* and this is the way Maurice must deal with his sins. He must take God by the heart.

It is not that Thérèse failed to take sin seriously. She

---

[70] Yellow Notebook, July 17, 1897.

172

was far too conscious of what it did to Jesus on Good Friday to do that, and she would go to any lengths to lessen His suffering. Like her patroness, St. Teresa of Ávila, she would gladly die a thousand deaths to save one soul from hell. Thérèse never made little of sin, but she made vastly more of God's inexhaustible mercy. With St. Paul she firmly believed that "where sin abounded, grace did more abound." She would come back to this subject again before she died, because she wanted to convince Maurice that *"confidence, nothing but confidence"* is the way to take God by the heart.

It has been said that in her letters to Maurice, Thérèse gave a whole course in her Little Way. In this letter she alluded to the elevator, a favorite image for the part God plays in the salvation of the *"little soul"* which confides itself to His mercy. Although like a small child one may be too weak to climb the demanding staircase of perfection, God will come down, like the elevator, pick up His child in His arms, and carry him up to where he is trying to go.

She never forgot the impression made on her by the first elevator she ever saw. It was one of the many wonders of Paris which delighted the young girl from provincial Lisieux. She was fourteen at the time and very impressionable. She made her grand discovery in the hotel where she stayed with Papa and Céline. With wide-eyed wonder she stepped into this new invention and was thrilled to feel it lifting her past the floors above. That elevator remained in her memory for the rest of her life and is immortalized in her autobiography as a metaphor for God's grace.[71]

The theology embodied in this metaphor is the theology of the Little Way. The Little Way is not an easy path involving no effort on our part. Thérèse was careful to make that clear in this letter. *"I sense that we have to go to heaven by the same route,"* she told Maurice, adding *"that of suffering joined to love."* The Little Way cannot deviate from the Way of the Cross. But Thérèse did not expect its followers to *want* suffering or look for it, rather only to take the trials of life as they come and use them for their own salvation and that of others. Thérèse had composed a prayer called the Act of Oblation, in which she offered herself as *"a holocaust victim"* to God's merciful love. When she invited her sister to offer that prayer, Marie refused on the grounds that she had more than enough suffering already and didn't want any more. Thérèse replied that the Act of Oblation would not bring her any more. It only called upon her to accept and offer freely to God all that she had already to endure.

---

[71] Someone has consulted the roster of the hotel where the Martins stayed and discovered that Friedrich Nietzsche was a guest while they were there. One likes to imagine that he got in the elevator one day when Thérèse was trying it out. *"Bon jour, Monsieur,"* she would have said with her delightful smile to the father of modern atheism.

Maurice Bellière would carry an exceptionally heavy cross of his own, more pain than most may ever have to bear. Before he died he would taste humiliation and defeat. For the present, however, he had to go through the pain of tearing himself away from a beloved mother who did not want him to leave, and now, in addition, the awful grief of losing Thérèse was beginning to set in. The greatest gift she could bestow on him at this moment was the assurance of the special place he held in her heart. And so she concluded her letter with the words, so warm and filled with affection, "À Dieu, my dear and much loved brother; *believe that I shall be your* true little *sister for all eternity.*"

She meant the emphasis of those expressions to engrave them forever on his memory, to be a source of strength for him in the hard days ahead.

To my dear Sister Thérèse

My good and very dear little Sister,

I won! How easy it was! I have your photograph. From now on you live in my mind, after having lived up to now only in my heart. I'm expressing myself poorly, but try to understand that your letters, indeed your very thought, now become embodied, they take shape. Your thought is no longer how should I say, abstract, it is you *now. I had tried hard to imagine what you looked like. I must tell you that I did not miss the mark by too much, at least as far as the general effect goes, so that when I saw you for the first time it was as if I were recognizing you. In spite of the fact, dear sister, that you had "put on your grand air" as you say, I found—as I already knew anyway that I would—that you are very good-natured and loving, and—but yes!—smiling no matter what you say.*

Thank you for the kindness with which you have given me the joy of possessing you near me, almost really, always with me. What then will it be like when your very soul will be lighting up these features, smiling at my soul and brimming with life. This will be Paradise at last. In all truth, shall I ever again be able to be unhappy? What suffering could be possible once a corner of Heaven lights up a whole life! But you know, I'm afraid that Jesus will tell you all the grief I've caused Him, all my wretchedness, and I get frightened that your tenderness may cool. If you knew how wretched I am! If that should happen, as soon as He starts to speak put your hand over His mouth and come to my defense, for without you I don't have a leg to stand on.

But what's this I read at the bottom of the photograph: "The Lord has commanded His Angel to watch over you and to guard you in all your ways.[72] *Thanks be to God I breathe easy again! You will stand by me; you have to, because it's an order from God. Therefore you will embark for Africa with me. First you will be with me in the novitiate. You will be my pilot. I have your motto inscribed on my sail: "Beloved pilot—To Live by Love."*[73] *And in three years we shall set out for the desert, we shall be missionaries together. You will be in your element there. There will be no lack of suffering, but then I shall represent you in that because you will suffer no longer.*

And you don't know whether you'll be able to get used to Heaven, my brave little sister, because there's no more suffering there? Let me take your place. If I shall become worthy of it obtain suffering for me . . . in love . . . so that I may be separated from you as little as possible in Heaven on the last day.

I am grateful to Jesus Who graciously wants to keep

---

[72] Psalm 90:11. This quotation was written at the bottom of the photograph.

[73] From her poem "To Live by Love."

*you among us for a while. Yes, how He really loves us! I
have prayed very hard to Him, I have raised my voice and
shouted to Him. He has let Himself be conquered by our
sorrow and our tears. I was, however, resigned. At first
there was an outburst of sorrow, crying out at the top of
its voice, but later calm was restored. Finally I thought the
way you do: yes, it is useful for us that you go. And besides
you will be closer to me. But all the same: your presence,
at any rate your action, will no longer be felt as it is felt
now, and unaccustomed as I am to supernatural things, I
can't get into my head how you will be more really present to help me. But that makes no difference and I'm not
complaining. I am ready for your departure, but maybe
that's because it doesn't seem like it's ready to happen right
away, since you're still alive.*

*Dear Sister, you're happy to see me entering into Love
through confidence. I believe as you do that this is the only
way that can guide me to the Port. In my dealings with
people I've never accomplished anything through fear. I've
never been able to submit to harsh discipline. The punish-
ments of my teachers left me cold, whereas correction
given to me with affection and in a gentle way drew tears
from my eyes, and brought me around to apologies and
promises that I usually kept. It is almost like that with
God. If an irritated God was presented to me with His
hand always raised to strike me, I fell into discouragement
and accomplished nothing. But if I see Jesus patiently
waiting for me to come back to Him, and giving me a*

new grace after I have asked Him to forgive me for com-
mitting yet another fault, I am conquered and climb right
back into the saddle. What sometimes holds me back now
is not Jesus but my own self. I am ashamed of myself, and
instead of throwing myself into the arms of this Friend, I
scarcely drag myself to His feet. Often a first impulse
draws me into His arms, but suddenly I stop short at the
sight of my own wretchedness and I do not dare . . . Tell
me little Sister, is this wrong? I believe that the divine
Heart is saddened much more by the thousand little acts of
cowardice and the carelessness of His friends, than by
faults, even grave ones, that spring from our nature. You
understand me and you will make me generous and
blameless as far as Jesus is concerned. If only I were wor-
ried as much about "the point of honor" where Jesus is
concerned as I am when it comes to people!

  You speak to me, dear Sister, about Mother Agnes of
Jesus, who is also your own blood sister. Her memory is
often linked to your own in my prayers, for I don't forget
what I owe her. Give her a heartfelt thank you for me. I
prayed for her all the more lovingly once I knew the bond
that united you to her. Listen to what I'm going to tell
you: It's through you and through your family that I be-
came aware that there was a Carmel in Lisieux. Some of
my fellow seminarians from Lisieux were talking among
themselves one day about a family named Martin which
had given three daughters and more distant relatives to the
Carmel. One of the girls entered at fifteen, another after

admirably caring right up to the end for her saintly father. I was present, and later on when I got the idea of asking for a Sister in Carmel, trying to think where I might make my request, it came back to me that there was a Carmel in Lisieux; and just look at the coincidence: your own sister received my letter and it is you, the one of whom I had heard others speak, who were assigned to me. When I received your "dates" I was struck by their agreement and I came to some conclusions. Am I mistaken? Aren't you the one who in the world used to be called Miss Geneviève Martin? I ask your pardon if I'm being indiscreet, but you have told me to hold nothing back. Once again all the same, do pardon me.

Good-bye for a while, dear little sister, until I have some news from you. If you could only see how happy I am to hear from you! However, I would no longer be happy if I learned that this caused you fatigue. Don't listen only to your affection.

Dear and indeed very dear little Sister, from the bottom of my heart I am forever your very fortunate brother,

Maurice B. Bellière

A Picture Is Worth
a Thousand Words

By July 21, 1897, the friendship of Maurice and Thérèse had matured to a point where he was completely at ease in writing to her. In this letter a friend addressed a friend, exulting in the assumption that what he wrote would be understood by the one who read it, confident that the love his letter carried would be reciprocated. He knew by now that he could trust himself with her.

She had sent him her photograph and he wanted to share his reaction. After months of exchanging letters, now he was able to *see* her! Naturally he had formed his own picture of her. "I had tried hard to imagine what you looked like." When the photo arrived he was delighted to see that he "did not miss the mark by too much."

The photo was taken under difficult circumstances. Thérèse was at the end of her strength, and the time exposure required by the slow film in use then was nine seconds. To maintain her expression for nine seconds without moving tried both her strength and her patience, and three takes were needed before the final shot was made.

The photographer was Céline. When she developed

the film and showed the picture to the novices, they burst into laughter and teased Thérèse about putting on her "grand air." They were used to her pleasant expression and this photo appeared stiff and formal. Her so-called grand air, however, did not seem grand at all to Maurice. "I found—as I already knew anyway that I would—that you are very good-natured and loving, and—but yes!—smiling no matter what you say."

We have forty-seven photographs of Thérèse, almost all of them taken by Céline, who had become an accomplished photographer before she entered the Carmel. Whenever she took up anything, she made it her business to excel in it, and her pictures were excellent. She had a talent for oil painting, and her father had wanted to send her to Paris to study under a well-known artist there. She declined because she had already decided to enter religious life after her father died, and she feared that beginning a career in art might jeopardize her vocation.

It was a compromise, perhaps, that made her take up photography, which was in its infancy. To be a photographer was to possess a rare skill, and for such a skill to be practiced in a Carmelite cloister was unheard-of. That it was allowed in the Carmel of Lisieux is a tribute to the acceptance of progress which found a welcome there. Céline was the proud owner of an excellent camera and the tools for a darkroom in which to develop her work. All this came with her when she moved across town to the convent on the Rue du Carmel. As a result we possess a whole collection of photographic studies of Thérèse. No other saint is so well documented, with an autobiography, a voluminous correspondence, a large body of poetry and playlets, the firsthand testimony of a host of contemporary witnesses, and finally forty-seven photographs. The last few taken are of particular interest for the way they trace the dramatic progress of her tuberculosis, as day by day it took its relentless toll. All Céline's plates have been carefully preserved and restored to their original candor, enabling us to know Thérèse as only the camera could record her.

In this seventh letter Maurice continued to be bothered by his feelings of unworthiness. The ghost of his past sins rose up once more to trouble him. What will her reaction be when she comes into the presence of God and discovers what a wretched person he has been? If Jesus begins to tell her all about the real Maurice Bellière, she must put her hand over His mouth and stop Him.

But his hesitation was only momentary. Under the holy picture she sent him he read the scriptural words *"The Lord has commanded His Angel to watch over you and to guard you in all your ways."* This reassured him that she would never take back her love. She was his angel appointed by God to watch over him, and she had been *commanded* to stand by him.

It was of course not only his past sins that made Maurice feel unworthy of Thérèse's friendship; it was also his deeply felt mediocrity. No witness has testified to heroic virtue in this man. To the contrary, we shall learn later from some of his associates that he was by no means beyond criticism. He could in fact be difficult to work with. There is a vast gap between the virtue practiced by Thérèse and that of Maurice.

But the same can be said of others who were on terms of intimacy with her, who never felt that in following her Way they duplicated her virtue. Toward the end of her long life,[74] Céline, who dreamed such great dreams with her sister when they were adolescents and who received some of the most beautiful letters she ever wrote, had this to say of herself: "I see myself as the Queen of all those who are imperfect. My realm is very vast and I have subjects by the millions, but whatever they do they can never match their Queen for being imperfect. 'The leopard does not change his spots.' Happily, the following words of my little Thérèse console me: *'It's enough to be humble, to put up with our imperfections graciously.'* There is where the real sanctity lies." Until the day she died, Céline was short of temper and often lost her patience.

She was not the only family member with problems

---

[74] Céline died in her ninetieth year in 1959.

to endure. Léonie suffered greatly. She was a very difficult child and caused stress in the Martin home. Self-conscious and not so gifted as her sisters, she was often ill at ease in company. Furthermore, she was afflicted with a chronic eczema that added to the difficulty of her life. She tried four times before she finally succeeded as a Visitandine nun. In a letter to Pauline not long before she died,[75] she wrote: "I have suffered much on account of my inferiority, and have known what loneliness of heart can be. But now I am above all such nonsense and have only one ambition: to practice humility. How I love these words: *'The good God works in us; there is no need to see or feel Him.'* Happily for me that is true, for I have always been and am increasingly a blockhead, a log; and I ask Jesus to set the log on fire with the Spirit of Love."

It has been said of Léonie that few understood the Little Way so well or practiced it so faithfully as she. Thérèse loved her deeply and wrote words of encouragement to her in letter after letter. She never gave up on Léonie's vocation to the Visitandines, in spite of all the obstacles in her way.

It takes a long time to absorb the wisdom of Thérèse, to see and embrace the truth about oneself and about the tireless patience of God. Maurice, like most,

---

[75] She died at the age of seventy-eight on June 16, 1941.

would need years to understand the message of Thérèse and apply it in his life.

At the end of his letter he related how he had come
to hear of her and her family from some of his fellow
seminarians who came from Lisieux. His information
was a bit confused. "Am I mistaken? Aren't you the
one who in the world used to be called Miss Geneviève
Martin?" There was no Geneviève among the Martin
sisters. The one he had heard about was Céline, who
in religious life was called Sister Geneviève. She was
the one whom he described as staying home with admirable fidelity to care for their father in his old age.

We shall see how nicely Thérèse handled this confusion of identity and how she would use it to tell Maurice the story of her family and of her father's death.

July 26, 1897

JESUS+

My dear little Brother,

How much pleasure your letter gave me! If Jesus has heard your prayers and prolonged my exile because of them, He has also lovingly heard mine, because you are resigned to giving up, as you put it, "my presence, my perceptible activity." Ah! my brother, let me tell you something: the good God is saving some very delightful surprises for you who are not, as you wrote me, "very used to supernatural things." As for me, I am not your little sister for nothing, and I promise you that after my departure for eternal life I will give you a taste of the happiness that can be found from feeling a friendly soul close by. Then it's not going to be this correspondence, which leaves us more or less separated from each other and is always very incomplete, and which you seem to wish could continue. Rather, it will be the conversation of a brother and sister which will charm the angels, a conversation which others won't be able to criticize because it will be hidden from them. Ah! how good it will seem for me to be freed from this mortal envelope which would force me, if—to suppose the impossible—I found myself in the presence of my dear little brother with a lot of people around us—to look at him as if he were a stranger, someone to whom I am indifferent!

Please, my brother, don't imitate the Hebrews who hankered after "the onions of Egypt."[76] *I have for some while served you too much of this vegetable which makes one* shed tears *when we let it get too near our eyes before it is cooked.*

Now I dream of sharing with you "the hidden manna" which the Almighty has promised to give to "the victor." It is precisely because it is hidden *that this heavenly* manna *attracts you less than the "onions of Egypt." But I am sure of one thing, that as soon as I shall be allowed to offer you a nourishment that is totally spiritual, you will no longer miss that which I would have given you if I had long remained on earth. Ah! your soul is too great to be attached to any consolation of this life on earth. It is in heaven that you must live in advance, for it is said: "Where your treasure is, there also is your heart."*[77] *Your* unique treasure, *is it not* Jesus? *Since He is in heaven, that is where your heart must dwell, and I tell you in all simplicity, my dear little brother, I think it will be easier for you to live with Jesus once I am there at His side forever.*

It must be that you don't know me at all well, if you are afraid that a detailed account of your faults could lessen the tenderness that I feel for your soul! O my brother, believe me that I shall not need to "put my hand

---

[76] See Numbers 11:5.

[77] Matthew 6:21.

over the mouth of Jesus." He has forgotten your infidelities long ago. Only your desires for perfection remain to make His heart rejoice. I implore you, don't drag *yourself to His* feet *ever again. Follow that "first impulse which draws you into His arms." That is where you belong and I have decided, now more so than from your other letters, that you are* forbidden *to go to heaven by any other road than the one your poor little sister travels.*

I completely agree with you that "the heart of God is saddened more by the thousand little indelicacies of His friends than it is by the faults, even the grave ones, which people of the world commit." But my dear little brother, it seems to me that it is only *when his friends, ignoring their continual indelicacies, make a habit out of them and don't ask forgiveness for them, that Jesus can utter those touching words which the Church puts on his lips in Holy Week: "These wounds you see in the palms of my hands are the ones I received in the house of those who* loved *me."[78] For those who* love *Him, and after each fault come to ask pardon by throwing themselves into His arms, Jesus trembles with joy. He says to His angels what the father of the prodigal son said to his servants: "Put his best robe on him and put a ring on his finger, and let us rejoice."[79] Ah! my brother, how the goodness of Jesus,* His merciful love, are so little known! *It is true that to*

---

[78] Zechariah 13:6.
[79] Luke 15:22.

enjoy these riches we must be humbled and recognize our nothingness, and that is what so many are not willing to do. But my little brother, that is not the way you behave, so the way of simple love and confidence is just made to order for you.

I wish you would be simple *with God, but also . . . with me; does what I say surprise you? I raise the question because you ask my* pardon *for what you call your* indiscretion *in wanting to know whether, before she entered the convent,* your sister *was called Geneviève. That seems to me a perfectly natural question for you to ask, and to show you that I mean what I say I'm going to provide you with some details about my family, because you haven't been very well informed.*

The good God gave me a father and mother more worthy of Heaven than of earth. They asked the Lord to send them a lot of children and then to take them for Himself. The request was granted. Four little angels flew off to Heaven, and the five other children who remained took Jesus for their Spouse.

It was with heroic courage that my father, like a new Abraham,[80] climbed the mountain of Carmel three times to immolate for God what he held most dear. First there were his two eldest. Then the third of his daughters, on the

---

[80] A reference to the biblical story of Abraham's willingness to sacrifice his beloved son Isaac. See Genesis 22.

*advice of her director and led by our incomparable father,
made a try at the convent of the Visitation. (God was
content with her offer of herself. Later on she went back
to the world, where she lives as if she were in the cloister.)
There remained for the Chosen One of God only two children, one eighteen years old and the other fourteen. This
last one, "the little* Thérèse," *asked him to let her go off
to Carmel and obtained permission without difficulty from
her good father, who pushed his kindness to the point of
taking her first to Bayeux and then to Rome, in order to
overcome the obstacles which were delaying the immola-
tion of the one he called his Queen. When he had piloted
her into port, he said to the* only child he had left: *"If
you want to follow the example of your sisters I give you
my consent; don't be worried about me." The angel who
was to become the support of the old age of such a saint
replied that* after his departure for heaven *she too would
enter the cloister, which filled him with joy because he
lived only for God.*

*But such a beautiful life had still to be crowned by a
trial worthy of it. A short time after my departure, the
father whom we so justly cherished was struck by an attack of paralysis, which affected his limbs and recurred
several times. But it was not to stop there. That would
have been too easy a trial, for the heroic patriarch had
offered himself to the Lord as a victim. So the paralysis
changed its course and settled in the dear head of the victim whom the Lord had accepted. Space is lacking for me*

to go into the touching details. I only want to tell you that we had to drink the chalice to the dregs and be separated for three years from our beloved father, leaving him in the hands of people who were Religious Sisters but nevertheless strangers to him. He accepted this trial, while at the same time he was well aware of the humiliation of it. He even pushed heroism so far that he would not ask God to be cured.[81]

À Dieu, my dear little brother. I hope to write you again if the trembling in my hand doesn't get any worse, for I've had to write this letter in several stages.

Your little sister, not "Geneviève" but "Thérèse" of the Infant Jesus and of the Holy Face.

---

[81] Her father's first attack of paralysis occurred on May 1, 1887. When Céline told him that they were all making a novena to St. Joseph asking for a cure so that he might go back home, he replied: "No, you mustn't ask for that, but only ask for the Will of God."

The Humanity of Thérèse

If Maurice Bellière ever questioned the singular place he held in the heart of Thérèse, reading this letter would put an end to all his doubts. It was the ninth one she wrote him, and the next would be her last. She was at the end of her strength now. In nine weeks she would die. Her last line was very touching: "À Dieu, *my dear little brother. I hope to write you again if the trembling in my hand doesn't get any worse, for I've had to write this letter in several stages.*" She finally gave him some idea of how extremely sick she was. It no longer made sense to keep it from him.

The letter is the longest she ever sent him, and writing it was a heavy drain on the little strength she had left. It was written over several days in little pieces, yet the flow of it is never interrupted. Maurice was much in her thoughts during those final days, and from time to time when her energy picked up a bit she went on with what he needed to be told. Most of all he needed to be assured of her love for him, and to have it to remember when she was gone.

Thérèse had a highly developed capacity to deal with different persons in different ways, to accommodate herself to each one. It was one of the reasons she was chosen to train the younger Sisters. She used to say that souls are as different as faces, and she dealt with each novice according to her needs. She was kind with those who needed kindness, but firm with those who cut corners on Carmelite discipline or tried to manipulate her. One young sister used to avoid the regular session she was supposed to have with Thérèse, knowing how probing it would be. Without ever seeming to hunt her down, Thérèse always managed to be somewhere she least expected in her path. The sister later spoke of the tact with which Thérèse made sure that those encounters took place. Another sister was inclined to be depressed. One evening Thérèse noticed that she was particularly sad and, unable to speak to her because of the night silence, she went out of her way to give her a most friendly smile, one which that sister never forgot. Remembering the moment years later, she remarked: "Oh that smile of Sister Thérèse, it just seemed to take all my troubles away."

During the time that she was corresponding with Maurice, Thérèse also exchanged letters with another missionary, Father Adolph Roulland of the Foreign Missionary Society of Paris. After his ordination he was assigned to China, and before leaving he came to the Carmel to say Mass. Mother Gonzague had asked Thérèse to do for him what she was already doing for Maurice. At first she wanted to decline, feeling that she had already promised her first brother all her prayer and sacrifice for his vocation, but Mother pointed out that she could do the same for someone else and Thérèse agreed. After Mass the two met in the parlor, and Thérèse gave him an altar cloth she had embroidered for the occasion. When he left for China she wrote to him faithfully.

Roulland was a very different man from Maurice. His family background was strong and so was his character. He was solidly set in his vocation and his needs were different from Maurice's. Her letters to Roulland are interesting and filled with insightful teaching, beautifully and often humorously written, but they are nothing like the ones she wrote Maurice. She never developed the deep personal friendship with him that she had with Maurice. There would be no need to caution Roulland, as she did Maurice, that no one should read her letters except his spiritual director.

She would not dream of starting a letter to Roulland the way she began this one: *"How much pleasure your letter gave me!"* And she would hardly write him as she wrote Maurice, in response to his grief at the thought of losing her: *"I am not your little sister for nothing, and I promise you that after my departure for eternal life I will give you a taste of the happiness that can be found from feeling a friendly soul close by. Then it's not going to be this correspondence, which leaves us more or less separated from each other and is always very incomplete, and which you seem to wish could continue. Rather it will be the conversation of a brother and sister which will charm the angels, a conversation which others won't be able to criticize because it will be hidden from them. Ah! how good it will seem for me to be freed from this mortal envelope which would force me, if—to suppose the impossible—I found myself in the presence of my dear little brother with a lot of people around us—to look at him as if he were a stranger, someone to whom I am indifferent!"*

Those words implied much more than ordinary friendship, and reading them Maurice could not fail to realize that her love for him was special. Her love was human and deeply felt, and she wanted him to share what was most important in her life, her love for her Lord. This was her grand passion with everyone, but very specially with Maurice. She understood him, understood his human frailty, his weakness, and his needs. He was an open book to her, and she knew perfectly well what his reaction would be to the very first words of her letter: *"How much pleasure your letter gave me!"*

Her mention of *"the onions of Egypt"* indicates again how steeped she was in Scripture and how her agile mind could apply it to real-life situations. In wishing he could keep her with him in this world, he was acting like the ancient Hebrews who, once they had begun their journey to the Promised Land and were delayed in crossing the desert, regretted ever starting and wanted to turn back to the prosperous place from which they came. They grumbled to Moses about the wretched manna God provided, the same food day after day, and hankered for "the onions of Egypt." What they should have longed for and what Maurice needed was the *"hidden manna,"* the spiritual nourishment Thérèse would be able to give him once she stood close to Jesus. The wisdom she could then impart would make the letters she could no longer write seem like those *"onions of Egypt"* which, she reminded him with a touch of pleasant humor, cause tears to flow when they are peeled.

She would continue to insist upon one thing: *he must give up all worry about his past.* Whatever his infidelities were, he simply must believe that God has forgotten them. She was not the least concerned about what Maurice had done. If he would just throw himself into God's arms with confidence, everything he ever did would be forgiven—including those minor infidelities which continued as part of his life. They do not come between us and God, provided, she pointed out, that we don't commit them with crass indifference to God's love for us. *"But my little brother, that is not the way you behave, so the way of simple and loving confidence is just made to order for you,"* she wrote. *"I have decided, now more so than from your other letters, that you are* forbidden *to go to heaven by any other road than the one your poor little sister travels."*

The care that she lavished upon him in the last tortured days of her life is amazing. She paid attention to small details, correcting his confusion of her name with that of Céline and relating the whole story of her father, his heroic sacrifice, his lingering illness, and his humiliating death. Since Maurice was an adopted member of her family, he should know the significant events of the family history.

In this letter Thérèse revealed herself as a warm and sensitive human being, who knew how to share herself with another whom she trusted, admitting some of the pain she had experienced in her own family in order to encourage him in the obvious difficulties he himself had experienced in his. She was aware of Maurice's limitations and very understanding of them. She did not expect him to be perfect and never took it as her mission to try to make him so. She had one mission: to convince him—and to convince the world—that *"God is nothing but Mercy and Love."* She knew that in the end that is all he needed to know.

My very dear and very good Sister,

Caught up as I am in a thousand things, I would have no hope of getting a chance to speak with you if I didn't steal a few minutes tonight. I've been full of regret every day that I haven't been able to do so, but my thoughts often turned to you and my heart found your own in the Heart of the Friend Whom we share, the good Jesus Who certainly wants to preserve you for us, knowing how much we shall miss you and knowing too what a powerful help you are even while you are still with us here on earth. Still, I can tell you in all truth, dear little sister, that I am ready for whatever the Master wants from me—all the more so because I fully believe in your word and in your plans for the other life. Whatever you may say about those "raw onions," I found them a delicious dish of which I could never get enough.

There is no doubt that Jesus is the Treasure, but I found Him in you. And He was easier to approach. And it is still through you that He will come to me from now on, won't He? This is by way of telling you that from Heaven, just as here on earth, I expect EVERYTHING from you. And my confidence will be strong enough to count on your help whenever I need it, a help that will be seen clearly to come straight from that friendly soul whom Jesus has made my very own sister, in a union as close as can be.

My dear and very dear little sister, I know you well enough to realize that my wretchedness would never get in the way of your tenderness here below. But in heaven, where you will share in the Divinity, you will take on its prerogatives of justice and holiness, and everything that is sullied will become an object of horror for you. That is why I was afraid. But since I am hoping that you will continue to be the Spoiled Child, you will do what you would have wanted to do for me on earth, and I believe in and hope for—and I also expect from you—that loving confidence *which I still lack but ardently desire. I think that once someone has that, he will be completely happy here below and will not find the exile too long.*

How kind you are, little Sister, with that simplicity and openness which charm me, yet at the same time astound me! I am so little accustomed to finding this in people that I'm sometimes surprised to see it, but of course I'm extremely happy when I do. The details which you give me so artlessly have touched me deeply; especially, oh yes especially, the one revealing a further kindness on the part of my dear sister: the memorial card with the picture of your venerable father, on the very day of the anniversary of his death. *Thank you from the very bottom of my heart, and thank you too for the details about yourself. How well your dear father named you: his "Queen." Oh yes, and you have remained a Queen in every way, on the eve of receiving the last crown and the final anointing . . . a Queen forever. How good God has been to your family, but also what an admirable family you have!*

Happy are they who hear the word of God and happy are they who obey it so completely, beloved by God both in time and in the glory of Heaven!

So you have always been Thérèse, little Thérèse and not Geneviève. You were perhaps predestined by this name. May St. Teresa live on in Thérèse my dear little sister.

Do you want to tell me also how you became my sister? Was it by choice or by chance?

In spite of all the joy and happiness I get from your letters, I do not want at any cost, especially at this price, to have your writing make your illness worse. Dear little Sister, I beg you to spare yourself.

You will see a new name for my signature. Since Monday I am a member of the Third Order of St. Francis and my second patron, the patron of Africa and the patron of the Tertiaries, has become mine even more specially.

Dear little sister of my soul, please accept your brother's expression of respectful tenderness.

Louis of France

I Found Jesus in You

This letter is evidence of how Maurice had grown since Thérèse entered his life and how much promise he held for the future because he had begun to understand what Thérèse was teaching him.

He worried that two weeks had passed without giving him an opportunity to write her. At this juncture that was a long time, because she was now so weak that any day might be her last. He protested bravely that he was ready to accept God's Will if she was called home, yet he begged for a delay. He watched the mail every day for some word from her. While the last thing he wanted was to drain her meager strength, he could not keep from asking for another letter. Completely at ease with her, he asked for a personal confidence: "Was it by choice or by chance" that she became his sister? She evidently thought his curiosity natural, and she would not neglect to answer his question in her next letter.

Thérèse herself did nothing to conceal the closeness that she felt toward him. Treating him as the beloved brother he had become, she confided details about her family which she would hardly share with a stranger. In a gesture of particular friendliness, she sent him one of the memorial cards given to friends at the time of her father's death. He did not miss the significance of the gesture. "Thank you from the very bottom of my heart," he wrote, "and thank you too for the details about yourself." He would treasure that card for the mark of honor it paid him.

He had already told her of his devotion to St. Francis of Assisi. He knew it would please her to learn that he had joined the Third Order of St. Francis, a worldwide association of laypeople with a love for this well-known saint of the Middle Ages and a desire to imitate his spirit of poverty and his legendary joy. In joining this order Maurice took the name of Thérèse's father, who was called after the great St. Louis, King of France. She would smile at his signature, "Louis of France," as she would be pleased by his reference to Papa as the king who affectionately called her his little Queen.

Maurice's letter is highly personal. He did not hesitate to use the word "tenderness" twice, once in speaking of her tenderness toward him in spite of his wretchedness, and again in closing with an expression of his own "respectful tenderness" for her. In the course of their lively correspondence their relationship had deepened, and Thérèse would not find his use of the word inappropriate.

But of all the things he wrote on this day to give her pleasure, nothing would please her more than to hear him say: "There is no doubt that Jesus is the Treasure but I found Him in you." Almost always when she addressed God she called Him Jesus. It was the incarnate Son of God in the Person of Jesus Who took possession of her consciousness. Abbé Combes, the great scholar of Thérèse, called her "the Saint of Jesus." She was Sister Thérèse of the Child Jesus and of the Holy Face. She loved Him in the weakness of the cradle and she loved him in the sorrow of the cross. Her relationship with Him was utterly *human*. He was, she said, her only Teacher, her only Director, and she remained in His company constantly, without ever seeing Him in a "vision" or hearing Him in a "locution." The communication between them was completely *interior,* deep within her spirit, heart to heart.

When Maurice said, "Jesus is the Treasure but I found Him in you," Thérèse knew that all the effort she put into her letters to him—and in her condition the effort was exhausting—was finally bearing fruit. He was *finding* Jesus. He still had to become more convinced that the One he was finding was no one else but the God of merciful love and that he could with total confidence be at peace with his shortcomings, his past sins, his "wretchedness." In her next letter she would put to rest his one remaining concern: that when she got to heaven and became fully aware of what a sinful man he was, she would no longer love him.

Thérèse herself was not without doubt about her

own position. She was walking a lonely path in quietly but firmly rejecting the Jansenistic piety of this period. She wondered at times if she was deluding herself in striking out upon *"the little way of confidence and love"* and playing down the role of hard asceticism required in the Carmel. Was there pride in standing alone and in staking everything on trust in the mercy of God's Love? It would be a mistake to think she never had her doubts.

When she was a young sister in 1891, these doubts came to a crisis and she went through an anxious time. Rarely did she ever seek spiritual direction from a confessor. But it happened just then that a priest named Alexis Prou came to preach a retreat at the Carmel. The other sisters were not impressed by him, but Thérèse was. He enjoyed no reputation as a counselor to nuns, being a simple preacher to the rank and file laypeople to whom he gave parish missions. But something about him attracted Thérèse.

"I was then having heavy interior trials of all sorts (to the point of wondering sometimes if there was a Heaven)," she wrote in her autobiography. *"I was thinking that I would say nothing about my interior dispositions, not knowing how to express them. Having scarcely entered the Confessional, I felt my soul expand. After saying a few words I felt understood in a marvelous way and even* fathomed. *My soul was like a book which the Father read better than I could myself. He launched me full sail*

on the tides of confidence and love *which attracted me so powerfully but upon which I did not dare to advance. He told me that* my faults gave no displeasure to the Good God, and that standing in His place he spoke for Him *in telling me that He was content with me. Oh! how happy I was to hear those consoling words."*

She never forgot the experience of that confession, which opened a period of peace and joy in her life. She closed this passage with the remark: *"I am of such a nature that fear makes me recoil. With* love, *I not only advance, I* fly!"[82]

Her experience of doubt foreshadowed the Night of Nothingness which fell upon her on Easter of 1896 and lasted until her death. That was not something she might describe as a *"a very heavy interior trial."* It was a terrifying darkness which shook her faith to its foundations. She was in the midst of it, as we have noted, throughout the entire time of her correspondence with Maurice, though one would never surmise it from her letters. The only relief she had from those harrowing eighteen months was a dream she had only five days after her Night of Nothingness began on Easter Day.

She dreamed about Mother Anne of Jesus, a close companion and friend of St. Teresa of Ávila. Teresa had sent Mother Anne from Spain with a small group

---

[82] *Story of a Soul*, 173.

of sisters to establish the first Carmel in France. What was particularly consoling about the dream for Thérèse was that previously she had described herself as "indifferent" to Mother Anne. She never prayed to her and only thought of her when, occasionally, her name came up in conversation. She described the dream in this way:

"At the first glimmerings of dawn I was (in a dream) in a kind of gallery. Suddenly, without seeing how they entered, I saw three Carmelites dressed in their mantles and long veils. I understood clearly that they came from Heaven. The tallest of the saints advanced toward me, raised her veil and covered me with it. Without the least hesitation, I recognized Venerable Anne of Jesus, Foundress of Carmel in France. Her face was beautiful, suffused with an unspeakable gentle light.

"Seeing myself so tenderly loved, I dared to pronounce these words: 'O Mother! I beg you, tell me whether God will leave me for a long time on earth. Will He come soon to get me?' Smiling tenderly, the saint whispered: 'Yes, soon, soon, I promise you.' I added: 'Mother, tell me further if God is not asking something more of me. Is He content with me?' The saint's face took on an expression incomparably more tender. *Her look and her caresses were the sweetest of answers, however she said to me: 'God asks no other thing from you. He is content, very content!' After again embracing me with more love than the tenderest of mothers has ever given to her child, I saw her leave.*

My heart was filled with joy, and then I remembered my Sisters, and I wanted to ask some favors for them, but alas, I awoke!

"The storm was no longer raging, heaven was calm and serene. I believed, I felt *there was a* heaven *and that this* heaven *is peopled with souls who actually love me."*[83]

It is interesting that Thérèse never spoke of this experience as anything but a dream. It would not occur to her to think of it as a vision. Nonetheless, she found great solace in it.

She understood well that Maurice also would need something to hold on to in the hard years ahead of him, once she was gone. The next letter, her last, would be her final assurance of God's love for him, and of her own, *"to the last day."*

---

[83] *Story of a Soul*, 190.

August 10, 1897

Carmel of Lisieux
Jesus+
My dear little Brother,

I am now all ready to leave. I have my passport for
Heaven, and it is my dear father who has obtained this
grace for me. On the 29th he gave me the assurance that I
would soon go to join him. The next day the doctor, astonished by the progress the sickness had made in two days,
said to Mother that it was time to grant my wish to receive
Extreme Unction. So I had this happiness on the 30th, and
also that of seeing Jesus in the Blessed Sacrament leave the
tabernacle to come to me, Whom I received as Viaticum
for my long *voyage!* This Bread of Heaven has strengthened me. Just look, it seems as if my pilgrimage can't get
to its destination. Far from complaining about this, I
rejoice that God still lets me suffer for love of Him. Ah,
how good it is to let yourself go in His arms, with neither
fears nor desires.

I have to tell you, little brother, that we don't understand Heaven in the same way. You think that, once I
share in the justice and holiness of God, I won't be able to
excuse your faults as I did when I was on earth. Are you
then forgetting that I shall also share in the infinite mercy
of the Lord? I believe that the Blessed in Heaven have
great compassion for our miseries. They remember that

when they were weak and mortal like us, they committed the same faults themselves and went through the same struggles, and their fraternal tenderness becomes still greater than it ever was on earth. It's on account of this that they never stop watching over us and praying for us.

Now my dear little brother, I must tell you about the inheritance you *will come into after my death. Here is the share which our Mother will give you: (1) the reliquary which I received on the day I took the habit and which has never left me since then; (2) a little crucifix which is incomparably more dear to me than the large one, for the one I have now is no longer the first one that I was given. In Carmel we sometimes exchange holy objects; it is a way of keeping us from getting attached to them. Let me come back to the little Crucifix. It is not beautiful; the face of Christ has disappeared. You won't be surprised at this when I tell you that since I was 13 years old this souvenir from one of my sisters has followed me everywhere. It was especially during my voyage in Italy that this Crucifix became dear to me. I touched it to all the famous relics I had the joy of venerating, which were more than I can count, and moreover it was blessed by the Holy Father. Ever since I've been sick I hold our dear little Crucifix almost constantly in my hands, and as I look at it now I think with joy that after having received my kisses it will go to claim those of my little brother. Look then what a* heritage *you will have! In addition, our Mother will give you the* last *picture that I painted.*

Dear little brother, let me end where I should have begun, by thanking you for the great pleasure *you gave me by sending me your photograph.*

À Dieu, *dear little brother, may God give us the grace to love Him and to save souls for Him. This is the wish of*

Your unworthy little Sister of the Child Jesus and of the Holy Face. r.c.i.

A Promise Renewed

This was Thérèse's final letter to Maurice, the fourth she wrote him in less than a month. This one had to be brief, for she had come to the limit of her strength. It was in fact the very last letter she ever wrote. She would ask for her pencil only two more times, to put a few words on holy cards. The latter of these would also be for Maurice, the last picture she painted, which Mother Gonzague sent him after she died. On the back of it Thérèse wrote: *"Last souvenir of the sister of your soul."* She thought of him often in the weeks before her death— sometimes with pleasant humor. Pinned to the curtain of her bed were photographs of her two missionary brothers, and only a few days before she died she joked to one of the sisters: *"I'm better looking than they are."*

In this letter of farewell she listed the items she would leave him, what she termed his *"heritage,"* underlining the word for the touch of humor in it. There was the reliquary given to her on the day she took the habit as a Carmelite, the painted holy card, and, finally, the little crucifix that was dearer to her than anything in the world, which Léonie had given her when she was thirteen and with which she never parted. It traveled with her to Rome, where she offered it to the Pope for his blessing. In the long days and nights of her darkness she held on to it, remembering how dark it was for Him as He hung on the cross. She had kissed the Face of Jesus so often that the features were worn away. She was glad that in the years ahead that crucifix would receive the kisses of her brother. She had little to leave anyone, but to Maurice she left the one object she treasured most of all.

"I am now all ready to leave. I have my passport for Heaven, and it is my dear father who has obtained this grace for me. On the 29th he gave me the assurance that I would soon go to join him." It was on that day, twelve days before she wrote this letter, that she had celebrated the anniversary of Papa's death, and as she prayed to him she evidently felt he gave her the conviction that she would soon join him in heaven. She had received the Sacrament of the Sick, called in those days Extreme Unction, and Holy Viaticum, the Latin expression for the final Holy Communion given to a dying person as "food for the journey."

Her strength had revived a little after she received the Last Sacraments, enabling her to write one more letter. The second paragraph contained the real treasure in the inheritance she was leaving Maurice, the final assurance of a love that would never die. Once she crossed the threshold of death and entered the life which was in Jesus when He rose from the dead on

Easter morning, she would share that life forever. That is how she would be able to go with Maurice to Africa and remain at his side as long as he lived, as unconstrained as Jesus is by time and space. She would indeed then see Maurice as he really was, she would know everything that was bad and good in his life, she would know his failings and his sins. But they would make no difference. Nothing, she assured him, would ever diminish her love.

The paragraph is vintage Thérèse. It goes to the heart of her understanding of God and is to be ranked as one of her finest declarations. She fiercely believed every word she said in this passage, about God and about sins committed through human frailty. Her words place the Church's teaching on the Communion of Saints in a clear and realistic light.

"I have to tell you, little brother, that we don't understand Heaven in the same way. You think that, once I share in the justice and holiness of God, I won't be able to excuse your faults as I did when I was on earth. Are you then forgetting that I shall also share in the infinite mercy of the Lord? I believe that the Blessed in Heaven have great compassion for our miseries. They remember that when they were weak and mortal like us, they committed the same faults themselves and went through the same struggles, and their fraternal tenderness becomes still greater than it ever was on earth. It's on

account of this that they never stop watching over us and praying for us."

Maurice must never again worry about the sins which darkened his past, nor about the faults into which he would fall in the future through weakness. What a strange idea he must have of heaven, she wrote, if he felt that those who are there do not look with pity on the failed humanity of those coming after them. Did they not themselves commit the same sins during their lifetime? And what a twisted idea of God, to imagine that He who is Merciful Love could ever turn away from us because of our weakness and failures. It is impossible for God to hate anyone because God is Love, and the Love that is His very Being is exactly the same as His mercy. For Thérèse there is an equal sign between love and mercy in God. He turns away from sin but never from sinners. Sin grieves God, preventing His love from finding its way into the hearts of sinners. It was crystal clear to Thérèse that God not only wants our love but *needs* it. The reason He created us was that we should love Him. We are the only ones in the universe who can *love* Him, because we are the only ones who are free. Love can in no way be forced out of us because if it could be, it would not be love. The hallmark of all love is that it is free, given willingly, gladly, joyously, and as joyously received.

Her will and testament to Maurice was the simple

and sublime truth that God is nothing but mercy and love, and with her last breath she would convince him that it was the one thing he needed to know. Thérèse knew that once she reached heaven she would be able to excuse his faults even more readily than she could as she was writing this letter, because she would share in the *infinite mercy* of the Lord—she underlined the words to take away any doubt he might have.

This last of her letters was an expression of the kindness that filled her heart for someone she loved as a brother. But in addition to her love for Maurice, it reflected her worldview. Thérèse illuminated the world beyond the grave, enabling us to envision it in a new way, as the eyes of her faith saw it. Heaven, she knew, is filled with joy and compassion and bustles with activity on behalf of those left behind to walk the hard road of their earthly life. Those in heaven have been purged of all selfishness, and their love has become the love of God Himself. They watch over us with eager care and pray that we shall come to a good end. In the long view of Christian faith, the other world is more *real* than this one, for it never passes away.

The darkness through which she was passing was torture, but it never obscured her nocturnal vision of the glory of God's love. She could *feel* nothing, no consolation at all from her faith. Her trust in God was blind. But it grew stronger as her trial of faith went on. *"Ah, how good it is to let yourself go in His arms, with neither fears nor desires!"* Thérèse could get along without religious comfort. She could not do without religious faith.

My very dear little Sister,

The moment has come, then. You are about to leave for Heaven. You are going to see God and the Holy Virgin. How blest you are. Much loved Sister, go to feast your soul upon Love. Heaven will be the fulfillment, the perfection of what you had on earth. Heaven, which already is so dear to your soul, is already its life. Jesus will at last be yours, all yours, and soon there will be an exchange of the tender and fervent expressions of affection that will last as long as eternity. Love without anything standing in its way anymore, in all its fullness, seeing it, hearing it, breathing it in, feeling it all around you invading and powerful, shared with those who are waiting for you and eager to share their love with you.

Already they are initiating you into the happiness that is up there on high, since already your beloved father is so unable to hold back his impatience that he is letting you know of the Bridegroom's approach.

You are therefore expected, and the angels are preparing a place for you. What can this poor creature do from now on? Can he dream of holding you back and making your friends in Heaven sad? See, they're holding out their hands to you. Let yourself go, take your departure and fall asleep in their arms, in the arms of Jesus Who seems only to be waiting for your consent so He can take you to Himself.

*But when a dear friend goes off to see another friend
who is also very dear, it's customary, is it not, to entrust
the first one with a message for the second? So tell Jesus,
dear little Sister, to fill my good mother with His grace.
Sensing the closeness of what soon has to happen, she has
started to tell me that she will never give her consent.
There is no doubt that I'm not going to back off, but your
affectionate heart knows how painful it is to crush the soul
of anyone so dear. Jesus can take care of all that; plead my
cause with Him, dear little Sister. I commend myself also
to the* Blessed Virgin, *and to the saints whom you know,
to Cardinal Lavigerie,*[84] *to the saints whose relics I shall
have the happiness of venerating after you yourself have
venerated them.*

*Oh, my good little sister, how clearly I saw the part
your heart played in the heritage I shall receive from you.
How dear to you those things you selected were, and how
grateful I am for the affection which prompted your choice
of them. Thank you. Oh yes, thank you from the bottom of
my heart for that cherished crucifix. (Oh, how dear it will
be to me after it was first so dear to you!) Until the day I
die it will remain my closest friend; yes, dear on so many
scores. How good you are to have thought of leaving it to*

---

[84] Cardinal Charles Lavigerie, the founder of the White Fathers, who had died
in 1892, was venerated as a very holy man, not only within the order but by
many outside of it who knew him. He was a close and trusted adviser of Pope
Leo XIII. He was a vigorous opponent of the slave trade in Africa and in 1888
founded the Anti-Slavery Society.

*me. The same goes also for the reliquary, which has been
the companion of your entire religious life. From heaven
you will see what veneration I will bestow upon it. And
then that picture, the* last *painted expression of your piety
which you left behind you. They will all be my dearest
treasure. Simply but with all my heart I say thank you,
dear little sister.*

*Tomorrow, or rather Thursday, I shall leave for
Lourdes with my mother. Be sure that I will pray for you
there with very special fervor. I hope to be a* bran-
cardier.[85] *Join in the pilgrimage with me. I shall be in
union with you constantly at the feet of the very gentle
Mother of Mercy.*

To the last day, if you CAN do it, *will you send me
some of your thoughts, dear little sister. This too will be
part of the inheritance. But please don't tire yourself. When
I return on the 25th I hope to find you still among us.*

*However, Jesus is calling you; go to God. Your little
brother sends you what is perhaps the* last good-bye, the
au revoir *until heaven. Because always and forever he
remains your brother,*

Louis

---

[85] A stretcher bearer for the sick.

Letting Go

This letter reached Thérèse six weeks before her death, when she was too sick to reply. Her illness was at a new stage. She had lost the use of her right lung completely, and the lower part of her left lung was also affected. The pain was acute. On some days, she would have to stop after each word to catch her breath. She cautioned that poisonous medicine should not be left within a sick person's reach. *"If I had not faith, I would have taken my own life without hesitation,"* she admitted. On August 19, she received Communion for the last time. Vomiting, breathing difficulties, weakness, and her frayed nerves made it impossible for her to continue writing.

Maurice had now come to grips with the reality of her condition, although he did not lose all hope of a miracle, for which he said he would pray on the pilgrimage he was about to make to Lourdes.

His mother was going with him to the famous shrine of the Blessed Virgin. As the time drew near for his departure to Africa, her opposition to his going stiffened. She had taken him into her heart when he was a baby only one week old, and she had given her whole life to raising him. She was proud of how well she had done her job and proud of his desire to be a priest, but she did not want to lose him forever to the missions. He could serve God just as well in a parish in their diocese. Let others give one of their sons to the missions; he was the only one she had. She opposed his plans fiercely, even threatening to disinherit him if he left her. For his part he was sure of God's call and he was going to answer it. But the last thing he wanted was to grieve the one he loved so dearly. He asked Thérèse to beg God to change her heart, that he might set out for Africa with her blessing.

More than ever he was in need of prayers on every score, as he stood on the threshold of his new vocation. Soon Thérèse would join the saints in heaven, and she must carry his needs with her. He charged her with messages for those whom they both loved.

While he would pray at Lourdes for a miracle, he knew in his heart that she was soon to die. The opening words of his letter were the sign of his acceptance. "The moment has come, then," he wrote. His thoughts turned to the future, and what it would hold was never in doubt for him. Thérèse would go at once to heaven, where she would be joined to Jesus in a union of love which would be inexpressibly tender and would last forever. Those whom she loved on earth and had preceded her into eternal life would be eagerly awaiting her arrival, and the reunion would be a feast of love. Especially her dear father, for whom she had grieved through his long and humiliating confinement in Bon Sauveur, would throw his arms around her in joyous welcome.

Maurice never doubted that all this would happen soon, but little did he dream that Thérèse, woman of faith that *she* was, was traveling through the last hard days of a terribly difficult journey, with a voice inside which kept saying: "When you die you will discover that after death there is *nothing*."

Dear little Sister of Jesus,

You must have realized that today I was especially united to you, and you must have known in whose soul it was that we met. Your saintly mother looked down upon you with more delight than usual, seeing that you will soon be reunited with her and joining in her happiness. Timidly, I introduced myself to her, asking a blessing from her and praying to her for you. Dear little Sister, you have undoubtedly heard her voice, closer now and insistent, calling you and laying claim to you. And you have answered her: "I will see you soon!" For the moment is approaching, dear sister of my soul. You are about to leave for your true home. At Lourdes, I have not asked for your cure, but I begged the sweet Queen of Virgins and Martyrs to help you with your final preparations and to open Heaven to receive you. I don't know how to pray, so I asked to be a stretcher bearer for poor sick people, and I offered that for you. Often when I was taking them to the baths at the Grotto, my thoughts turned to you and rose up to Mary, and I said: "Mother, this is for my Sister Thérèse." If some little suffering came to me, it was for you. On Sunday especially I offered even the sufferings of the sick for you, and when Our Lord in the Blessed Sacrament passed close to me, blessing the crowd of unfortunates who surrounded Him, I fervently implored Him to bless you. This is the way I prayed for you. And when I saw those sick people, whom a few hours before I had carried almost lifeless in my arms, some of them with horrible maladies . . . when I saw them made well again, cured and now forming the escort of honor for Jesus, I thought of you suffering on your poor bed and I asked some consolation for you from your Bridegroom, a final preparation, an additional tenderness. My prayer, then, was above all one of action. But that affective prayer which God also loves, which I do not know, little Sister, you will teach me when you shall be near me. I somehow knew that you had not yet left this earth, because I just did not feel it in my heart.

Thank you, little Sister, for your feast day souvenir, and for the thought dictated by your heart.[86] Thanks to Mother Agnes who wrote it. Thank you for the few lines you traced,[87] the last ones, dear and precious, with the holy prayer that you loved so much. Thank you for this most recent act of tenderness.

Dearly beloved little sister, the language of earth must be tiring for you. Your unworthy and wretched brother would not want to distract you from Jesus. He tells you once more: À Dieu, until we meet again, for-

---

[86] This message, dictated by Thérèse to Mother Agnes, has not been found.

[87] We are not sure what those "few lines" were. He may be referring to the words on the back of a holy card, *"Last souvenir of the sister of your soul,"* the very last words she ever wrote him, or he may be speaking of a brief letter that has been lost.

ever in the union of our apostolate and of the love of
Jesus.

I am resigned, you see, and sometimes I almost long for
that more intimate union which Jesus is preparing for us.

Forever in His lovable Heart,

Your brother,
Louis

I should have liked to bring you back some souvenir
from Lourdes, but your poverty prevented me. I have
nothing to give you, only my prayer—which doesn't
amount to anything, without generosity and without
merit.

"Why I Love You, Mary"

This was the last letter from Maurice that Thérèse would receive. We may be sure she read it more than once in her final days.

In it he invoked the memory of her mother, the twentieth anniversary of whose death was on the very day he wrote the letter. Thérèse would be recalling that her mother had made a pilgrimage to Lourdes herself not long before she died, to ask the Virgin Mary for a cure of the breast cancer which was spreading ominously and would soon claim her life. While the cure was not granted, she left Lourdes fortified by the grace to face death with courage, and ready to commend her beloved husband and their five young daughters to Mary's maternal care.

Thérèse must have been consoled to see how changed Maurice was from the man who first wrote to the Carmel almost two years before. In those days he was pleading for prayers that *he* desperately needed. Now he was praying for her. His was not the prayer of words but that of action, as he gladly gave himself in service to the poor, carrying them in his arms to be immersed in the waters of the shrine at the very spot where Mary had once appeared to a young girl named Bernadette. He had grown more solid in his faith, more heedless of himself as he reached out to others.

The Little Way was taking hold. He was willing to let go of Thérèse, thinking ahead to the new relationship that would exist between them once she died.

The pilgrimage in which he was partaking was a memorable one. Thérèse's cousin-in-law, Dr. Francis Néele, made the same pilgrimage, and in a letter to her uncle reported that forty thousand pilgrims were in attendance and nearly fifty cures took place, "which in anyone's memory was never seen in Lourdes."

That Maurice was at Our Lady's shrine would be reassuring to Thérèse, who commended him every day to the care of the Blessed Mother. Her love for Mary was lifelong and profound. It was also down-to-earth and realistic, shunning the pious exaggeration fashionable at the time. The last poem she wrote was "Why I Love You, Mary." She worked on it for the whole month of May in 1897. It was an attempt to sum up all that she believed about the Blessed Mother. She told Céline: *"I have always dreamed of saying in a song to the Blessed Mother everything I think about her."* What she thought about Mary was entirely based upon the Gospels, to which she went for her facts. She stopped where the Gospels stopped, refusing to go beyond them to indulge imagination. When the poem was finished, it was two hundred lines long. In a faltering hand she signed it *"la petite Thérèse."*

The poem is a masterpiece of clarity that presents the Virgin Mother as she really is, clearing away all the accretions of a piety which had become insipid. In a remarkable manner, it foreshadows the Marian doctrine of the Second Vatican Council. For Thérèse, Mary was "more a mother than a queen," and she had no wish to embellish her image. She often said that she was never interested in anything but the truth. Mary was one of us, not someone above us. What kind of mother would she be, Thérèse asked, if her children could not imitate her? By virtue of her Immaculate Conception she was singularly filled with the grace of God and untouched by the original sin which is our common lot. But she was human and walked the ordinary ways we all must travel. If she was preserved from sin, she was not spared the suffering which is its consequence. Just like the rest of us, she was often puzzled by the Will of God. She obeyed it blindly, without knowing where God was leading her, wanting only to be "the servant of the Lord" at any cost. When she was asked to be the mother of Jesus, with no prophecy to light the future that was ahead of her, her answer was a simple yes, "let it be done." She suffered pain as we all do, from privation and the cold, from misunderstanding, from anxiety and care. Thérèse's Mary was the woman set before us in the Gospels, unspoiled by selfishness, utterly open to God's wishes, simple and pure as a child. She was the woman of faith par excellence, who walked in the dark wherever God wanted to lead her. She endured the awful pain of Calvary without the knowledge that there was to be a Resurrection, giving her Son the only thing she had to give Him, her steadfast mother's love. It was there at the foot of the Cross that Jesus made her the mother of us all, when He said to John: "Son, there is your mother."

Mary is the model of the whole Church, and she was the shining example which Thérèse tried all her life to follow. Mary, too, had walked through a terrible darkness not unlike that which overshadowed the last year and a half of Thérèse's life. Mary's faith, like that of Thérèse, was a blind faith. A priest who knew Thérèse well called her "a ravishing miniature of the Virgin Mary."[88]

How consoled Thérèse must have been that Maurice was in Lourdes at this critical moment, imploring Our Lady's support for her and asking her protection for himself as he prepared to set forth for Africa to give his life to the work which God carved out as his destiny.

---

[88] Father Hodierne, who became the chaplain of the Carmel after the death of Thérèse.

My dear and more than dear little Sister,

Rejoice with me. The one you love so much and for whom you have offered so many prayers and good deeds has at last had his dearest desires fulfilled, at least almost completely. Little Sister, your brother has been a missionary for a day! Tell me, to whom does he owe it? To Jesus first of all Who chose him, but after Him to my good little sister from the Carmel in Lisieux, to my Sister Thérèse of the Child Jesus. You have succeeded completely, for it is you who have done it all. From the way I was acting it looked as though I would derail what you were doing, but your Jesus is so good. He loves you so much that He could not say no to your suffering which was begging mercy for me. Thank you from the bottom of my heart, kind little Sister. I owe you this immense honor of being today a missionary of Jesus. And see how good He is! He has willed for you to be present for this triumph of grace, since He has preserved you until now. You will depart soon, little Sister. Soon you will come to your brother who waits for you here. Jesus is waiting for you and so am I. Come quickly. If only you knew how beautiful Africa is! How much the poor Arabs need help! If you only knew above all (oh, what an egoist I am!) how your brother needs to know you are near him. He can't fathom how he ever landed in such a holy house! Who led him here? How did he tear himself away from such strong and charming ties? He understands none of this and never thought he would find himself at such a feast. He sometimes even wonders if he's dreaming.

You have prayed much, very much for my poor mother, haven't you? She has been admirable. Ask your reverend Mother; my letter to her will fill out this one. Oh, that hour of parting, that last blessing, with my friends sobbing around me, my Mother strong to the end, sending me off to God. I will never forget it. If you could know these tricks of the devil, these temptations, the thousand things he used to break down my resolution! Once more he has lost, thank God. Now I am hard at work. I must go forward, and already I am happy.

It is rough at the beginning, but so much the better. When it is the hardest I think how much harder it is for you. For example, we sleep on a simple straw mattress and in May we shall be sleeping on a plank. That brings me closer to you and I am happy, extremely happy.

When you leave for heaven let me know. I'm waiting impatiently for you; from now on what more is left for me except the immediate presence of your dear soul close, so close, to mine, for I am always in need of some help. The moment you really get to know me you will see how miserable I am.

After your departure there will be your inheritance[89]

---

[89] The crucifix and reliquary.

which shall be counted among my dearest treasures. Your last painting is here, your photograph is there, surrounded by a few others of a very small circle: my mother and some friends, and also your good father in a frame that is quite handsome—and that is all, my books, and my crucifix waiting for yours to arrive. Here I have no relics except a piece of linen from Blessed Margaret Mary. I'm also waiting for your own to come. You see this is your inheritance. Is this bad, is it greediness? It is especially for you that I wait. Where are you in your illness? Will you be coming soon?

Today I am sending my guardian angel to yours, and I say the same prayer to him that you were recently singing yourself,[90] asking him to let you know that tomorrow I begin my Retreat, which will end on the tenth with the taking of the habit (a white robe, with a rosary around the neck. This is the Arab dress: a woolen garment, a cloak, and a hat—with the rosary added. All black and white). If you are still on earth, I shall have the joy of sending you flowers on October 15. If not, accept right now these flowers of my respectful and brotherly affection, with my liveliest thanks forever.

Brother Louis

Forgive me if in any way I cause you pain—I don't mean to.

---

[90] An allusion to her poem "To My Guardian Angel."

Death of Thérèse

his letter has a special pathos. It was written two days after Thérèse died. Maurice knew that she was dying and that his letter might not reach her in time, but he always felt that somehow he would know when death came to take her. He had said as much in his letter written from Lourdes: "I somehow knew that you had not yet left this earth, because I just did not feel it in my heart."

His departure for Africa had been heart-wrenching, and his description of it was vivid. His friends were weeping and his mother, who had showed such strong opposition to his becoming a foreign missionary, now put up a brave front. His remark about "strong and charming ties" was no exaggeration. He had friends who loved him, and he would always bear a deep affection for the woman he called his mother, who finally gave him her blessing as he set sail for Africa. Maurice was leaving behind everything he held dear, and now he was to suffer the loss of his newfound sister. The valor of this man, who never thought himself valorous, evokes admiration.

His one consolation was that Thérèse would be with him. Nothing was more real to him. She would stand by him to make him strong, she would pray for him, and she would give him a love far richer than the love he was renouncing. He expected her to join him as realistically as if she had travel plans to take a ship and meet him in Algiers. It never crossed his mind that she would not keep her promise. Whatever may be said of the doubts he harbored concerning himself—and Maurice was a very self-doubting man—he had none at all about the reality of eternal life. His faith on that score never faltered. And so he would wait for her and she would come to him. This encounter with her after her death was the dream that gave him strength.

Thérèse died as he was crossing from Marseilles to Algiers—the same night, he would later recall, that he was standing at the ship's rail, gazing at the stars and praying for her. She died in terrible agony.

Her lungs hemorrhaged for the first time on Good Friday of 1896, and the tuberculosis which caused the hemorrhage lasted eighteen months until her death. Slowly it undermined her young body, every cell of which fought back fiercely. To the end her vitality astonished those around her, but it was all in vain. The disease was well named "consumption" for it *consumed* those whom it attacked. In the last days she was skin and bone. One morning, Sister Aimée lifted her in her arms while her bed was being remade. Mother Gonzague was called to see how thin she was; the bones were almost protruding through her back. "What's this," she said gently, "our little girl so thin?"

Still attempting to maintain her good humor, Thérèse replied: *"A skeleton!"*

Her breath had become alarmingly short, something she always feared. Her great obsession was that she would die of suffocation. It seemed to those around her that Thérèse, who lived to love Jesus, was now living his Passion. Asphyxiation is what ultimately caused the death of Christ on the cross. Céline would recall the image of her sister one afternoon, gasping for breath, trying to find some relief. She was seated in bed with her arms extended outward, as if in the form of a cross, leaning on her and Pauline. "For us she was a striking image of Jesus on the cross," Céline said. And as with Christ, Céline realized, there was no consolation for her sister. "[Her] broken words, all bearing the stamp of perfect conformity to God's will, were heartbreaking to hear. Like Jesus, God seemed to have abandoned her."

On the morning of the 29th the death rattle began in her throat. The community was summoned to say the Prayers for the Dying. At midday Thérèse questioned Mother Gonzague if the end was at hand: *"Is this the agony?"* The doctor came, but there was nothing he could do. When he left, she remarked: *"I can't take any more! . . . Oh, pray for me! . . . Jesus! . . . Mary! . . . Yes, I will it, I really do will it. . . . Oh Mother, what this does to the nerves!"*

The following night the Prioress told Marie and Céline to take turns watching their sister. Pauline was sleeping in the next cell. Thérèse's sleep was peopled with nightmares. The morning dawned overcast and it began to rain. *"It is pure agony,"* she said, *"without a touch of consolation."*

All through the day she gasped for breath. *"If you knew what it is to suffocate! . . . But God will not abandon me, for sure. . . . He has never abandoned me! . . . Mother, offer me quickly to the blessed Virgin. I am a baby who can't take any more!"*

Marie, her godmother, was so distraught by the struggle that she hesitated to come back into the infirmary. Pauline went to pray before a statue of the Sacred Heart on the first floor, that her sister might not despair in the last moments.

In the early evening, the bell rang, summoning the community again. Thérèse welcomed the sisters with a weak smile. She was holding her crucifix in a firm grasp. The "terrible death rattle" tore at her chest. Her face was flushed, her hands purplish, her feet ice cold. She was sweating so profusely that the mattress was soaked through.

Suddenly she sat up. Her eyes grew luminous with a look the nuns never forgot. Her gaze was fixed above the statue of Our Lady of the Smile. She spoke her last words: *"Oh, how I love You! . . . My God. . . . How I love You!"* She obviously "saw" God. It was the only vision she ever had and it was said to last only a few moments, "for the space of a Credo." Then she sank back on the pillow, her eyes closed. Her face was serene, with just the suggestion of a smile. There was a beauty about her again which gave her the appearance of a very young girl. It was about twenty past seven in the evening of September 30, 1897.[91]

Céline bolted into the cloister in tears. The rain was falling. She later recalled how she said to herself: "If only there were stars in the sky!" A few moments later the clouds parted and the stars came out. The Guerins, on their way home from the Chapel of the Carmel, also noticed the sudden change. They too saw the stars, the same stars Maurice watched from the ship which was carrying him to Algiers, as he prayed for her.

When his ship docked in the morning she was there, waiting for him.

---

[91] The dialogue here is excerpted from *The Last Conversations*, in which were recorded a number of things Thérèse said in her final days. Pauline and Céline and a few other sisters took notes. Apparently they were beginning to think that they had a saint on their hands.

III
AFRICA

~

The Correspondence of
Maurice Bellière to
Mother Gonzague and
Father André Adam

Maison-Carrée, Algeria
October 14, 1897

Venerable and very dear Mother,[92]

*I just wrote to you and to my dear Saint to congratu-
late you for the Feast of Saint Teresa, but there was no
point in mailing my letters once I received the news which
the one from Mother Agnes brought me yesterday. Hearing
it did not surprise me, since her death was expected at any
moment; nor was I at first overcome, accustomed as I am
during this past month to watching all that was dearest to
me disappear. I said to myself: Well, I must face it, the last
of life's treasures is gone and there is nothing left for me
now.*

*Later on, a completely natural sorrow overwhelmed
me, brought on by the void which now engulfs me—
which the absence of that cherished sister made complete.
Then calm returned, with the thought of the immense
happiness which crowns her glorious martyrdom. First I
wanted to cry with you, Mother, but I think I should
rather join in the chorus of your thanksgiving, for now we
have a saint in heaven who loved us while she was on
earth. Now she becomes a powerful helper up there beyond. Never again shall I doubt my salvation.*

I did not realize she had died, but since I have been

---

[92] Mother Gonzague.

here I have experienced a certain calm, a joy I did not know before, which has kept me from even a moment's worry or regret. I was wondering to what I owed this happiness. Now I wonder no longer. The saint was near me with her comforting tenderness and strength.

How beautiful and consoling the description of her death was! Please tell Mother Agnes how grateful I am to her for sending it to me. If I had been in France when she died I would, like the good people of Lisieux, have hurried to venerate the Saint. At the very moment of 7:30 on Thursday night I was well out to sea, a hundred miles from France. That night—I don't recall the hour—I thought of her and was repeating the prayer she asked me to say for her every day until I died. Perhaps she was listening in heaven.

She was waiting for me here when I arrived on the first! And she was helping me during my Retreat, and she was present on Sunday when the reception of the Religious Habit made me a missionary. She will always be with me here below, at every conquest and victory. But just the same, Mother, it will be good for me on occasion to hear an echo from the Carmel over here. I continue to be your affectionate and respectful son, and on that basis I place a claim on the prayers for me you are in the habit of saying, and upon the kind words you have sent in the past— which doubtless now more than ever will give me courage and joy.

Mother, thank you for the souvenir you are sending me.

Indeed, my little sister once told me that you were keeping her small crucifix and her reliquary for me. Perhaps you have some relics of herself. *Oh, please do include something of herself in the package you are sending!*

In the past you mentioned a project you were planning with Mother Agnes for the future, after the death of my sister, in which you thought I might be associated. Dear and Reverend Mother, I offer you both of my hands for whatever you may wish to ask of me, in anything you are hoping to accomplish.

In Jesus and Mary, and also in Our Saint, I am forever, very dear Mother, your grateful and respectfully devoted son.

M. B-Bellière
Missionary of Africa

243

Missions to Fulfill

By the time Thérèse died on the night of September 30, she had firmly rejected the conventional understanding of heaven as eternal rest. She looked forward on her deathbed to a life of intense effort until the last day of history, laboring side by side with Jesus for the salvation of others. Her vocation was "to be Love in the heart of the Church," and love knows no rest. October 1, chosen to be Thérèse's feast day because it was her first day in heaven, was Maurice Bellière's first day in Africa. She had promised to go there with him and she lost no time. She watched him as he came down the gangplank at six o'clock in the morning. Her worldwide mission began with him, her first missionary.

The confreres from the White Fathers' seminary welcomed the newcomers warmly and brought them directly to Maison-Carrée. Before he went to bed that night Maurice wrote to Mother Gonzague, giving her an account both of his sad departure from Marseilles and of his joyous arrival in Africa. He told her he had grown confident of his missionary vocation. Some sixty men were in the band which set out from Marseilles. They came from a half dozen European countries as well as from Egypt and Canada. The dream of the community was to phase out of Africa once the native clergy was numerous and strong enough to serve the African Church. They knew, of course, that that day was still far in the future.

Maurice had just written to Mother Gonzague and to Thérèse, but before he could mail either letter, word arrived from Pauline that Thérèse had died. He wrote immediately to Mother Gonzague, expressing his sorrow and, by the same token, the reassurance he felt that his sister had not reneged on her promise to be with him. He shared the mixed emotions he experienced on hearing of her death, convinced that she was the reason for the "calm" and "joy" he felt from the moment he set foot on African soil. Sure of her sanctity and her larger importance to the Church, he requested what is called a first-class relic of his saint, "something of herself," a lock of her hair, for example.

Soon many would agree that Thérèse was a saint, in such huge numbers that a Vatican official would remark that if they did not hasten her canonization, the people themselves would canonize her by popular acclaim. The instrument of her spreading fame was her autobiography, which was distributed to Carmelite convents throughout the world and passed on from one person to another. This was the project Maurice referred to in his letter when he offered his assistance. He had been asked to share his letters from Thérèse. He was enthusiastic and viewed this effort as an "apostolate."

As the work progressed, Pauline sent him preliminary drafts of the book and eventually the full version. Writing to her on December 3, he was full of enthusiasm in his reaction: "What should I say? I should sing a chant of joy—if only I could sing! Our Mother Gonzague will tell you how truly delighted I am. The wonderment, the gratitude, and all the many feelings which crowd in on me! They cluster together in a happiness that is deeply intimate, profound, and unknown before! For it seemed to me, too, that an invisible hand *'touched musical chords in my soul which until then had remained forgotten.'* " (He was quoting Thérèse's own words in the autobiography, where she described her first reaction to Pauline's request that she become Maurice's partner in prayer.)

He continued: "I had hardly gotten through the first part when I stopped short, startled. 'God is there!' I cried. 'The two missionaries who were sought from heaven with prayers and tears . . . I am the first of them!! What a blessing for me!' And I thought of the joy your beloved Father would have felt, if he had lived four more years to see so dear a wish fulfilled by his 'Queen.' "

Maurice was beside himself with joy as he read the autobiography. Heretofore he had known Thérèse only through the letters she had sent him. Now he held in his hands this classic of spiritual literature, written by a young woman who had become his dearest friend. His eyes opened in wonder before the childhood she described, the marvels God had worked in her soul. She stood before him in a new and brilliant light. How could he be so fortunate as to have known her? With no self-consciousness she described God's love for her, and her love for Him, and revealed the depth and breadth of her apostolic longings. In writing *The Story of a Soul* she had no inhibitions. She opened the door of her heart and set all its secrets free.

Through the years Maurice would pray constantly to Thérèse and count heavily on her help. He devoured everything the Carmel sent him about her. He pored over her letters, knew them almost by heart, and made them the object of his prayer and reflection. He kept close the photograph that Céline had taken. "I know she is near me, and I now have the habit of consulting her when there is a decision to be made," he wrote. "As if she were physically beside me, I say to her: 'Look, show me what I have to do.' Her portrait is always before me and finds me often on my knees, praying to her with faith and confidence." Thérèse was never far from Maurice. He would introduce her to Africa in his seminary days and later would speak of her to his converts, giving them her picture to keep in their huts.

Maurice continued to keep in touch with Mother Gonzague and Pauline and occasionally with Céline and Marie. He considered himself a member of the

247

Martin family. Unfortunately, a good part of the correspondence has been lost. His friend and the executor of his will, Father André Adam, destroyed many of the letters between Maurice and Pauline because he considered the correspondence too sentimental. We can be grateful that he did not do the same with the correspondence between Maurice and Thérèse.

Maurice was facing four years of preparation in the seminary of the White Fathers. He had a year to do in the novitiate, and, since he had finished one year of theology in his diocesan seminary in France, he had only three years of study remaining before his ordination as a priest. He entered the novitiate as an eager candidate. He was said to be a passable but not a brilliant student. An evaluation given by his professors just before he received the diaconate toward the end of his seminary course spoke of him as "a good confrere" who got on well with his classmates and enjoyed the company of others.

He fell in love at once with Africa. "If you could know how beautiful it is!" he wrote. But the life was not easy. The routine of the novices and the whole atmosphere of Maison-Carrée were spartan and demanding. The days were passed mostly in reflection on the Scriptures and in spiritual exercises. The only formal study was a basic language course to give the young men a start in the languages they would need. What a novice needed most was to acquire the knowledge of God. He was to strengthen his interior life, until his sole aim was to love God and bring that love to others.

Manual work and group recreation were part of the daily schedule, and laughter often broke out, especially over the ludicrous attempts of these men from different countries to master the strange languages of Africa. To relieve the tension of their strenuous life, holidays were celebrated by long walks to mission posts, where they could observe the work of the White Fathers in the field. These were arduous treks of twenty miles and more under a broiling sun, from which they returned happy but exhausted. They slept as soundly on the wooden plank of the novitiate as they would have slept in a featherbed. They were young and filled with heroic dreams. To be a White Father was to belong to the shock troops of the Church, and they were glad to have their mettle tested. Esprit de corps and the grace of God kept them going. With his gift for the dramatic and his eye for comedy, Maurice blended in well. Deep down, however, he was a serious man, eager to give the best that was in him. Thérèse had touched his life and imparted to him some of her own courageous spirit.

He left the novitiate for the seminary in Carthage in August 1898. It was around this time that he began to experience difficulties with his health, which were sufficiently serious for him to say in a letter to Pauline in April 1899: "I would so much like to live another two years to receive the crown of Ordination; and then, if even after saving only one soul, to be buried in the sands of the desert. When you pray to our Saint, please tell her to speak to Jesus about this and to arrange it with Him."

In the same letter he wrote: "I see again the hand of God in choosing that saint to be my sister. I recognize that she comes from Him. She has been watching over me and she guards me still. It is true. She wrote me in pencil toward the end of her life: *'When my dear little brother leaves for Africa, I shall follow him, not only in thought and in prayer . . . my* soul *will be with him forever, his faith will know very well how to discover the presence of a little sister whom Jesus gave him, to be a support . . . until the last days of his life.'* Hasn't she kept her word! I wonder at God's goodness to me. As soon as I leave France she takes me by the hand. I set out for Africa, and she leaves the world so that she can be waiting for me on the 1st of October when I disembark in Algiers in the morning, and her soul is right with me to *'teach me the same way* (as hers), *that of suffering united to love.'* For she told me that I must go to heaven *'by the same way'* as herself, *'by the elevator of love.'* It is thus that I explain the marvels which Jesus has done for me and in me since that time."

Maurice finished his course in the seminary and was ordained a priest on June 29, 1901. The following morning he offered Mass with the sisters at the nearby Carmelite convent, founded in 1885 by Cardinal Lavigerie to pray for God's blessing on the missions of Africa. It was the first place he wanted to say Mass after his ordination.

Like the rest of his class he went home for a holiday before taking up his first assignment. His reunion with his mother, who had not seen him for four years, must have been a very emotional experience, and the reception given him by his friends would have been that accorded a returning hero. There is no record of his visiting the Carmel in Lisieux, but he had long ago promised to go there for Mass, and a note he wrote later to Céline makes it appear certain that he went there and met her personally.

His first assignment was not to a mission but to Bishop Livinhac's office in Algiers. His knowledge of English made him useful to this superior of the White Fathers, who often dealt with British government personnel. Moreover, Maurice's health problems might have been a handicap at that moment in the grueling work of the missions. This assignment lasted for one year, from August 1901 to July 1902. It was an interesting one which gave him an overall vision of his community's work. The Bishop was fond of Maurice and would prove to be a good friend later. Some interesting people came to the Bishop's residence. One of them was the famous Father Charles De Foucauld, the Hermit of the Sahara, who was very friendly with some of the White Fathers and who stayed with the Bishop for a week during Maurice's time as secretary. De Foucauld was the rich young man whose conversion took place on the same day that Thérèse's Christmas miracle occurred in 1886.[93]

---

[93] De Foucauld came from a highly placed and very wealthy family and had begun to carve out a brilliant career in the military. He was a convinced agnostic who had abandoned his Catholic faith, a bon vivant of some renown whose extravagant parties attracted a host of fellow revelers. On Christmas Day 1886 something made him enter the confessional of a certain Abbé Huvelin in a Paris church. The abbé was well regarded as a spiritual director and counted among his penitents the great British Catholic intellectual, Baron Friederich von Hügel. When De Foucauld left his confessional he was a convert to the faith he had rejected and went on to become the well-known Hermit of the Sahara.

That was the day of Thérèse's Christmas miracle, which she spoke of as her "conversion" and the greatest grace of her life.

On that same day another young man wandered into the Cathedral of Notre Dame while Vespers was being sung. He, too, had given up the faith of his birth, but something profound happened to him during the celebration of Vespers and he emerged from the cathedral to begin a new life as one of the outstanding Catholic laymen of his time. He carved out an enduring place in French literature as a playwright, a poet, and a very influential spokesman for the Church. For several years he was France's ambassador to the United States in Washington. His name was Paul Claudel.

God dispensed three stunning graces on that Christmas Day 1886. One wonders whether those were the only ones, what others He gave on that day, and where He gave them. Surely He did not confine His generosity to France.

An interesting biography of Charles De Foucauld, called *The Sands of*

After a year in his first assignment, Maurice was deemed ready for missionary work. He went home once more for a brief holiday and then set out for south central Africa, to begin the apostolate for which he was ordained. He sailed with ten companions from Marseilles on July 29, 1902, all of them bound for various destinations on the continent of Africa. Today a jet takes eleven hours to fly the distance he traveled, but his voyage by ship lasted sixty-seven days. It brought him south across the Mediterranean to Egypt, through Port Said and the Suez Canal into the northern end of the Red Sea. He sailed past Egypt, the Sudan, and Ethiopia, into the Gulf of Aden, around Cape Guardafui, and down the Indian Ocean along the coast of Africa to Dar es Salaam on the shore of Tanzania. It was an exciting journey for a young man who had spent almost all his life in a small provincial town in Normandy, taking him past all those "faraway places with the strange sounding names." The long voyage was filled with the excitement of going at last to his life's work. That work would be hard, far harder than he might imagine, but this only fired his romantic dreams of sacrifice and spiritual conquest. He and his companions were raised on stories of the he-

---

Tamanrasset, has been written by Marion Preminger, the wife of the famous movie producer Otto Preminger (Garden City, N.Y.: Doubleday, Image, 1961).

roic missionaries who had preceded them. They were buoyed by the camaraderie of men from other nations, forged into a band with a single purpose. Their differences of origin, family background, and personal temperament would try their spirit of collaboration, but that was simply a part of the challenge which they took up generously.

Once they had landed on the coast of Africa and begun the long inland journey of two weeks, they came up against the difficult reality of what lay before them. In places the jungle was so thick they had to hack their way through with machetes. The heat and humidity were formidable, and the mosquitoes seemed organized to drive them out of Africa. A description by a confrere, Père Guillemé, gives us some notion of the conditions they sometimes faced. At one time on a journey Maurice found himself traversing the Lwanga Valley. Exploring it in 1900 the intrepid Guillemé had found it "a land of few enchantments." He reported that he and his companions had "sweated profusely, been assailed by tse-tse flies,[94] drained by the intense heat, and devoured by thirst. In the night, there were hordes of mosquitoes to give us little rest, and if we did succeed in drowsing off it was to awaken with a

---

[94] This was the insect whose venomous bite spread the dreaded and fatal sleeping sickness (maladie du sommeil).

start to the lugubrious scream of hyenas or the terrifying roar of lions." A land of few enchantments indeed. Until they set foot on shore they had been tourists. Now they were missionaries and the pleasures of travel were over.

Maurice's immediate destination was Chiwamba in Nyassa, a mission territory established shortly before by Père Guillemé. Having worked for many years in the Congo, this man was well seasoned and widely respected by his confreres, the natives, and the English administration. Mr. McDonald, the governor, himself not a Catholic, was very partial to the missionaries, helping them in every way he could. Maurice and he would become good friends.

Guillemé arrived in the spring of 1902, to be joined soon by Fathers Guyard and Perrot. Within three months they had constructed provisional buildings of wood, hay, and reeds: a long hut to house the missionaries, a hall for catechism classes, a school, a kitchen, and a warehouse. The plan was for Chiwamba to be the nucleus for other stations in the region. Père Louveau and Brother Wilfred arrived in early September from Ubemba, just as Père Alfred Honoré came from Europe. They were joined in October by Maurice and Brother Sebastian.

In founding the White Fathers, Cardinal Lavigerie had made a rule that there should be at least three missionaries at a station, enough to form a community of prayer and mutual support and to carry the heavy workload. Eventually there would be four men at Chiwamba, an arrangement very agreeable to Maurice who was by nature gregarious and to whom friends were always important. In 1905, when he was at Likuni, he spoke of "the *entente cordiale,* the good humor, and lively spirit" which prevailed.

The support the men gave one another was critical to the success of their work. In Chiwamba they had no one to help them as they struggled with the new language. At first the natives did not understand a word they said, and only slowly were they able to build enough vocabulary to be able to communicate. The school opened in November, with students who had never seen the inside of a classroom. The teacher was Maurice, who has left us this account of his experience: "It is a pleasure to see the group of young scholars arriving, running and shouting. They are there well before the hour, sitting in line, their backs turned to the first warm rays of the sun and their arms folded on their bare chests, trying to keep off the biting cold of morning. Father appears; the joyous band gathers about him and a fire is lit around which they all sit. The class goes on with varying results. . . . Finally the bell rings ending the hour and they all take off for a noisy game of ball."

We may imagine the difficulty of teaching and preaching when they were so poorly equipped. The teachers had to prepare all their instructions carefully and learn them by rote. In conversation they were limited to brief memorized snatches, doing the best they could. They were obliged to be good-humored in putting up with the laughter of their students and to manage as well as they might with their tongues virtually tied.

Mealtimes hardly were a diversion for these young men. They never had enough to eat and the fare was monotonous. Chicken was almost always the main course, but by the time it reached the table it had first been boiled to make soup and had lost most of its flavor. Vegetables were scarce. For a Frenchman, life at the table was a trial.

The daily strain of operating under these liabilities took its toll, but there were other obstacles. The missionaries walked from village to village to catechize, trying to cover each village once a week. In the rainy season traveling was all the more difficult. They often arrived soaked and sweating, needing to change at once into dry clothes to avoid catching a fever. While the climate was relatively benign in Nyassa compared with some other regions of Africa, it nevertheless was difficult for Europeans. The mission was hit hard by the young age at which many of the fathers died. Guyard died in 1903 at age thirty, Louveau in 1906 at thirty-five. With ordination at twenty-five or twenty-six, the ministry of the priests averaged hardly half a half a dozen years. This took its toll on the order. By 1885, we know, the White Fathers had reached a membership of two hundred and thirty priests and brothers. In the eighteen years of the order's existence, almost thirty percent of those members had already died. Eleven were martyred by the people they came to serve, and fifty-six had succumbed to fatigue, fevers, and privations of all kinds. In 1885 Cardinal Lavigerie wrote, "One could call it a Society of Martyrs."

These were the men Thérèse thought of in May 1897 when, in the throes of her sickness and utterly exhausted, she rose from her bed to pace up and down in the infirmary. One of the nuns asked her why in the world she was out of bed and pacing the floor, and she replied: *"I'm walking for a missionary."* When they gave her medicines that tasted like poison, she took them graciously, even though she knew they were useless. She wanted to share the hardships of the missionaries and hoped to lighten their burden. *"I have arranged with God by doing this,"* she said, *"to help the poor missionaries who have neither the time nor the means to take care of themselves."*

From my bedside.
My dear André,

   Today is your feast day and it's from my sickbed that I rise and come to you in spite of that, to wish you as joyous and hopeful a day as my desires and my sufferings want you to have.

   I speak of suffering and that's what I'm doing right now. The good God has put me out of commission since the 25th, and at first it was extremely serious. I was hit with the local disease, the one that claims the most victims here, and from which you usually die: black water fever. It's very simple: your blood is poisoned by malaria, you urinate black, and if you have a little strength left after that your chances are about one in a hundred.

   Otherwise no. On Wednesday I was about to get up on the machila[96] *to go to the district center where they were expecting me, when I noticed that . . . my urine was black. Hum! That's it . . . I lie down and become concerned about myself. Today the sickness has slowed. If I hadn't noticed anything until night, I was done for. Nor-*

---

[95] Notre Dame de la Delivrande, Our Lady of Deliverance.

[96] A kind of stretcher with a seat on which the natives carried a passenger who would find travel in the jungle difficult.

mally the recovery takes several months. For me it will be only a few weeks, but those will be filled with a thousand boring precautions. For now I'm fed up with being on the shelf.

Dec. 3 An anniversary which reminds me of various circumstances, both happy and otherwise. You remember '96?[97] At least today I'm glad to see myself standing again and confident that things are going well. Cured—but convalescent, which is almost worse!

Dec. 9 As you can see I'm mending in stages—that's the way it has to be. You will at least know that I'm getting over my sickness and soon there will be no sign of it. Nonetheless, don't be too surprised if one of these days you get a telegram telling you that your brother has gone to the next life. I expect it any day. So I will prepare seriously for death on the Retreat which starts on the 16th and ends at Christmas, God willing. However, I would find it a bit early, because I haven't done anything yet, and they would look askance at me when I arrived at the gates of St. Peter. So I'll get to work after this Retreat, so that if I drop dead it will be with my weapons in my hands, on active duty. This sickness is a friendly warning from Providence and I want to take advantage of it. "I am already being poured out like a libation and the time of my dissolution is near. The tendency of the flesh is toward death,

---

[97] A time when he worried that he would not be accepted for the missions.

but that of the spirit toward life *and peace. Run so as to win. I don't run like a man who loses sight of the finish line. I don't fight as if I were shadow boxing. What I do is discipline my own body and master it, for fear that after having preached to others I myself should be rejected.*

"Therefore, I am ruined if I do not preach the gospel. Isn't that why I have made myself the servant of all? All things to all men."[98]

I have no other raison d'être in this life. In your prayers keep this intention in mind.

13 Dec. Include another intention: that I may give what they expect from me in the new situation they have put me in. In a little while I leave for Blantyre. The responsibility there will be heavy, complex, and delicate. I shall have to deal with our relationship with the government and all that . . . and with both the Secretary of the Interior and the Minister of Foreign Affairs. I need the good God to pilot my ship. Ask Him to do this for your brother. I have as my consolation that I always tell myself to do God's Will, by being obedient and sticking to my program: ask nothing, refuse nothing.

I shall be the Procurator there in charge of directing the

---

[98] The allusions in this paragraph and the preceding one are to St. Paul's letters. Maurice gives them in Latin, a language with which priests were familiar in those days and might use with each other when quoting Scripture in a letter. See 2 Timothy 4:6; Romans 8:6; 1 Corinthians 9:24, 26–27; 1 Corinthians 9:16, 19, 23.

arrival of personnel and of goods. But while doing this I won't neglect the spiritual work. I expect at the same time to make the missionary work among the Blacks advance.

So, I shall be closer to you, even though I'm moving 200 miles to the South—but I'm only four days from Chinde, which is three or four weeks away from France, eight days from Zanzibar. It's good for the mail—very direct.

> *À Dieu, happy New Year to you and to all,*
> *I embrace you very tenderly,*
> *your brother Maurice*

P.S. You know you are as good as Aubrée[99] for handling my affairs. I understand that Mother is asking for your help. Okay!

---

[99] Father Aubrée was a classmate of Maurice in the diocesan seminary. They were good friends and Maurice had him as a beneficiary in his will.

A Land of Few Enchantments

In 1997, this letter from Maurice to his friend Father André Adam came to light. Written in 1903, it is included here because it affords a glimpse into the soul of Maurice six years after the death of Thérèse and the kind of stress under which he was laboring at this time. The letter was found pressed between the pages of a book in Father Adam's library, buried there for more than ninety years. The handwriting was recognized at once as that of Maurice. The letter started in pencil and was finished in ink, written in stages on four different days.

The character of this man, his simple faith in God, his courage under fire, his love for the people he had come to serve in Africa are all evident in these brief pages. They were written to the best friend he had in the priesthood, with whom he had shared years in the seminary preparing to serve the Diocese of Bayeux, the friend who would prove his loyalty later.

Heavy responsibilities were laid upon the shoulders of Maurice, who was now twenty-nine years old. The illness which he recounts, a result of black water fever, usually signaled the approach of death. When the urine turns black, almost always death follows quickly. Maurice was aware of his situation and fully expected to die. His chances were one in one hundred, but because the symptom was noticed immediately and remedies speedily applied, he survived. As soon as he recovered, he lost no time in returning to work. His initial enthusiasm to be a missionary had not lessened over the years although he would never again be the man he was upon his arrival in Africa.

We don't have much detail about his time in the missions, and there is little from Maurice's own pen. What we know comes from the sparse records which were kept at his mission station. But opinions on Maurice were varied. For instance, Père Honoré, the official keeper of the diary at Chiwamba, could be hard on Maurice in what he wrote to the authorities in Algiers. At one time when the latter was placed temporarily in charge of the mission, we find this entry: "Two Brothers were engaged in the making of bricks, but Père Bellière as Superior has reserved the overseeing of the work to himself. He spends a great part of the day visiting workers in all directions, smoking his pipe and giving advice to Fr. Lucien, who knows much better than he how bricks should be made and how to supervise workers in this part of the world."

Although we cannot dismiss this characterization, the entry betrays more than a little bias. The caricature of Maurice smoking his pipe and giving out orders hardly belonged in a report to headquarters and must have had its origin in a serious personality clash between the two. Honoré at the time was having grave health problems and was suffering from depression. He was so discouraged that at one point there was thought of sending him back to France for rest. His health improved, however, and he stayed in Africa for a long career as a missionary. He died in 1950 at Likuni after suffering for many years from leprosy, and left an excellent record behind him.

Not long after the mission center was founded at Chiwamba, Père Guillemé made the decision to move it north to Likuni, partly because Governor McDonald moved his headquarters to that vicinity, but also because the natives of the region were more friendly and open to evangelization. Maurice was appointed the superior, and Brother Sebastian was to join him. Brother Sebastian also kept a diary, and in it we find nothing but praise for Maurice. The two were friendly and worked well together. At one point Maurice was called away to serve temporarily at a place called Nguludi. The reason for his transfer was the need which suddenly arose there for an English-speaking priest, but according to Brother Sebastian the move was made also to offer some measure of relief or distraction to Maurice who, Brother tells us, was showing signs of fatigue, which may have been because of the black water fever.

After Maurice's recovery, in June 1904, Bishop Dupont came to Likuni. He was returning to the missions after an absence of five years in Europe. The Bishop had spent many years in Africa and had established a formidable reputation. The natives called him Bwana Moto Moto. *Moto* means fire, and its duplication signified the superlative. It was said of him that the work he achieved a beast could not accomplish.

By the time he came to Likuni he was an old and worn-out man, but his temperament had not changed. He drove himself mercilessly. He was making a tour of the missions and chose Maurice to accompany him as his secretary. They encountered fierce hostility from the Muslims and apathy on the part of the natives. The climate was beastly in the Lwanga Valley, Guillemé's "land of few enchantments," the land of the dreaded tse-tse fly.

Dupont did not spare Maurice and was extremely hard on him. The trip was a bad experience, more than Maurice could stand. By the time he returned to Likuni on November 8, 1904, to resume his duties as superior, his health was in desperate condition and he needed to get away. He undertook a number of exploratory trips in search of likely places to establish missions, often in the company of Père Perrot. Maurice's reports were optimistic, but the high spirits were apparently a cloak to cover his discouragement.

The Bishop would offer a different version of the facts: "In the company of Père Perrot, Père Bellière has gone to Blantyre and Zomba without permission and without a stated purpose. They have spent six weeks [actually it was four] with the different English authorities. On returning they stopped for a few hours [at Mua] without going to see their confreres, but instead stayed with the English. These things are noticed and comments are made." Maurice was obviously avoiding Père Louveau, the superior at Mua, with whom he was also having a conflict. The Bishop spoke of "serious difficulties."

In a letter to Bishop Livinhac on September 25, 1905, Dupont painted a dark portrait: "Père Bellière, feeling his position to be untenable, has asked to be relieved, adding that if I don't want him to be, he will write to you to recall him at once."

Père Larue was called to Likuni from Kilubula to replace Maurice, but when he arrived in November Maurice had already left. Larue offered the opinion that the attitude of Père Louveau had discouraged "his very sensitive confrere, Bellière."

The last entry of Maurice in the diary of Likuni is dated September 26, 1905. It is a simple notation: "A letter from Ubemba from Bishop Dupont." Doubtless that letter brought a request that he defer his departure until Larue came, but he could hold out no longer. He left for Maison-Carrée to surrender his arms to his old boss and good friend Bishop Livinhac. He never arrived. After this came a long silence.

Dupont's harsh evaluation of Maurice must receive

its own evaluation in the light of the Bishop's demanding standards of what a missionary should be. He was unsparing in his expectations of himself and never thought he should expect less from those who did not have his incredible stamina and iron will. Père Guillemé, himself a tireless worker, wrote of the Bishop: "It is infinitely regrettable that he came back from Europe with [his old] ideas, for the Vicariate was quickly ruined, the British administration was turned off, and the missionaries were discouraged."

Maurice left Likuni on October 22, 1905. It was almost eight years since his arrival in Africa as a seminarian full of dreams. How sadly different was his departure as a broken priest. He carried with him the letters he had received from Thérèse, the early version of her autobiography, and an oval photo of her. On the back of it he had written a prayer which was popular then. Thérèse had copied it as a young girl and no doubt it was she who had sent it to him. It ends with the words "I ask of You, Jesus, a heart that loves You, a heart that cannot be conquered, always ready for battle after each tempest, a heart that is free, never seduced, a heart that is straight and never walks on crooked paths."

Soon he would take a path which knows no turning. He would walk at last the Way of the Cross.

IV
The Passion and Death of Maurice Bellière

~

October 22, 1905–
July 14, 1907

No glory decorates Maurice's final years. Having left his mission post without authorization to return to France, he was summoned back to face an inquiry before the Community Council in Algiers. The Council's record for December 16, 1905, declares: "Père Bellière just arrived from Marseilles after having quit the Mission of Nyassa under conditions that were hardly regular, which his letters and those of Bishop Dupont do not sufficiently clarify. As the matter is grave, this Priest must appear at the Motherhouse to give an explanation."

Whatever questions were asked of him in that inquiry, Maurice's answers were less than satisfactory. The Council stopped short of a severe penalty but was firm in its judgment: "The explanations given by Père Bellière indicate that he acted with an astonishing flightiness and unconsciousness, and without taking account of the seriousness of his action. The Council therefore acknowledges extenuating circumstances and does not impose dismissal from the Society. However, to provide an example and to maintain discipline, it decides that this Father shall be sent back to his mission, despite the humiliation which he can feel from returning to confreres who are aware of his unjustified departure. The Superior General will communicate this decision to Bishop Dupont, and will ask him to take this missionary back and place him in the second rank in one of the posts in the northern part of his Vicariate."

The decision was a bitter pill for Maurice. He left Africa in disgrace on January 4 and went home for some days of rest, having agreed to return to the missions on January 27. Bouts of fever dogged him, however, from which he was unable to recover. The doctor whom he consulted said he wasn't ready to return. To do so would place his health in serious jeopardy.

Six months went by without improvement, and on August 17 he was sent to a sanitarium which the White Fathers had just opened for their sick priests in Autreppe, Belgium. He remained there for only two weeks. The doctor at the sanitarium advised him to go home to breathe the healthy air of Normandy and get further rest.

By now he must have realized that he would never be well enough for missionary work. He was slipping badly both physically and psychologically. Either on his own initiative or at the suggestion of others, he left the White Fathers. His separation from the society could hardly have been a dismissal, for the community would certainly feel obliged to care for a priest whose health was broken by the missions. It is probable that friends advised him to return to his Diocese of Bayeux, where he could be with his mother and get the care he needed. Her sadness at seeing him in such a pitiable state was made all the more painful by the fact that her own health was failing fast and she could not care for him. She died some five months later, on January 15, 1907, at age sixty-three.

There is a gap in the record of his final days. At some point he left his mother's home and began to drift about. Slowly he was going out of his mind and was no longer responsible for his actions. His old friend from seminary days in Sommervieu, Father Adam, went in search of him and finally found him, lost and wandering. He brought him to Caen and committed him to Bon Sauveur, the institution for the insane run by the Bon Sauveur Sisters.

Bon Sauveur was, and still is, a large and well-supervised facility in the center of Caen. The sisters and staff were far in advance of their time in the care of the mentally ill. Patients were allowed the greatest measure of freedom possible and treated with dignity. Maurice was admitted on June 8.

He died in Bon Sauveur on July 14, 1907, five weeks after his thirty-third birthday.

V

EPILOGUE

*A*n hour's drive northwest from Lisieux will take you past some of Normandy's loveliest dairy farms to the ancient city of Caen. It was the capital of William the Conqueror (1027–1087), and it is there that one may visit the tomb of that famous man. It retains its quaintness from the Middle Ages, with broad boulevards and picturesque buildings, and graceful steeples rising from its many churches.

Still there, unchanged, is the mental hospital called Bon Sauveur, under the care of the same community of sisters who had charge of it in the time of Maurice Bellière. If the day is pleasant and you walk about the well-kept grounds, you will see patients like those whose lot he shared so many years ago. The French word for them is *les aliénés,* those who have gone out of their minds.

Aliéné was the last word typed on Maurice's release from the White Fathers' sanitarium in Autreppe. Some in the time of Thérèse spoke insensitively of Bon Sauveur as "the madhouse," and when she heard the word it was a knife thrust in her heart. For three and a half years her father was also a patient there. The family tried hard to keep him at home, but with the advance of his illness he became unmanageable and had to be put away. It was only three months before his death that he was well enough to be released in the care of Céline. When Thérèse learned of his death, the blood drained from her face, and to Pauline's suggestion that she send a note to Céline she replied simply: *"I can't."* It was two days before she could bring herself to write a word of consolation to the closest of her sisters.

With what memories of Papa she must have looked upon Maurice's final years and stood at his bedside in Bon Sauveur, pondering the mystery of the Providence which arranged for the two men she loved above all others to spend their last days there. She had made a solemn promise to be with her beloved brother *"to the end,"* and it was a promise she would never break.

In the record of his mission at Likuni, written not long after his death, it is noted that Maurice died of sleeping sickness, *maladie du sommeil.* No diagnosis is available from the hospital because French law holds the records of mental patients confidential for one hundred years, but the White Fathers somehow learned the cause of his death. He was not the only one of them to die from the dreaded *maladie.* The disease was carried by the tse-tse fly, to whose venomous sting Maurice had been exposed in parts of Africa where his travels took him, especially in Lwanga where he went with Bishop Dupont in the fall of 1904. In all cases the disease was fatal. The patient suffered acute pain, slowly drifting into a somnambulant state with eyes half closed, able neither to sleep nor to stay fully awake and twitching grotesquely. Mercifully, Maurice was in Bon Sauveur only one month when death took him from his misery.

The period of incubation of this sickness could last more than five years, which means it would have begun to affect his behavior long before it would be discovered. This no doubt accounted for the cryptic and somewhat guarded statement of the Council of the White Fathers: "The explanations given by Père Bellière indicate that he acted with *an astonishing flightiness and unconsciousness,* and without taking account of the seriousness of his action. The Council therefore acknowledges *extenuating circumstances."* This was not the confrere they had known. The man who fled in haste from Likuni had lost his hold upon himself and was already marked for death, but the sleeping sickness would take three years to run its course.

Ten miles directly north of Caen, the little fishing town of Langrune lies on the coast of Normandy. Its name in French means "Greenland," reflecting the tradition that it was settled by Vikings in the distant past. The first thing to catch your eye on entering the town is its exquisite little church, a Gothic gem of rough-hewn, blue-gray granite, built in the eleventh century. It was there that Maurice said his prayers as a boy, there that he felt in his heart the first stirrings of a vocation to the priesthood, and there that he dreamed of the missions far away. To this day it serves the Catholics of Langrune as their parish church.

Behind the church is the little parish cemetery where you will come upon Maurice's grave. If you had gone there twenty years ago you would have found it overgrown with weeds and surmounted by a bent and broken stone on which were carved the names of Maurice and his aunt. But if you go there now you will find the grave well cared for, with a handsome monument of polished marble placed above his body. Nearby a plaque on the outer wall of the church announces that this is where Maurice once worshiped as a boy. Proudly chiseled on it are the words that tell us who he was: MAURICE BELLIÉRE, SPIRITUAL BROTHER AND PROTÉGÉ OF SAINT THÉRÈSE.

It was the publication of their correspondence in 1976 that brought about the change. Until their letters came to light, Maurice was a forgotten man. Now people visit his grave, to pay their respects and offer prayers.

It is a moving experience to read the epitaph. To be the spiritual brother of the greatest saint of modern times, and to have the title conferred by the saint herself, is no small mark of honor. *"It was by choice that I became your sister,"* she had written to him. Long after the marble into which his epitaph was cut has crumbled into dust, Maurice Bellière shall be known as the spiritual brother and protégé of St. Thérèse. It remains his title forever.

It is clear from everything we know of him that he was not a great man. Neither before he encountered Thérèse nor after did he rise above the average of those with whom he served on the missions, and they did not regard him as beyond the kind of criticism they might direct at any in their company. He turned up in the life of Thérèse not as a knight in shining armor but as a weak and needful man, sensitive, impressionable, and keenly aware of his sins. She asked of him no great achievement and set no goal too high for him to reach. It was not his virtue that evoked her love for him. She loved him in his human frailty the way he was, as a sister loves a brother. She never criticized him and never doubted the deep inner worth that lay beneath his limitations. She knew that God could use him for His purposes because his heart was good, no matter how far short he might fall of his own ideals.

Maurice was the quintessential "little soul" to whom Thérèse was attracted, the prototype of most of us. He deserves our attention for that very reason—not because he was great but because he was not. Millions of people in the century since her death have been drawn to Thérèse and want to know more about her. Almost all of them are ordinary. She is the friendliest of saints, in whose company an ordinary person feels at home. She is the democrat of mysticism, who uncovers and appeals to the mystic that lies within every human being. She makes the quest for holiness easy, in the sense that she makes clear that God asks of us no more than we can give. She does not try to force high standards on us. She *draws* us, asking only that we trust in the God who is *"nothing but Mercy and Love."* This is all she ever desired for Maurice.

If his achievements were not heroic, and if his life seems to have ended in disappointment, his ideals were great and his dreams could soar. When all has been truly said, his end was no disaster. At one point when he was a seminarian, he wrote to Mother Agnes in his lofty romantic style: *"In Africa life is short* and I dare to think that *'my exile will be brief.'*[100] *But as long as I die on the job it is all right. So much the better if I lose my head."* He was referring to martyrdom from the blow of a machete, delivered by an enemy of the Gospel which he was sent to preach.

It does not stretch facts to say that God gave him both his wishes. He "lost his head," not from the machete of an enemy of the Gospel but from the bite of a tse-tse fly. His other wish, "to die on the job," was also granted. He died on the job, although far away from Africa in a hospital bed in Caen, with the sister who loved him at his side.

---

[100] A quotation from Thérèse's poem "To Live by Love."

Recommended Reading
on St. Thérèse

Story of a Soul—her Autobiography. Translated by Father John Clarke, O.C.D. ICS (Institute for Carmelite Studies) Publications, Washington, D.C. Translated by John Beevers. Doubleday, New York, 1957. (A classic, with millions of readers in all the major languages of the world.)

The Letters of St. Thérèse of Lisieux, 2 volumes. Translated by Father John Clarke, O.C.D. ICS Publications, Washington, D.C., 1982, 1988.

The Poetry of St. Thérèse of Lisieux. Translated by Father Donald Kinney, O.C.D. ICS Publications, Washington, D.C., 1996.

The Story of a Life, by Guy Gaucher. HarperCollins San Francisco, 1993. A splendid biography (her "Autobiography" is the story of her *soul*, not of her life).

The Power of Confidence, by Father Conrad De Meester, O.C.D. Translated by Susan Conroy. A masterful study of the origin and development of St. Thérèse's Little Way. Highly recommended. To be published by Alba House, Staten Island, New York, in the Fall of 1998. *Highly Recommended.*

Under the Torrent of His Love, by Father Marie-Eugène of the Child Jesus, O.C.D., 1995. A brief and very deep reflection on her spirituality.

The Passion of St. Thérèse of Lisieux, by Guy Gaucher. Crossroad Publications, New York, 1990.

Thérèse, by Dorothy Day. Templegate, Springfield, IL, 1979. A beautiful and convincing biography from one of this century's outstanding converts and social activists.

The Hidden Face, by Ida Friederike Gorres. Pantheon, New York, 1957. The author, a psychiatrist, offers profound insights into the psychological development of Thérèse. Her book stands tall in the literature on the Saint.

Thérèse of Lisieux: The Story of a Mission, by Hans Urs Von Balthasar. Sheed and Ward, New York, 1954. A great study by a great scholar.

The Spirituality of St. Thérèse: An Introduction, by Abbé André Combes. P. J. Kenedy and Sons, New York, 1950.

The Heart of St. Thérèse, by Abbé André Combes. P. J. Kenedy and Sons, New York, 1951.

Saint Thérèse and Suffering, by Abbé André Combes. P. J. Kenedy and Sons, New York, 1951. (The three books by Abbé Combes are of enduring value. He was one of the top scholars who exhaustively studied her life in the early part of this century.)

St. Thérèse of Lisieux: A Spiritual Renaissance, by Father Henry Petitot, O.P. Burns, Oates and Washbourne, London, 1927. Although written seventy years ago, Father Petitot's book retains a high place on the list of books about St. Thérèse.

The Story of a Family, by Father Stéphone-Joseph Piat, O.F.M. P. J. Kenedy and Sons, New York, 1948. The history of the Martin family, carefully researched and charmingly told.

ɛ̃ WATERLILY FIRE
Poems 1935–1962 ɛ̃

ઉ~ WATERLILY FIRE
Poems 1935–1962 ઉ~

Muriel Rukeyser

THE MACMILLAN COMPANY   NEW YORK

Macmillan New York, London
A Division of The Crowell-Collier Publishing Company
1962 ઉ~

~ ACKNOWLEDGMENTS

For permission to publish the poems in the last part of this book, I wish to acknowledge the kindness of the following magazines: *Poetry, The Vassar Review, American Judaism*. These publishers have granted permission to print poems which first appeared in books: New Directions, Harper & Brothers, Simon & Schuster, Inc. This selection was made from the following books: *Theory of Flight, U.S.I., A Turning Wind, Beast in View, The Green Wave, Elegies, Selected Poems, One Life, Body of Waking*. This volume is published by arrangement with New Directions.

811
R

First Printing

The Macmillan Company, New York
Brett-Macmillan Ltd., Galt, Ontario

Printed in the United States of America

Library of Congress catalog card number: 62-13595

DESIGNED BY RON FARBER

• My thanks to MARIE DE L. WELCH and to M. L. ROSENTHAL —both poets, critics, friends—who helped me select the poems in this book. •

CONTENTS

∾ I.
From THEORY OF FLIGHT ∾

ಶ EFFORT AT SPEECH
BETWEEN TWO PEOPLE ಶ

: Speak to me.   Take my hand.   What are you now?
I will tell you all.   I will conceal nothing.
When I was three, a little child read a story about a rabbit
who died, in the story, and I crawled under a chair :
a pink rabbit : it was my birthday, and a candle
burnt a sore spot on my finger, and I was told to be happy.

: Oh, grow to know me.   I am not happy.   I will be open:
Now I am thinking of white sails against a sky like music,
like glad horns blowing, and birds tilting, and an arm about me.
There was one I loved, who wanted to live, sailing.

: Speak to me.   Take my hand.   What are you now?
When I was nine, I was fruitily sentimental,
fluid : and my widowed aunt played Chopin,
and I bent my head on the painted woodwork, and wept.
I want now to be close to you.   I would
link the minutes of my days close, somehow, to your days.

: I am not happy.   I will be open.
I have liked lamps in evening corners, and quiet poems.
There has been fear in my life.   Sometimes I speculate
On what a tragedy his life was, really.

: Take my hand.   Fist my mind in your hand.   What are
      you now?
When I was fourteen, I had dreams of suicide,
and I stood at a steep window, at sunset, hoping toward death :
if the light had not melted clouds and plains to beauty,
if light had not transformed that day, I would have leapt.
I am unhappy.   I am lonely.   Speak to me.

: I will be open.   I think he never loved me:
he loved the bright beaches, the little lips of foam

3 ಶ

that ride small waves, he loved the veer of gulls:
he said with a gay mouth: I love you.   Grow to know me.

: What are you now?   If we could touch one another,
if these our separate entities could come to grips,
clenched like a Chinese puzzle . . . yesterday
I stood in a crowded street that was live with people,
and no one spoke a word, and the morning shone.
Everyone silent, moving. . . . Take my hand.   Speak to me.

ಶ BREATHING LANDSCAPE ಶ

Lying in the sun
and lying here so still
an egg might slowly hatch in this still hand.

The people pass
abruptly they nod : they smile
trailed in the air, silence follows their faces.

I know, lying
how the hills are fixed
and the day-moon runs at the head of the fixed hills.

Nothing crossed the field
all day but a bird
skirting the tall grass in briefest transit.

Their stern ideas
are a long work to each
and even armored we hardly touch each other.

The wind leans,
the air placed formally
about these faces and thoughts in formal dance.

4 ಶ

Silence hangs in the air.
Nothing speaks but the sound
of certain rivers continuing underground.

&ᴥ SAND-QUARRY
WITH MOVING FIGURES &ᴥ

Father and I drove to the sand-quarry across the ruined marsh-
 lands,
miles of black grass, burned for next summer's green.
I reached my hand to his beneath the lap-robe,
we looked at the stripe of fire, the blasted scene.

"It's all right," he said, "they can control the flames,
on one side men are standing, and on the other the sea;"
but I was terrified of stubble and waste of black
and his ugly villages he built and was showing me.

The countryside turned right and left about the car,
straight through October we drove to the pit's heart;
sand, and its yellow canyon and standing pools
and the wealth of the split country set us farther apart.
"Look," he said, "this quarry means rows of little houses,
stucco and a new bracelet for you are buried there;"
but I remembered the ruined patches, and I saw the land ruined,
exploded, burned away, and the fiery marshes bare.

"We'll own the countryside, you'll see how soon I will,
you'll have acres to play in" : I saw the written name
painted on stone in the face of the steep hill:
"That's your name, Father!"   "And yours!" he shouted, laughing.
"No, Father, no!"   He caught my hand as I cried,
and smiling, entered the pit, ran laughing down its side.

·❧ SONG FOR DEAD CHILDREN ❧·

We set great wreaths of brightness on the graves of the passionate
who required tribute of hot July flowers :
for you, O brittle-hearted, we bring offering
remembering how your wrists were thin and your delicate bones
    not yet braced for conquering.

The sharp cries of ghost-boys are keen above the meadows,
the little girls continue graceful and wondering;
flickering evening on the lakes recalls those young
heirs whose developing years have sunk to earth
    their strength not tested, their praise unsung.

Weave grasses for their childhood : who will never see
love or disaster or take sides against decay
balancing the choices of maturity;
silent and coffin'd in silence while we pass
    loud in defiance of death, the helpless lie.

·❧ NOTES FOR A POEM ❧·

Here are the long fields inviolate of thought,
here are the planted fields raking the sky,
signs in the earth :
water-cast shuttles of light flickering the underside of rock.
These have been shown before; but the fields know new hands,
the son's fingers grasp warmly at the father's hoe ;
there will be new ways of seeing these ancestral lands.

    "In town, the munitions plant has been poor since the war,
    And nothing but a war will make it rich again."
    Holy, holy, holy, sings the church next door.

Time-ridden, a man strides the current of a stream's flowing,
stands, flexing the wand curvingly over his head,
tracking the water's prism with the flung line.
Summer becomes productive and mature.
Farmers watch tools like spikes of doom against the sure
condemning sky descending upon the hollow lands.

The water is ridged in muscles on the rock,
force for the State is planted in the stream-bed.
Water springs from the stone—the State is fed.

Morning comes, brisk with light,
a broom of color over the threshold.
Long flights of shadows escape to the white sky :
a spoon is straightened.   Day grows.   The sky is blued.
The water rushes over the shelves of stone
to anti-climax on the mills below the drop.
The planted fields are bright and rake the sky.
Power is common.   Earth is grown
and overgrown in unrelated strength, the moral
rehearsed already, often.
(There must be the gearing of these facts
into coördination, in a poem or numbers,
rows of statistics, or the cool iambs.)
The locked relationships which will be found
are a design to build these factual timbers—
a plough of thought to break this stubborn ground.

WOODEN SPRING

How horrible late spring is, with the full death of the frozen
    tight bulbs
brownly rotting in earth;   and each chord of light
rayed into slivers, a bunch of grapes plucked grape by grape apart,
a warm chord broken into the chilled single notes.

(Let us rely on cerebral titillation
for the red stimulus of sensuous supply;)
here is no heat, no fierce color : spring is no bacchante this year
eager to celebrate her carnal dedication.

The ghosts swim, lipless, eyeless, upward :
the crazy hands point in five directions down :
to the sea, the high ridge, the bush, the blade, the weak white
    root :
thumping at life in an agony of birth, abortive fruit.

Spring is very mad for greenness now
(: I suppose it would be beautiful, if we let ourselves be :),
but we must strip nascent earth bare of green mystery.
Trees do not grow high as skyscrapers in my town,

and flowers not so lovely as the pale bewildered youth,
hands pointing in five directions upward and out;
and spring in the fields and cities spreads to the north and south,
and is comforted in desire for the sun's mouth.

Earth does not seem wooden to the comforted spring :
(spring could not seem so dull, I comforted :
but there must be abstraction, where fields need not sprout, waves
    pound,
there must be silence where no rushing grasses sound,
life in this lack of death, comfort on this wide ground).

❧ SONNET ❧

My thoughts through yours refracted into speech
transmute this room musically tonight,
the notes of contact flowing, rhythmic, bright
with an informal art beyond my single reach.
Outside, dark birds fly in a greening time :
wings of our sistered wishes beat these walls :
and words afflict our minds in near footfalls
approaching with a latening hour's chime.

And if an essential thing has flown between us,
rare intellectual bird of communication,
let us seize it quickly;   let our preference
choose it instead of softer things to screen us
each from the other's self : muteness or hesitation,
nor petrify live miracle by our indifference.

❧ FOUR IN A FAMILY ❧

The father and mother sat, and the sister beside her.
I faced the two women across the table's width,
speaking, and all the time he looked at me,
sorrowing, saying nothing, with his hard tired breath.

Their faces said : This is your home;   and I :
I never come home, I never go away.
And they all answered : Stay.

All day the city turned about this room,
and silence had remained between our faces,
divisions outside to concentrate a world
tally here only to dead profits and losses.

We follow barrier voices, and we go fast,
unknown to each other, they race, I turn away.
No voice is strong enough to cry me Stay.

My sister, I wished upon you those delights
time never buries,
more precious than heroes.

Strange father, strange mother, who are you, who are you?
Where have I come,
how shall I prosper home?

৶ THE GYROSCOPE ৶

But this is our desire, and of its worth. . . .
Power electric-clean, gravitating outward at all points,
moving in savage fire, fusing all durable stuff
but never itself being fused with any force
homing in no hand nor breast nor sex
for buried in these lips we rise again,
bent over these plans, our faces raise to see.
Direct spears are shot outward from the conscience
fulfilling what far circuits?   Orbit of thought
what axis do you lean on, what strictnesses evade
impelled to the long curves of the will's ambition?
Centrifugal power, expanding universe
within expanding universe, what stillnesses
lie at your center resting among motion?
Study communications, looking inward, find what traffic
you may have with your silences : looking outward, survey
what you have seen of places :
                              many times this week I seemed
        to hear you speak my name
                              how you turn the flatnesses
        of your cheek and will not hear my words
                              then reaching the given latitude

and longitude, we searched for the ship and found nothing
and, gentlemen, shall we define desire
including every impulse toward psychic progress?
Roads are cut into the earth leading away from our place
at the inevitable hub.　　All directions are **out,**
all desire turns outward : we, introspective,
continuing to find in ourselves the microcosm
imaging continents, powers, relations, reflecting
all history in a bifurcated Engine.
Here is the gyroscope whirling out pulsing in tides illimitably
widening, live force contained
in a sphere of rigid boundary;　　concentrate
at the locus of all forces, spinning with black speed
revolving outward perpetually, turning with its torque
all the developments of the secret will.
Flaming origins were our fathers in the heat of the earth,
pushing to the crust, water and sea-flesh,
undulant tentacles ingrown on the ocean's floor,
frondy anemones and scales' armor gave us birth.
Bring us to air, ancestors! and we breathed
the young flesh wincing against naked December.
Masters of fire, fire gave us riches, gave us life.
Masters of water, water gave us riches, gave us life,
masters of earth, earth gave us riches, gave us life.
Air mocks, and desire whirls outward in strict frenzy, leaping,
elastic circles widening from the mind,
turning constricted to the mind again.
The dynamics of desire are explained
in terms of action outward and reaction to a core
obscured and undefined, except, perhaps, as "God in Heaven,"
"God in Man,"
Elohim intermittent with the soul, recurrent
as Father and Holy Ghost, Word and responsive Word,
merging with contact in continual sunbursts,
the promise, the response, the hands laid on,
the hammer swung to the anvil, mouth fallen on mouth,
the plane nose up into an open sky.
Roads are cut, purchase is gained on our wish,
the turbines gather momentum, tools are given :

whirl in desire, hurry to ambition, return,
maintaining the soul's polarity;   be : fly.

❧ SUNDAYS, THEY SLEEP LATE ❧

The days are incestuous, each with its yesterday,
and they, walking heavily in the streets, atone for the moment's
sin : their memories laboring under the weight of today
in its perverse alliance with the past.   Laments

are heard, droning from the city on all other mornings
but Sundays, they sleep late, and need not cry to wake,
sniffling in the pillow, realizing the day's churnings
of minute resolving to minute, and the whole day slack,

of wind bled of vigor, the talk in the parlor
of people pasturing on each other's minds, and sunset
evolving in the air, a quiet change against the duller
signs in pandemonium of day's gradual transit:

the klaxon voices through the roads, the picnickers joking
(returning from the fields), who wept before they dressed.
On Sundays their dreams are longer, and their waking
is a long exhalation of their weeks, decompressed.

There are these things to be remembered : the nine boys waiting,
battle-fronts of the rising army with holes bitten by death,
the man in the prison overland, and history beating
out the recurrent facts of power, suppression, wrath.

The days are incestuous.   They witness the daily binding
of minutes linking backwards.   Their remembering atones
in no part for the things they remember.   They sink in blinding
sleep too long, they dissolve in sleep their remembering bones.

·❧ THE SURROUNDED ❧·

They escape before, but their shadows walk behind,
filling the city with formidable dark,
spilling black over the sun's run gold, speeding a rumor
of warfare and the sciences of death, and work
of treason and exposure, following
me for an easy mark.

The sky is travelled by brightness, clouds ignite,
flame is incised upon the martyred air;
the city dissolves in foaming craters, stars
falling in multitudes dazzle the sky with fire,
and I pursue them, I am pursued, and
they are everywhere.

Now there is no more brightness, and no shadow
but the shadow of a thought, and I'm in jail enough
to know conviction with prisoner certainty,
haunted by protest, lacking completion's proof
surrounded by shadows
more plausible than love.

·❧ MOVIE ❧·

Spotlight her face   her face has no light in it
touch the cheek with light   inform the eyes
press meanings on those lips.

                    See cities from the air,
fix a cloud in the sky, one bird in the bright air,
one perfect mechanical flower in her hair.

Make your young men ride over the mesquite plains;
produce our country on film : here are the flaming shrubs,

the Negroes put up their hands in Hallelujahs,
the young men balance at the penthouse door.
We focus on the screen : look   they tell us
you are a nation of similar whores   remember the Maine
remember you have a democracy of champagne —

And slowly the female face kisses the young man,
over his face the twelve-foot female head
the yard-long mouth enlarges and yawns

                                        The End

Here is a city   here the village grows
here are the rich men standing rows on rows,
but the crowd seeps behind the cowboy the lover the king,
past the constructed sets America rises
the bevelled classic doorways   the alleys of trees are witness
America rises in a wave a mass
pushing away the rot.

                    The Director cries Cut!
hoarsely CUT   and the people send pistons of force
crashing against the CUT! CUT! of the straw men.

Light is superfluous upon these eyes,
across our minds push new portents of strength
destroying the sets, the flat faces, the mock skies.

৯ CATS AND A COCK ৯

                         for Eleanor Clark
What hill can ever hold us?
                    Standing high
we saw December packed, snow upon snow,
empty until the cars, leaping in beams below,
opened the shadow of the trees in fans

enormous on the plain, fragile and magnified.
Print of the delicate branch sweeping our feet
in hundred hugeness, passing to white again.

Up the dark hill a pack of cats :
bursting from hollows, streaming to the crest,
streaming all night toward dawn
when green invaded east.
We stood to hear the rigid cock cry Five
a black cock crowing over cold water,
when all those cats found their sole proud objective
and whirled away to slaughter.

      .   .   .   .   .

      We walk the streets
      of the dark city
      placards at back
      light in our heads,

      Moon rides over us
      town streams below :
      Strike and support us
      the strike-songs go.

      Ceilings of stars
      disturb our faces,
      tantrums of light
      summon our eyes;

      The daystar stands
      hungry for day :
      we file, regarding
      this twin morning.

      Shall that bind us,
      parade and planet,
      mobile and point?
      No, not yet,

> there is labor
> before a reunion.
> Poets, pickets,
> prepare for dawn!

. . . . .

Come chop the days
lop off the moving hours,
we had not known there were disparate things.

Forget these syntheses and fade
peerless and distant into a distant grave
still hoping unity indeed be made?

I wish you to be saved . . . you wish . . . he wishes . . . she . . .
in conjugation of a destiny.
We were figures rubbed by wind passing upon a frieze,
galloping figures at a column's base
hungrily running from death and marble space.

I give you cats : I give you a cock on a hill :
these stream in beauty : that stands blocked in pride
I pledge you death until
they fight and acquiesce, or one has died.

Earnestly and slowly I continue :
no one could guess how the impact of a word
heard plain and plainly understood
can have attacked us so and so deferred.

Fight them down, deliver yourself, friend!
see, we all fight it down : poetry, picket-line,
to master pride and muscle fluid with sun,
conflicting graces moving to one end.

. . . . .

Witness the unfailing war, season with season,
license and principle, sex with tortured sex,
class versus class, and help us to survey
this city for faces, this hill for tracks.

16 ह

Sickness will bind itself upon our tissue
clipping off with restriction blood and heat and milk,
becoming real against all disbelief
a sly ghost coughing to advertise its bulk.

Climax to Egypt, our milestone pyramid
forces out history and we remember
conflict of thousands of April processions,
rival winds ripping at the heart's deep chamber.

No natural poison : a vicious, banker's thrust
nudges toward dissolution during war,
this peak of open battle points disgust
of decay, counterattacks backing us to our door.

This is when death thrives in the rot
and formal nightmare, zebra of sleep,
presents us madness, diffusion to remember,
to cherish, loss if we lose; and dust to keep.

Resent the nightmare, assume a waking stance,
this clock of revolt, held in the hand and striking,
clapping, the violent wings of a struck bird,
speaks your top hour, marks your fatal chance.

.   .   .   .   .

"Still elegiac! : between two battles, when one is happy
to be alive !"—Rosa Luxemburg

Here was a battle forced by the brain's fortitude,
mapping machines of peace before crisis had come;
and by this planning we create a world
new-hearted, secure from common delirium.

If the strike was won, the prisoners freed at last,
the cataract tapped for power, parade-songs sung :
Prepare for continuance, open your brilliant love,
your life, — front April, give it tongue !

.   .   .   .   .

Below the flowering hedge
rest in the light, forget
grief's awful violet
and indecision's wedge
driven into your pride,
and how the past has died.

Here is transition :
pain, but no surgeon's knife
: anaesthetize your life?
you lose the vision
of how you simply walk
toward a younger folk,

simply, a flaming wire
advancing on the night,
reducing midnight
to clear noon-fire ;
moving upon the future
and large, clean stature
nearer to all your nature.

.   .   .   .   .

The latchpieces of consciousness unfasten.
We are stroked out of dream and night and myth,
and turning slowly to awareness, listen
to the soft bronchial whisperings of death.

Never forget in legendary darkness
the ways of the hands' turning and the mouth's ways,
wander in the fields of change and not remember
a voice and many voices and the evening's burning.

Turn and remember, this is the world made plain
by chart and signal, instrument and name :

to some we say Master, others call Sister,
to some we offer nothing but love :

flier in advance, the cloud over his mouth ;
the inventor who produces the moment of proof ;
a sun and moon and other several stars ;
and those who know each other over wars.

Cats stream upon a hill,
the poet-cock breaks his throat now to say :
Moment of Proof, May dawn transposing night,
partisan dawn's on the side of day!

                    .   .   .   .

What hill can ever hold us?
                              Deeply night
found you intent upon this city river,
asleep at heart (turn light to her at last,
it shall be to her
as wellwater) :
going all day along the gilded air
you saw at midnight
(going, down to the river, haunted by fog-horns) :
steam escaping over the spouting manhole,
a rout of white cats racing through the street.
Wet street, and the fight was ended there,
cats and that cock, fearful antagonists
resolved in fog, a quick pack running uphill
to a cock rigid with joy; running, but not to kill.

                    .   .   .   .

    "Forehead to forehead I meet thee, this third time,
                    Moby Dick!"—Herman Melville

Moment of proof, when the body holds its vision.
masses recognize masses, knowledge without all end ;
face fathoms other face, all the hills open sunrise,
mouth sets on mouth ; Spring, and the tulips
                    totter in the wind.

Forfeit in love, forfeit in conflict, here
met and at last marked clear in principle,

desire meets desire, the chase expands, and now
forever we course, knowing the marks of growth,
                seeing the signals.

Now we remember winter-tormented cities,
the August farm's overgrown hollow, thick with goldenrod,
the impetus of strain, and places where
love set its terminals, the vivid hunger
                and satisfying food.

Mayday is moment of proof, when recognition
binds us in protest, binds us under a sun
of love and subtle thought and the ductile wish.
Tomorrow's Mayday. — How many are we?
                We'll be everyone.

No hill can ever hold us, peak enlists peak,
climax forces out climax, proud cock, cats streaming,
poets and pickets contriving a valid country,
: Mayday moment, forever provoking new
                belief and blooming.

❧ II.
From U. S. 1 ❧

❧ GAULEY BRIDGE ❧

Camera at the crossing sees the city
a street of wooden walls and empty windows,
the doors shut handless in the empty street,
and the deserted Negro standing on the corner.

The little boy runs with his dog
up the street to the bridge over the river where
nine men are mending road for the government.
He blurs the camera-glass fixed on the street.

Railway tracks here and many panes of glass
tin under light, the grey shine of towns and forests:
in the commercial hotel (Switzerland of America)
the owner is keeping his books behind the public glass.

Postoffice window, a hive of private boxes,
the hand of the man who withdraws, the woman who reaches
        her hand
and the tall coughing man stamping an envelope.

The bus station and the great pale buses stopping for food;
April-glass-tinted, the yellow-aproned waitress;
coast-to-coast schedule on the plateglass window.

The man on the street and the camera eye:
he leaves the doctor's office, slammed door, doom,
any town looks like this one-street town.

Glass, wood, and naked eye : the movie-house
closed for the afternoon frames posters streaked with rain,
advertise "Racing Luck" and "Hitch-Hike Lady."

Whistling, the train comes from a long way away,
slow, and the Negro watches it grow in the grey air,
the hotel man makes a note behind his potted palm.

Eyes of the tourist house, red-and-white filling station,
the eyes of the Negro, looking down the track,
hotel-man and hotel, cafeteria, camera.

And in the beerplace on the other sidewalk
always one's harsh night eyes over the beerglass
follow the waitress and the yellow apron.

The road flows over the bridge,
Gamoca pointed at the underpass,
opposite, Alloy, after a block of town.

What do you want — a cliff over a city?
A foreland, sloped to sea and overgrown with roses?
These people live here.

❧ PRAISE OF THE COMMITTEE ❧

These are the lines on which a committee is formed.
  Almost as soon as work was begun in the tunnel
  men began to die among dry drills.   No masks.
  Most of them were not from the valley.
  The freights brought many every day from States
  all up and down the Atlantic seaboard
  and as far inland as Kentucky, Ohio.
  After the work the camps were closed or burned.
  The ambulance was going day and night,
  White's undertaking business thriving and
  his mother's cornfield put to a new use.
  "Many of the shareholders at this meeting
  "were nervous about the division of the profits;
  "how much has the Company spent on lawsuits?
  "The man said $150,000.   Special counsel:
  "I am familiar with the case.   Not : one : cent.

" 'Terms of the contract.   Master liable.'
"No reply.   Great corporation disowning men who
    made . . ."
After the lawsuits had been instituted . . .
The Committee is a true reflection of the will of the people.
Every man is ill.   The women are not affected,
This is not a contagious disease.   A medical commission,
Dr. Hughes, Dr. Hayhurst examined the chest
of Raymond Johnson, and Dr. Harless, a former
company doctor.   But he saw too many die,
he has written his letter to Washington.
The Committee meets regularly, wherever it can.
Here are Mrs. Jones, three lost sons, husband sick,
Mrs. Leek, cook for the bus cafeteria,
the men : George Robinson, leader and voice,
four other Negroes (three drills, one camp-boy)
Blankenship, the thin friendly man, Peyton the engineer,
Juanita absent, the one outsider member.
Here in the noise, loud belts of the shoe-repair shop,
meeting around the stove beneath the one bulb hanging.
They come late in the day.   Many come with them
who pack the hall, wait in the thorough dark.
This is a defense committee.   Unfinished business:
Two rounds of lawsuits, 200 cases
Now as to the crooked lawyers
If the men had worn masks, their use would have involved
time every hour to wash the sponge at mouth.
Tunnel, 3 miles long.   Much larger than
the Holland Tunnel or Pittsburgh's Liberty Tubes.
Total cost, say, $16,000,000.
This is the procedure of such a committee:
To consider the bill before the Senate.
To discuss relief.
    Active members may be cut off relief
        16-mile walk to Fayetteville for cheque—
        WEST VIRGINIA RELIEF ADMINISTRATION, #22991,
        TO JOE HENIGAN, GAULEY BRIDGE, ONE AND $5\%_{100}$,
        WINONA NATIONAL BANK.   PAID FROM STATE FUNDS.

25 ❧

Unless the Defense Committee acts;
the *People's Press*, supporting this fight,
signed editorials, sent in funds.
Clothing for tunnel-workers.
  Rumored, that in the post-office
  parcels are intercepted.
  Suspected : Conley.   Sheriff, no hotelman,
  head of the town ring—
  Company whispers.   Spies,
  The Racket.
Resolved, resolved.
George Robinson holds all their strength together:
To fight the companies   to make somehow a future.
"At any rate, it is inadvisable to keep a community of dying
persons intact."
"Senator Holt.   Yes.   This is the most barbarous example
of industrial construction that ever happened in the world."
Please proceed.
"In a very general way Hippocrates' *Epidemics* speaks of the
    metal digger who breathes with difficulty, having a pain
    and wan complexion.
    Pliny, the elder. . . ."
"Present work of the Bureau of Mines. . . ."
The dam's pure crystal slants upon the river.
  A dark and noisy room, frozen two feet from stove.
  The cough of habit.   The sound of men in the hall
  waiting for word.

  These men breathe hard
  but the committee has a voice of steel.
  One climbs the hill on canes.
  They have broken the hills and cracked the riches wide.

  In this man's face
  family leans out from two worlds of graves—
  here is a room of eyes,
  a single force looks out, reading our life.

Who stands over the river?
Whose feet go running in these rigid hills?
Who comes, warning the night,
shouting and young to waken our eyes?

Who runs through electric wires?
Who speaks down every road?
Their hands touched mastery;   now they
demand an answer.

❧ THE DISEASE ❧

This is a lung disease. Silicate dust makes it.
The dust causing the growth of

This is the X-ray picture taken last April.
I would point out to you : these are the ribs;
this is the region of the breastbone;
this is the heart (a wide white shadow filled with blood).
In here of course is the swallowing tube, esophagus.
The windpipe. Spaces between the lungs.

Between the ribs?

Between the ribs. These are the collar bones.
Now, this lung's mottled, beginning, in these areas.
You'd say a snowstorm had struck the fellow's lungs.
About alike, that side and this side, top and bottom.
The first stage in this period in this case.

Let us have the second.

Come to the window again.   Here is the heart.
More numerous nodules, thicker, see, in the upper lobes.
You will notice the increase : here, streaked fibrous tissue—

Indicating?

That indicates the progress in ten months' time.
And now, this year — short breathing, solid scars
even over the ribs, thick on both sides.
Blood vessels shut.   Model conglomeration.

What stage?

Third stage.   Each time I place my pencil point:
There and there and there, there, there.

    "It is growing worse every day.   At night
    "I get up to catch my breath.   If I remained
    "flat on my back I believe I would die."

      It gradually chokes off the air cells in the lungs?
      I am trying to say it the best I can.
      That is what happens, isn't it?
      A choking-off in the air cells?

Yes.
      There is difficulty in breathing.
Yes.
      And a painful cough?
Yes.

      Does silicosis cause death?

Yes, sir.

&sw; GEORGE ROBINSON :   BLUES &sw;

Gauley Bridge is a good town for Negroes, they let us stand
     around, they let us stand
around on the sidewalks if we're black or brown.
Vanetta's over the trestle, and that's our town.

The hill makes breathing slow, slow breathing after you
     row the river,
and the graveyard's on the hill, cold in the springtime blow,
the graveyard's up on high, and the town is down below.

Did you ever bury thirty-five men in a place in back of your
     house,
thirty-five tunnel workers the doctors didn't attend,
died in the tunnel camps, under rocks, everywhere, world
     without end.

When a man said I feel poorly, for any reason, any weakness
     or such,
letting up when he couldn't keep going barely,
the Cap and company come and run him off the job surely.

I've put them
DOWN from the tunnel camps
to the graveyard on the hill,
tin-cans all about — it fixed them!—

TUNNELITIS
hold themselves up
at the side of a tree,
I can go right now
to that cemetery.

When the blast went off the boss would call out, Come, let's
     go back,
when that heavy loaded blast went white, Come, let's go back,
telling us hurry, hurry, into the falling rocks and muck.

The water they would bring had dust in it, our drinking water,
the camps and their groves were colored with the dust,
we cleaned our clothes in the groves, but we always had the
    dust.

Looked like somebody sprinkled flour all over the parks and
    groves,
it stayed and the rain couldn't wash it away and it twinkled
that white dust really looked pretty down around our ankles.

As dark as I am, when I came out at morning after the tunnel
    at night,
with a white man, nobody could have told which man was white.
The dust had covered us both, and the dust was white.

✿ ALLOY ✿

This is the most audacious landscape. The gangster's
stance with his gun smoking and out is not so
vicious as this commercial field, its hill of glass.

Sloping as gracefully as thighs, the foothills
narrow to this, clouds over every town
finally indicate the stored destruction.

Crystalline hill: a blinded field of white
murdering snow, seamed by convergent tracks;
the travelling cranes reach for the silica.

And down the track, the overhead conveyor
slides on its cable to the feet of chimneys.
Smoke rises, not white enough, not so barbaric.

Here the severe flame speaks from the brick throat,
electric furnaces produce this precious, this clean,
annealing the crystals, fusing at last alloys.

Hottest for silicon, blast furnaces raise flames,
spill fire, spill steel, quench the new shape to freeze,
tempering it to perfected metal.

Forced through this crucible, a million men.
Above this pasture, the highway passes those
who curse the air, breathing their fear again.

The roaring flowers of the chimney-stacks
less poison, at their lips in fire, than this
dust that is blown from off the field of glass;

blows and will blow, rising over the mills,
crystallized and beyond the fierce corrosion
disintegrated angel on these hills.

?❧ THE DAM ❧?

All power is saved, having no end.   Rises
     in the green season, in the sudden season
     the white the budded
                         and the lost.
     Water celebrates, yielding continually
     sheeted and fast in its overfall
     slips down the rock, evades the pillars
     building its colonnades, repairs
     in stream and standing wave
     retains its seaward green
     broken by obstacle rock; falling, the water sheet
     spouts, and the mind dances, excess of white.
     White brilliant function of the land's disease.

     Many-spanned, lighted, the crest leans under
     concrete arches and the channelled hills,
     turns in the gorge toward its release;

kinetic and controlled, the sluice
urging the hollow, the thunder,
the major climax
        energy
total and open watercourse
praising the spillway, fiery glaze,
crackle of light, cleanest velocity
flooding, the moulded force.

> *I open out a way over the water*
> *I form a path between the Combatants:*
> *Grant that I sail down like a living bird,*
> *power over the fields and Pool of Fire.*
> *Phoenix, I sail over the phoenix world.*

Diverted water, the fern and fuming white
ascend in mist of continuous diffusion.
Rivers are turning inside their mountains,
streams line the stone, rest at the overflow
lake and in lanes of pliant color lie.
Blessing of this innumerable silver,
printed in silver, images of stone
walk on a screen of falling water
in film-silver in continual change
recurring colored, plunging with the wave.

Constellations of light, abundance of many rivers.
The sheeted island-cities, the white surf filling west,
the hope, fast water spilled where still pools fed.
Great power flying deep: between the rock and the sunset,
the caretaker's house and the steep abutment,
hypnotic water fallen and the tunnels under
the moist and fragile galleries of stone,
mile-long, under the wave. Whether snow fall,
the quick light fall, years of white cities fall,
flood that this valley built falls slipping down
the green turn in the river's green.
Steep gorge, the wedge of crystal in the sky.

How many feet of whirlpools?
What is a year in terms of falling water?
Cylinders; kilowatts; capacities.
Continuity: $\Sigma Q = 0$
Equations for falling water. The streaming motion.
The balance-sheet of energy that flows
passing along its infinite barrier.

It breaks the hills, cracking the riches wide,
runs through electric wires;
it comes, warning the night,
running among these rigid hills,
a single force to waken our eyes.

They poured the concrete and the columns stood,
laid bare the bedrock, set the cells of steel,
a dam for monument was what they hammered home.
Blasted, and stocks went up;
insured the base,
and limousines
wrote their own graphs upon
roadbed and lifeline.

Their hands touched mastery:
wait for defense, solid across the world.
Mr. Griswold. "A corporation is a body without a soul."
Mr. Dunn. When they were caught at it they resorted to
    the methods employed by gunmen, ordinary machine-gun
    racketeers. They cowardly tried to buy out the people
    who had the information on them.
Mr. Marcantonio. I agree that a racket has been prac-
    tised, but the most damnable racketeering that I have
    ever known is the paying of a fee to the very attorney
    who represented these victims. That is the most outrag-
    eous racket that has ever come within my knowledge.
Miss Allen. Mr. Jesse J. Ricks, the president of the
    Union Carbide & Carbon Corporation, suggested that the

stockholder had better take this question up in a
private conference.
The dam is safe. A scene of power.
The dam is the father of the tunnel.
This is the valley's work, the white, the shining.

High	Low	Stock and Dividend in Dollars	Open	High	Low	Last	Net Chge.	—Closing—		
								Bid	Ask	Sales
111	61¼	Union Carbide (3.20)	67¼	69½	67¼	69½	+3	69¼	69½	3,400

The dam is used when the tunnel is used.
The men and the water are never idle,
have definitions.

This is a perfect fluid, having no age nor hours,
surviving scarless, unaltered, loving rest,
willing to run forever to find its peace
in equal seas in currents of still glass.
Effects of friction : to fight and pass again,
learning its power, conquering boundaries,
able to rise blind in revolts of tide,
broken and sacrificed to flow resumed.
Collecting eternally power. Spender of power,
torn, never can be killed, speeded in filaments,
million, its power can rest and rise forever,
wait and be flexible. Be born again.
Nothing is lost, even among the wars,
imperfect flow, confusion of force.
It will rise. These are the phases of its face.
It knows its seasons, the waiting, the sudden.
It changes. It does not die.

A FLASHING CLIFF

Spinning on his heel, the traveller
sees across snow a flashing cliff.
Past the plain's freeze, past savage branches
immune in ice, a frozen waterfall,
clamped in December, glistens alive.

Love, will you recognize yourself displayed?
Or is the age defective, cold as storm
to lock fast water in iron artifice,
whitening cataracts?—contempt and loss,
and nothing, in the great world, can lie calm,

travel alive, but is frozen solid,
and will not face its mirror nor speak its pain.
Will you fight winter to break in immense speed
resisting and sensitive, a waterfall-flash
sparkling full across the vicious plain?

Fight down our age, the mad vindictive time?
No victory's here. Now, any passion suffers
against proud ice, flashing, angry, and jailed.
You, maniac, catalept!
And, love. You are all rivers.

HOMAGE TO LITERATURE

When you imagine trumpet-faced musicians
blowing again inimitable jazz
no art can accuse nor cannonadings hurt,

or coming out of your dream of dirigibles
again see the unreasonable cripple
throwing his crutch headlong as the headlights

streak down the torn street, as the three hammerers
go One, Two, Three on the stake, triphammer poundings
and not a sign of new worlds to still the heart;

then stare into the lake of sunset as it runs
boiling, over the west past all control
rolling and swamps the heartbeat and repeats
sea beyond sea after unbearable suns;
think : poems fixed this landscape : Blake, Donne, Keats.

❧ LOVER AS FOX ❧

Driven, at midnight, to growth, the city's wistful turnings
lead you living on islands to some dark single house
where vacant windows mark increased pursuit,
chasing the runner outward beyond bounds
around the wildest circle of the night.

Circling returns! the city wreathed in rivers,
streaked skies surrounding islands of blank stone—
into this mythic track travelling breakneck,
a streaming furnace of escape, you, fox,
pursued, brick-red and vicious, circling bricks,

are followed as nimbly all mottled cloudy night;
fastened upon your path, the Floating Man
face down above the city, as shadow, changing shape,
as shadow of clouds, flying, and swiftly as
indifference running mad around the world.

Speed now! see city, houses across the water,
mosaic and bright over the riverfall
remote from the bursting eye, the open nostril,
flared lip (an image of angels singing speed),
caught in a nightlong visionary chase.

See the entire scene bright as you fly
round lots pauper all year, shacks lame with weather,
this sour fertile time teeming and ramshackle
before you, loving, clean sight in spyglass air.
And around town again. River, river.
Why do people live on islands?

❧ THE DROWNING YOUNG MAN ❧

The drowning young man lifted his face from the river
to me, exhausted from calling for help and weeping;
"My love!" I said; but he kissed me once for ever
and returned to his privacy and secret keeping.

His close face dripped with the attractive water,
I stared in his eyes and saw there penalty,
for the city moved in its struggle, loud about us,
and the salt air blew down; but he would face the sea.

"Afraid, afraid, my love?"   But he will never speak,
looking demands for rest, watching the wave come up,
too timid to turn, too loving to crying out,
lying face down in tide, biting his nervous lip.

Take him by shoulder and jaw, break his look back on us,
O hard to save, be saved, before we all shall drown!
But he has set his look, plunged his life deep for peace,
his face in the boiling river, and is surrendered down.

❧ BOY WITH HIS HAIR CUT SHORT ❧

Sunday shuts down on this twentieth-century evening.
The El passes. Twilight and bulb define
the brown room, the overstuffed plum sofa,
the boy, and the girl's thin hands above his head.
A neighbor radio sings stocks, news, serenade.

He sits at the table, head down, the young clear neck
    exposed,
watching the drugstore sign from the tail of his eye;
tattoo, neon, until the eye blears, while his
solicitous tall sister, simple in blue, bending
behind him, cuts his hair with her cheap shears.

The arrow's electric red always reaches its mark,
successful neon! He coughs, impressed by that precision.
His child's forehead, forever protected by his cap,
is bleached against the lamplight as he turns head
and steadies to let the snippets drop.

Erasing the failure of weeks with level fingers,
she sleeks the fine hair, combing: "You'll look fine tomorrow!
You'll surely find something, they can't keep turning you down;
the finest gentleman's not so trim as you!" Smiling, he raises
the adolescent forehead wrinkling ironic now.

He sees his decent suit laid out, new-pressed,
his carfare on the shelf. He lets his head fall, meeting
her earnest hopeless look, seeing the sharp blades splitting,
the darkened room, the impersonal sign, her motion,
the blue vein, bright on her temple, pitifully beating.

✑ NIGHT-MUSIC ✑

for Marya Zaturenska

TIME EXPOSURES

When the exposed spirit, busy in daytime,
searches out night, only renewer.
That time plants turn to. The world's table.
When any single thing's condemned again.
The changeable spirit finds itself out,
will not employ Saint Death, detective,
does its own hunting, runs at last to night.
Renewer, echo of judgment, morning-source, music.

Dark streets that light invents, one black tree standing,
struck by the street-light to raw electric green,
allow one man at a time to walk past, plain.
Cities lose size. The earth is field
and ranging these countries in sunset, we make quiet,
living in springtime, wish for nothing, see
glass bough, invented green, flower-sharp day
crackle into orange and be subdued to night.

The mind, propelled by work, reaches its evening:
slick streets, dog-tired, point the way to sleep,
walls rise in color, now summer shapes the Square
(and pastel five o'clock chalked on the sky).
We drive out to the suburbs, bizarre lawns
flicker a moment beside the speeding cars.
Speed haunts our ground, throws counties at us under
night, a black basin always spilling stars.

Waters trouble our quiet, vanishing down
reaches of hills whose image legend saves:
the foggy Venus hung above the flood
rising, rising, from the sea, with her arms full of waves
as ours are full of flowers.

Down polished airways a purple dove descending
sharp on the bodies of those so lately busy apart,
wingtip on breasttip, the deep body of feathers
in the breastgroove along the comforted heart.

The head inclined offers with love clear miles
of days simple in sun and action, bright
air poised about a face in ballet strictness
and pure pacific night.

But in our ears brute knocking at all doors,
factories bellow mutilation, and we live needly still
while strength and hours run
checkless downhill.

Flattered by grief, the changeable spirit
puts on importance. Goes into the street,
adventures everywhere but places fear
is absent. Everywhere the face's look
is absent, the heart is flat,
the avenues haunted by a head whose eye
runs tears incessantly, the other eye
narrow in smiling. Everywhere, words fail,
men sunk to dust, houses condemned, walls ruined,
and dust is never an anachronism.
Everywhere the eye runs tears. And here
the hand, propelled somehow, marches the room
pulling dark windowshades down around the gaze.

And now, stately, jotting on lipstick, she
prepares to sexualize her thistle thought.
Loosens her earrings, smiling. Drives
herself far into night. Smiles, fornicating. Drives
herself deep into sleep. Sees children sleep.

ADVENTURES, MIDNIGHT—II.

With those two I went driving in the dark,
out from our town in a borrowed car whose light
ate forests as we drove deeper into the park.

Beloved, spoke the sweet equivocal night—
those two stood clapped, each breast warmly on
      breast,
I stood apart to remove them from my sight:

The creased brook ran in continual unrest,
rising to seastorm in the rioting mind.
Here night and they and I—and who was merriest?

He turned his face away refusing, and so signed
for her to stop who too was comfortless
and equally needy, as tender and as blind.

On the road to the city stood the hedge whose
      darkness
had covered me months ago with that tall stranger
as foreign to me as this loneliness,

as enemy to me as tonight's anger
of grief in the country, shut with those two in
      the park:
this crying, frantic at removal, the dark, the
      sorrowful danger.

੨ WOMAN AND EMBLEMS ੨

WOMAN AND BIRD

A bird flew out of a cloud
(with a beak, flying),
broke its beak on my bone,
cried bird-cries over crying.

Sky, stranger, wilderness
(flying starry through flesh),
make an end; be me, bird.
It reverses my one wish.

Bird screams slavery among bones.
(I watch with a bird's eyes.)
Quarrel, wings; if I travel,
bird stays—stand, bird flies.

Bird sets feathers where flesh was
(my claws slide away on space).
Bird, here—now, bird, we fly!
Mourns, mourns, it turns a captive face.

THE BIRTHDAY

A sound lying on the fantastic air
opens the night and the child is born;
as the wind moves, the solemn crying
pioneers in the air, changes

to flame crusading among the grasses
fire-whitened, aroused before it,
rippled crops—and blazing races
into a central arena

where it stands as a fighting-cock
conqueror head, aggressive spur,

and the gilt feather, the bronze, the greenish,
flicker and threaten.

The feathers of the fighting-cock
become a tree, and casting seed,
raise potent forests at its side—
birth among burning.

The great magnetic branches sign
meaning on the record sky—
now rise, moon, stiffen, bird, and flames,
kill and engender.

Reversal, chameleon,
pursuing images—
recurrent birth offering other names,
a spool of brightness.

WOMAN AND MUSIC

This is a tall woman walking through a square
thinking what is a woman at midnight in a park
under bells, in the trivial and lovely hours
with images, violins, dancers approaching?

This is a woman sitting at a mirror
her back to the glass and all the dancers advancing,
or in a chair laughing at a bone
sitting upright in a chair
talking of ballet, flesh's impermanence.

This is a woman looking at a stage—
dancing—and all the parks, walks, hours
balanced against a tallest blue decor,
dancing—and all the parks, walks, hours
descend in brilliant water past the eyes
pursuing and forgotten and subdued
to blinding music, the deliberate strings.

&❧ III.
From A TURNING WIND &❧

The fear of poetry is the
fear : mystery and fury of a midnight street
of windows whose low voluptuous voice
issues, and after that there is no peace.

That round waiting moment in the
theatre : curtain rises, dies into the ceiling
and here is played the scene with the mother
bandaging a revealed son's head. The bandage is torn off.
Curtain goes down. And here is the moment of proof.

That climax when the brain acknowledges the world;
all values extended into the blood awake.
Moment of proof. And as they say Brancusi did,
building his bird to extend through soaring air,
as Kafka planned stories that draw to eternity
through time extended. And the climax strikes.

Love touches so, that months after the look of
blue stare of love, the footbeat on the heart
is translated into the pure cry of birds
following air-cries, or poems, the new scene.
Moment of proof. That strikes long after act.

They fear it. They turn away, hand up palm out
fending off moment of proof, the straight look, poem.
The prolonged wound-consciousness after the bullet's shot.
The prolonged love after the look is dead,
the yellow joy after the song of the sun.

⁊ TARGET PRACTICE ⁊

Near Mexico, near April, in the morning.
Desert where the sun casts his circles of power
on acquiescent sand shifting beneath them. Car
speeding among white landscapes;   suddenly
the permanent scene at the dead-center.

Photo, in circles of speed, how at raw barnside
father and son stand, man with his rifle up
levelled at heartpoint of a nailed-up bird
spread, wings against the wood. The boy's arm thrown
up over his eyes, flinching from coming shot.

Bullseye, you bullet! pinning down the scene.
And speed you car over the waste of noon
into the boundaries of distance where
the first ring lessens into memory.
Until, a little lower than the sun,

centered in that last circle, hangs a free
fierce bird down-staring on the target of land,
circle on circle of power spread, and speeding
eyes passing from zone to zone, from war to where
their bullets will never bring him down.

⁊ NUNS IN THE WIND ⁊

As I came out of the New York Public Library
you said your influence on my style would be noticed
and from now on there would be happy poems.
                    It was at that moment
the street was assaulted by a covey of nuns
going directly toward the physics textbooks.

Tragic fiascos shadowed that whole spring.
The children sang streetfuls, and I thought:
O to be the King in the carol
kissed and at peace;   but recalling Costa Brava
the little blossoms in the mimosa tree
and later, the orange cliff, after they sent me out,
I knew there was no peace.
                    You smiled, saying : Take it easy.

That was the year of the five-day fall of cities.
            First day, no writers. Second, no telephones. Third
            no venereal diseases. Fourth, no income tax. And on
            the fifth, at noon.
The nuns blocked the intersections, reading.
I used to go walking in the triangle of park,
seeing that locked face, the coarse enemy skin,
the eyes with all the virtues of a good child,
but no child was there, even when I thought, Child!
The 4 a.m. cop could never understand.
You said, not smiling, You are the future for me,
but you were the present and immediate moment
and I am empty-armed without, until to me is given
two lights to carry : my life and the light of my death.

If the wind would rise, those black throbbing umbrellas
fly downstreet, the flapping robes unfolding,
my dream would be over, poisons cannot linger
when the wind rises. . . .

All that year, the classical declaration of war was lacking.
There was a lot of lechery and disorder.
And I am queen on that island.

Well, I said suddenly in the tall and abstract room,
time to wake up.
Now make believe you can help yourself alone.
And there it was, the busy crosstown noontime
crossing, peopled with nuns.

Now, bragging now,
the flatfoot slambang victory,
thanks to a trick of wind
will you see faces blow, and though their bodies
by God's grace will never blow,
cities shake in the wind, the year's over,
calendars tear, and their clothes blow. O yes!

❧ DEMOCRITUS LAUGHED ❧

Democritus laughed when he
saw his whole universe
combined of atoms, and
the gods destroyed —
He killed the ghostly
vengeance deep at the source,
holding bright philosophical sand
up for a threat —
laughing his soldier laughter
with ages of troops after
who grin with reason in
the trenches of
metaphysics, astronomy, disease,
philosophy, the state, and poetry,
the black-and-white war on sin,
the dead wars, the impossible dark wars,
the war on starve, the war on kill, the war on love,
the war on peace.

❧ CORRESPONDENCES ❧

Wars between wars, laughter behind the lines.
Fighting behind the lines. Not children laughing,
but the trench-laughter of the wounded, of radios,
of animal cartoons, the lonely broadcast
on the taxi dashboard, behind the wrecking crew
lit by a naked bulb — to the forgetful bars
prisms and amber shaken with laughter, to the ships at sea.
To the maleficent walls of cities, and an old actress
trying against the trying wind under the skyscrapers,
blind ageing face up, still the look of the lioness,
walking close to the buildings, along the wall,
she licks her lips in panic of loneliness.
She understands the laughter that rides around the streets,
blowing the news to the stone-lands, the swamp-lands, the
        dust-land,
where omens of war, restless in clouds of dust,
mean dust is never an anachronism
and ruin's news.

The actress knows. Laughter takes up the slack,
changes the fact, narrowing it to nothing,
hardly a thing but silence on a stage.
Crack of laughter. Walls go white, and the plain open note
talks in a houseful of noise. Reply : Now hide!

Over the air, the blindfold answer, the news of force,
the male and hairless hand of fear
in a shiny leather sleeve
armed.

The radiations of harm : black grooves in photographs,
blackness in spokes playing from Hitler's head.
A head with one nightmare.
Expect failure of plans, the floodgates closing,
failure of traffic-control, loss of voice, fog.

Wires dead, defection of your central power-plant.
A code : Laughter. What alphabet are they using?

Many wished for little.
Many asked unity.

We had our characters as we had our cities,
or as a lyric poet has his voices, audible
as separate lives, maturing in poise, and symbols
coming to their "great period," too big to kill,
able to batter at the jetties of hell.

Rites of initiation of our lives:
by filth in childhood,
by wealth in the middle,
by death at the end.
We knew the dear, the enemy, we saw the spy
whisper at ear, the agency suggest,
and where no secrecy and treason were
we saw the novelist, pimp of character,
develop the age so it be understood
to read like his book, a city of the dead.

But the century had its rites, its politics,
machineries whose characters were wars.
Ceremonies of further separation. And now, our backs to brick,
war closes in, calling us to the guns
to make accounting how our time was spent.
And the planes fall. Soon the whole incident is
over, all but the consequences.

Laughter, and childhood; and laughter; and age; or death.
Call to the male puppet, Croak,
and to the female puppet, Shriek,
and turn on me your gun for luck.

Take us our sacrifices, a wish for the living,
this foil of thought, this soil from which we sprang,

fugal music of peace, the promises well-kept,
the big and little diaries of the dead.
The song of occupations and the ghosts,
the historian, pimp of centuries, the general, pimp of wars,
the Floating Man, gentle above the cities,
afraid to touch, a cloud before his head,
laughing the laugh of a man about to be drafted,
the flier, mock-protagonist of his time,
refugees who reserve a final condemnation
and see a richer horror in the sky.

Humor, saliva of terror, will not save the day
or even one moment when the cities are
high in a boneyard where clowns ride up and down
and a night crew works quickly before morning;
while news arrives of the death of others,
laughter of brothers and the brother wars,
works of an age among such characters.

Violent electric night! and the age spiralling past
and the sky turning over, and the wind turning the stars.

❧ GIBBS ❧

It was much later in his life he rose
in the professors' room, the frail bones rising
among that fume of mathematical meaning,
symbols, the language of symbols, literature . . . threw
air, simple life, in the dead lungs of their meeting,
said, "Mathematics *is* a language."

Withdrew. Into a silent world beyond New Haven,
the street-fights gone, the long youth of undergraduate
riots down Church Street, initiation violence,

secret societies gone : a broken-glass isolation,
bottles smashed flat, windows out, street-fronts broken:

to quiet,
the little portico, wrought-iron and shutters' house.
A usable town, a usable tradition.
In war or politics.
Not science.
Withdrew.
Civil War generates, but
Not here. Tutors Latin after his doctorate
when all of Yale is disappearing south.

There is no disorganization, for there is no passion.
Condense, he is thinking.   Concentrate, restrict.
This is the state permits the whole to stand,
the whole which is simpler than any of its parts.
And the mortars fired, the tent-lines, lines of trains,
earthworks, breastworks of war, field-hospitals,
Whitman forever saying, "Identify."
Gibbs saying
"I wish to know systems.

To be in this work.   Prepare an apocryphal
cool life in which nothing is not discovery
and all is given, levelly, after clearest
most disciplined research.
The German years
of voyage, calmer than Kant in Koenigsberg, to states
where laws are passed and truth's a daylight gift.

Return to a house inheriting Julia's keys,
sister receiving all the gifts of the world,
white papers on your desk.
Spiritual gift
she never took.
Books of discovery,
haunted by steam, ghost of the disembodied engine,
industrialists in their imperious designs

made flower an age to be driven far by this
serene impartial acumen.
                         Driving
his sister's coach in the city, knowing the
rose of direction loosing its petals down
atoms and galaxies.   Diffusion's absolute.
Phases of matter!   The shouldering horses pass
turnings (snow, water, steam) echoing platted curves,
statues of diagrams, the forms of schemes
to stand white on a table, real as phase,
or as the mountainous summer curves when he
under New Hampshire lay while shouldering night
came down upon him then with all its stars.
Gearing that power-spire to the wide air.
Exacting symbols of rediscovered worlds.

Through evening New Haven drove. The yellow window
of Sloane Lab all night shone.

Shining an image whole, as a streak of brightness
bland on the quartz, light-blade on Iceland spar
doubled! and the refraction carrying fresh clews.
Withdrew.
                    It will be an age of experiment,
or mysticism, anyway vastest assumption.
He makes no experiments.   Impregnable retires.
Anyone having these desires will make these researches.
Laws are the gifts of their systems, and the man
in constant tension of experience drives
moments of coexistence into light.
It is the constitution of matter I must touch.

Deduction from deduction : entropy,
heat flowing down a gradient of nature,
perpetual glacier driving down the side
of the known world in an equilibrium tending
to uniformity, the single dream.

                                        He binds
himself to know the public life of systems.
Look through the wounds of law
at the composite face of the world.

                    If Scott had known,
he would not die at the Pole, he would have been
saved, and again saved — here, gifts from overseas,
and grapes in January past Faustus' grasp.
Austerity, continence, veracity, the full truth flowing
not out from the beginning and the base,
but from accords of components whose end is truth.
Thought resting on these laws enough becomes
an image of the world, restraint among
breaks manacles, breaks the known life before
Gibbs' pale and steady eyes.
                                        He knew the composite
many-dimensioned spirit, the phases of its face,
found the tremendous level of the world,
Energy : Constant, but entropy, the spending,
tends toward a maximum — a "mixed-up-ness,"
and in this end of levels to which we drive
in isolation, to which all systems tend,
Withdraw, he said clearly.

The soul says to the self : I will withdraw,
the self saying to the soul : I will withdraw,
and soon they are asleep together
spiralling through one dream.
                                        Withdrew, but in
his eager imperfect timidities, rose and dared
sever waterspouts, bring the great changing world
time makes more random, into its unity.

🦢 RYDER 🦢

Call himself unbegun, for the sea made him;   assemblage of
    waters gave him his color.
But not the sea;   coast-line, coast-water, rising sfumato from
    smoke-holes of the sea,
pitching onto the black rock of the ocean-edge.   But not the
    coast-line;
the Atlantic coast, flinging him headlong from its rigors into his
    art.
Great salt-swept boldface captain, big-boned New Englander
    drowning deep
among the mysteries of the painful western adventure, circling
in unappeased circles into America.

Tempests, phantasmagoria!   Impervious, first of all
to paint the tragic landscape that breeds us here,
the deep life, the terrible foreboding whose soil
is in our mind, the imagination of this geography.
Whose whaling port acknowledges the fearful
content of evil and the swift-lit blessed light,
Melville's 'latent horror of life' in the whale water
that Ryder, whose racecourse with its big horse Death
runs round the brain, knew.
                  In his room
wreckage of boxes, propped-leg, easel, couch, ashes, coal-keg, shells,
bronzed tarnished coffee-pot, books, paints, piled broken furniture,
varnish drippings, matches, cans, newspapers stacked up,
plaster falling with a scurrying like mice, paper bannering from the
    walls,
the stains, the path cleared to the stuffed chair crammed with
    poems,
money, checks, poems, the bathtub filled with clothes—
the unseen room, after a moment there.
He stood
            laying the paint on
                        stacking color on,

more pigment, dark and stormy, thickness, depth, more black,
 stove-ashes maybe,
and at the last slashed poker through the cloth, a knife of lightning,
 white as space, leaping white! out of darkness!
Out black night leaping, rider to flame.

He walks through the rainy streets, the great grey sweater;
fog walking through rain, wool worn on his giant head,
his giant beard stowed in the collar. Walks black pavement.
Is seen on corners beaten by storms of night.
He gives a painting to the tubercular seamstress
"to look at while she lives," talks poetry
and philosophy to the woman at the newsstand.
He believes with his eye, he lives in the foreboding
empty tempests of the mind, thunder revolving
among his blackest noons; remembers voyages
to fabulous harbors whose event was sea.

He looks through the plateglass window at his formal dinner,
turns down the street, "I have been there," looks through glass
at formal painting, inch by inch, reaching the corner
stands back, "That's a fine place." And moves away
to mystic reconciliations, feeling the world enlarge
and never complete itself, a bone riding a horse
around a track, dead angels from the sea resurrected
to lend a metaphor of waves, to sound the abstract
Jonah who rolls under a pitch of ocean,
knows God with his arms up among the teeth of waves,
the moon stark in the sky as a center of whirlpool.
All these invoke the image, a sea-belief in the sea
whose waters open swallow the army whole and save the tribe.

He is your irresponsible pioneer. He is deprived. Fearful of sex.
  Desire, God's blossoming rod
points to assemblages of waters, heroes Macbeth kneedeep,
the foggy Dutchman riding, salt eyelids see
the fall of waters, the distinction and power, the shock,
the helplessness immanent in things.

Ghosts of oxen, stiff-grappled claws of a dead bird,
romantic wish that mourns from an Opera seat
over the spotlit love, wishes housekeeper love,
Elaine of wish, bends over an empty big suit of armor,
over the giant fallen bones of the dead horse.

Historic disherison : Ryder, emblematist,
divorced from the arts, believing in art alone,
master of meaning and never mastering means,
wasteful and slow, without tradition.   He shortens
the life of his paintings in their friable colors
by ignorance, by storms.   Refusing the dead life
like a nest of tables whose next is always smaller
refined and congruent, slashes American sky
by derelict lightning, turning all landscape into
sublunar ocean.   He is chained under water,
chained under rain, under paint, no hold on daylight,
his fixed moon stares into a tragic coast
whose people are little figures pasted on.
"Not you," he cries, "the human document."
These are not paintings for comfort hung on walls.
Paint over it, paint.   It is a monument
cracking and supernatural, an obelisk at the sea,
three sides shadowed with names, the sea-slab empty.
A big-boned charging figure under rain
seen by the visionary moon and dark,
unbegun among assemblages of waves.
His head that was moon the center of the storm.
His boulders that were eyes washed by the drift of ocean.

❧ CHAPMAN ❧

Returns to punishment as we all return, in agonized initiation
        proving America,
a country returning to moments of conversion, in agony supporting
        its changes, receiving
the past, the clews of instinct, and the rich return:
conviction in our people's face, all in pain.
He dances in Boston, the young and turning side
turned to a room of marvellous skirts whose rustle
like burning paper alters, rustling black to flame.
He looks across all rooms to a sibyl-minded woman
the dark   the clew to life   whose afternoons
he shares through Dante's climbing Paradise
to break his youth, the handsome turning side
dancing and turning again to her dark head
in rings of darkness whose God is ringed in light
which coils and revolves around him—
in the smoky garden
after the word was spoken
the blow to the rival's smoky head echoing in the hand
ringed round with darkness;
dark passages through streets unknown; and now, at home,
he sees his braced arm, ringing with the shock,
given before him to the ringing fire.

Blaze of hard-coal.   Disapparition of flesh.
He draws his hand out of flame; charred to the bone,
white knuckles and finger-bones exposed.
His soul rises screaming in the shape of an eagle.
He says, quietly and exactly, "This will never do."
"The one time in my life I lived was twenty days of pain."
And later, after the healing, after the marriage,
alone among red desert, the wild bushes' grey-green,
the red buttes cancelling half the sky, he writes
"It was not waste land in Colorado.   Not waste time, for
"you are here and many lives packed into one life,

"the green shoot out of the heart of the plant, springing up
    blossoms in the night;
"many old things have put on immortality,
"and lost things have come back knocking within
"from before the time I was conceived in the womb,
"there were you also.
"And of the pain! it was false,
"and the rending, unnecessary.
"The breaking down of dams that ought never be up,
"but being up it was the sweeping away
"that the waters might flow together."

The life all burning on the public hill,
the men living tramort, travelling through their deaths,
arrive with marks by which they know one another
at the center of systems.   By a breach of childhood
symptoms of health declare all the signs leading through,
until the crisis comes,
air seethes, and all the bushes flicker up,
memories parasite in the life underground
irrupt with convulsions and the speech of fire.

At the focus, the cool life is insufficient.
He knows his conversion.   He speaks of Whitman as tramp:
"By an act as simple as death, he puts off effort and lives in peace."
Knowing by what redemption he claims his house,
he stands on the balcony of a burning building.
The ghosts come near the blood.   Sits at the bedside reading
to the dropped quiet head, Dante and fire and coexistent death
at his wife's bedside.
Fire, rage, splendor;   and terror
who judges the judgment of men.
He is broken, his face is broken back,
his spirit's legs are broken, crutches hold him,
a second wife holds him while he becomes
incredible to himself, fulgurite fused by lightning,
health shaking its flag of death in his frenetic head.

Death of his son, and he heals, he is born again,
fed on his agonies, wanting again
his gritty taste of truth.

There are those who are many-born.   There is the man
who will plunge his hand in the fire this evening, who goes out
        every day
seeing Prometheus in mirrors, finding
comets, men of the people, conscious, who take their place
in national revulsion producing a nation's poems,
belong to the present, are not sterilized
by breaks from the past.
He fights for the acute senses, terror, passion, and need.
"I make it a policy to say nothing I will not regret."
Speaks from a cart-end, manhandles his hecklers,
knows the struggles of treason making it easy for death
to arrive when the living have passed the perfection of youth.

The century bursts upward in shocks of flame,
fireworks' starfish of imperial spirit,
ordeals by fire : he fights the finished wars,
looks back to slavery.   They burn the shingles down,
the lynched face broken back, mouth filled with fire,
firebrand full in face.   The ashes rise.
Chapman arrives to face his empty hall,
courtly, one-handed, turning his handsome side
upon the hall to face his audience,
one Negro woman come to hear.   Undoings
walking in all forms, treacheries of the deep
spirit caught in the net.   Our need is of new life.
There are these tendencies in America:
they planned John Brown;   they do what will be done.

Birth after birth, in the spanned democratic
passage of birth, the incubation motive,
desire's experience, tense for finality.
He is reborn too often;   the shock cannot take.
He loosens;   fights for war;   fights Harvard's plans:

a stone for both sides — he rants, upholstered deep
in Harvard Club armchairs — a monument to Zero.
He is charred out, is calling vengeance on Jews,
he is old and charred.   He has been many-born.
Blinks in the fire-world, sees started birds
blinked red and black, the wing a dark log burning
against the sun;   flashes of cypress and swamps,
a watery forest of red birds.
Goes down
his altering ash smothers the shock of peace,
he carries flame
but selling-out is not a dramatic moment,
is the chain of memories parasite,
the thin flame of existence travelling down
until the yellow and alizarin red
flares out.   The whole of any life, he said,
is always unmistakably one thing.
And a dream-voice said Freiheit
a crackling globe flew down
fire and punishment, returning grace;
vortex of parable through modes of life
simple and imperceptible transitions
in countries of transition giving other lives
the long remorseless logic of their love.

❧ ANN BURLAK ❧

Let her be seen, a voice on a platform, heard
as a city is heard in its prophetic sleep when
one shadow hangs over one side of a total wall
of houses, factories, stacks, and on the faces
around her tallies, shadow from one form.

An open square shields the voice, reflecting it
to faces who receive its reflections of light as

change on their features. She stands alone, sending
her voice out to the edges, seeing approach people
to make the ring ragged, to fill in blacker
answers.
          This is an open square of the lit world
whose dark sky over hills rimmed white with evening
squares lofts where sunset lies in dirty patterns
and rivers of mill-towns beating their broken bridges
as under another country full of air.
Dark offices evening reaches where letters take the light
even from palest faces over script.
Many abandon machines, shut off the looms,
hurry on glooming cobbles to the square. And many
are absent, as in the sky about her face, the birds
retreat from charcoal rivers and fly far.

The words cluster about the superstition mountains.
The sky breaks back over the torn and timid
her early city whose stacks along the river
flourished darkness over all, whose mottled sky
shielded the faces of those asleep in doorways
spread dark on narrow fields through which the father
comes home without meat, the forest in the ground
whose trees are coal, the lurching roads of autumn
where the flesh of the eager hangs, heavier by
its thirty bullets, barbed on wire. Truckdrivers
swing ungrazed trailers past, the woman in the fog
can never speak her poems of unemployment,
the brakeman slows the last freight round the curve.
And riveters in their hardshell fling short fiery
steel, and the servant groans in his narrow room,
and the girl limps away from the door of the shady doctor.
Or the child new-born into a company town
whose life can be seen at birth as child, woman, widow.
The neighbor called in to nurse the baby of a spy,
the schoolboy washing off the painted word
"scab" on the front stoop, his mother watering flowers
pouring the milk-bottle of water from the ledge,

who stops in horror, seeing. The grandmother going
down to her cellar with a full clothes-basket,
turns at the shot, sees men running past brick,
smoke-spurt and fallen face.
                    She speaks of these:
the chase down through the canal, the filling-station,
stones through the windshield. The woman in the bank
who topples, the premature birth brought on by tear-gas,
the charge leaving its gun slow-motion, finding those
who sit at windows knowing what they see;
who look up at the door, the brutalized face appraising
strangers with holsters;   little blackened boys
with their animal grins, quick hands salvaging coal
among the slag of patriotic hills.

She knows the field of faces at her feet,
remembrances of childhood, likenesses of parents,
a system of looms in constellation whirled,
disasters dancing.
                    And behind her head
the world of the unpossessed, steel mills in snow flaming,
nine o'clock towns whose deputies' overnight power
hurls waste into killed eyes, whose guns predict
mirages of order, an empty coat before the blind.
Doorways within which nobody is at home.
The spies who wait for the spy at the deserted crossing,
a little dead since they are going to kill.
Those women who stitch their lives to their machines
and daughters at the symmetry of looms.

She speaks to the ten greatest American women:
The anonymous farmer's wife, the anonymous clubbed picket,
the anonymous Negro woman who held off the guns,
the anonymous prisoner, anonymous cotton-picker
trailing her robe of sack in a proud train,
anonymous writer of these and mill-hand, anonymous city-walker,
anonymous organizer, anonymous binder of the illegally wounded,
anonymous feeder and speaker to anonymous squares.

She knows their faces, their impatient songs
of passionate grief risen, the desperate music
poverty makes, she knows women cut down
by poverty, by stupid obscure days,
their moments over the dishes, speaks them now,
wrecks with the whole necessity of the past
behind the debris, behind the ordinary
smell of coffee, the ravelling clean wash,
the turning to bed, undone among savage night
planning and unplanning seasons of happiness
broken in dreams or in the jaundiced morning
over a tub or over a loom or over
the tired face of death.
                        She knows
the songs : *Hope to die, Mo I try, I comes out,*
Owin boss mo, I comes out, Lawd, Owin boss mo
food, money and life.
                      Praise breakers,
praise the unpraised who cannot speak their name.
Their asking what they need as unbelieved
as a statue talking to a skeleton.
They are the animals who devour their mother
from need, and they know in their bodies other places,
their minds are cities whose avenues are named
each after a foreign city. They fall when cities fall.
They have the cruelty and sympathy of those
whose texture is the stress of existence woven
into revenge, the crime we all must claim.
They hold the old world in their new world's arms.
And they are the victims, all the splinters of war
run through their eyes, their black escaping face
and runaway eyes are the Negro in the subway
whose shadowy detective brings his stick
down on the naked head as the express pulls in,
swinging in locomotive roars on skull.
They are the question to the ambassador
long-jawed and grim, they stand on marble, waiting
to ask how the terms of the strike have affected him.

Answer : "I've never seen snow before. It's marvellous."
They stand with Ann Burlak in the rotunda, knowing
her insistent promise of life, remembering
the letter of the tear-gas salesman : "I hope
"this strike develops and a damn bad one too.
"We need the money."
                              This is the boundary
behind a speaker : Main Street and railroad tracks,
post office, furniture store. The soft moment before storm.
Since there are many years.
And the first years were the years of need,
the bleeding, the dragged foot, the wilderness,
and the second years were the years of bread
fat cow, square house, favorite work,
and the third years are the years of death.
The glittering eye all golden. Full of tears.
Years when the enemy is in our street,
and liberty, safe in the people's hands,
is never safe and peace is never safe.

Insults of attack arrive, insults
of mutilation. She knows the prophetic past,
many have marched behind her, and she knows
Rosa whose face drifts in the black canal,
the superstitions of a tragic winter
when children, their heads together, put on tears.
The tears fall at their throats, their chains are made
of tears, and as bullets melted and as bombs let down
upon the ominous cities where she stands
fluid and conscious. Suddenly perceives
the world will never daily prove her words,
but her words live, they issue from this life.
She scatters clews. She speaks from all these faces
and from the center of a system of lives
who speak the desire of worlds moving unmade
saying, "Who owns the world?" and waiting for the cry.

ᢍ IVES ᢍ

Knowing the voices of the country, gathering
voices of other harvest, farm-hands who gather in
sources of music on the blueberry hills,
the village band, lines at the schoolhouse singing—
lit cheeks and lips over the blown-glass lamps
in the broad houses, along the pebble beach,
or up the baldface mountain's granite sky
above New England, voices of wilderness,
scorch of the sun where ranges all run west,
snow-glare on seaward slopes, sea-breeze and tea,
the voices of stinted music in the towns.
There are strange herbs in the pasture, and the stiff
death angels on the red assyrian stones.
Daguerreotypes and family quiet, wells,
woodwork and panelling, the cloaks of the forest,
all the blinds drawn on the imagination's
immediate mystery of the passer-by.
Intense as instruments to split these sounds
into component memory, and reduce
memory to uncompromising sound.

To whom do I speak today?   I've heard their oarlocks turning
at dawn on the river, in the warm bankside light
heard cut trees fall, hickory pull the head
toward violent foreground laughter of torn wood,
watched steeples diminishing in low day before sunset,
and found the evening train riding the bend.
That train will never speak again of tracks
routed to outland counties, but the firm
sumac and corn, broadleaf tobacco farms,
a churchyard murmur for the air of truth,
acres where birds I did not know till now
fly sharp-reflected in water, a field of sky;
over the human lake, the gods make the swallows fly.

To whom do I speak today?   Call off your wit and write
for silent implicated men, a crabbed line

of intercepted music with the world between.
Networks of songs, white seagull in white air,
cliff edge and stripe of sand's immovable gulls
hung over women's morning festivals.
Affection of villages whose boy guitarist,
blond, with his rolled sleeve and the girl behind
sings into fire-darkness goodbye after pleasure
and the streets, our liberty, the village store,
songs of the sorrow and mystery of pavilions'
slow carousel-music, bulbs and mirrors in sunlight,
processions of godly animals revolving;
or big October mornings, cider and perry noon
when the child comes open-mouth round the corner singing;
that music of the imagination here
which is the only sound lives after war.

Acoustics of sideshows! and the organist
playing the mirror of the mind again.
Concord whose choice between repose and truth
colors our memory, whose outer islands of thought
are fugal movements in one dignity.
Rebellion of outposts whose deepest results arrive
when the rebellion, not from worst to greatest,
but great to greater goes.   The sequent movements
of that developing know supernatural
Hawthorne as dripping wet with guilt, a ghost
personal at first, and national at twilight,
and tries to be universal suddenly at midnight;
know in their pace the supernatural future
and the future of human coarseness, and Emerson's
future, eternity, whose forecast is the past,
and Alcott's suffering, whipping his innocent
boy next to the guilty, since guilt need not suffer;
and Thoreau who did not die of his consumption
but lived with it.
                              Raise us an instrument
limitless, without the scarecrow keyboard
can give repose and fame to successful pianists
playing to camouflage dullness.   A scale for truth,

obscurities of a village organist
who satisfies his life on Sunday.

Songs.
Young men singing on stoops, the sickle pears of Concord,
the wheels scraping the curb, lockets of childhood
faith, barn dances, ballads;   or those revealing men
I gave a mask, and they to me the secrets
of sensual thought, music and thunderbolt.
The concentrated man bent over drums,
a skeleton over drums, a fritter of triangles
played without aim, spasms of arabesques
in decoration of nothing.   I speak a flute over frost,
hypnotisms of trumpets, the plain and open voice
of the walk toward the future, commonplace transcendent
chores and melodeons, band-concert morning
or the ultimate Negro over his white piano
meaning O Saint!   O Blues!

This is Charles Ives.
Gold-lettered insurance windows frame his day.
He is eclectic, he sorts tunes like potatoes
for better next-year crops, catching the variable
wildest improvisations, his clusters of meaning;
railing against the fake sonorities, "sadness
"of a bathtub when the water is being let out,"
knowing the local hope knocking in any blood.
"Today we do not choose To die or to dance,
"but to live and walk."
Inventor, beginner of strong
coherent substance of music, knowing all
apple-reflecting streams, loons across echoing lake,
cities and men, as liners aloof in voyage,
and their dead eyes, so much blue in the ground
as water, as running song he loves and pours
as water into water, music in music.
Walks
at starfall or under the yellow dragons of sunset

among the ritual answers and the secular wish,
among spruce, and maroon of fallen needles, walks
the pauper light of dawn imagining truth,
turning from recommended madness, from Europe
who must be forced to eat what she kills, from cities
where all the throats are playing the same tune
mechanically.

          He was young.   He did not climb
four flights on hands and knees to the piano.   Heard
the band in the square, Jerusalem the Golden
from all the rooftops, blare of foreground horns,
violins past the common;   in the street
the oral dissonance, the drum's array.
Far breaking music indistinct with wheels'
irregular talk, the moving world, the real
personal disagreement of many voices;
clusters of meaning break in fantastic flame,
silver of instruments rising behind the eye.

He gathers the known world total into music,
passion of sense, perspective's mask of light
into suggestion's inarticulate
gesture, invention.   Knowing the voices, knowing
these faces and music and this breeding landscape
balanced between the crisis and the cold
which bears the many-born, he parcels silence
into a music which submerges prayer,
rising as rivers of faces overhead,
naming the instruments we all must hold.

❧ IV.
From BEAST IN VIEW ❧

ᨠ AJANTA ᨠ

I—THE JOURNEY

Came in my full youth to the midnight cave
Nerves ringing; and this thing I did alone.
Wanting my fulness and not a field of war,
For the world considered annihilation, a star
Called Wormwood rose and flickered, shattering
Bent light over the dead boiling up in the ground,
The biting yellow of their corrupted lives
Streaming to war, denying all our words.
Nothing was left among the tainted weather
But world-walking and shadowless Ajanta.
Hallucination and the metal laugh
In clouds, and the mountain-spectre riding storm.
Nothing was certain but a moment of peace,
A hollow behind the unbreakable waterfall.
All the way to the cave, the teeming forms of death,
And death, the price of the body, cheap as air.
I blessed my heart on the expiation journey
For it had never been unable to suffer:
When I met the man whose face looked like the future,
When I met the whore with the dying red hair,
The child myself who is my murderer.
So came I between heaven and my grave
Past the serene smile of the *voyeur*, to
This cave where the myth enters the heart again.

II—THE CAVE

Space to the mind, the painted cave of dream.
This is not a womb, nothing but good emerges:
This is a stage, neither unreal nor real,
Where the walls are the world, the rocks and palaces
Stand on a borderland of blossoming ground.
If you stretch your hand, you touch the slope of the world
Reaching in interlaced gods, animals, and men.

There is no background.   The figures hold their peace
In a web of movement.   There is no frustration,
Every gesture is taken, everything yields connections.
The heavy sensual shoulders, the thighs, the blood-born flesh
And earth turning into color, rocks into their crystals,
Water to sound, fire to form; life flickers
Uncounted into the supple arms of love.
The space of these walls is the body's living space;
Tear open your ribs and breathe the color of time
Where nothing leads away, the world comes forward
In flaming sequences.   Pillars and prisms.   Riders
And horses and the figures of consciousness,
Red cow grows long, goes running through the world.
Flung into movement in carnal purity,
These bodies are sealed—warm lip and crystal hand
In a jungle of light.   Color-sheeted, seductive
Foreboding eyelid lowered on the long eye,
Fluid and vulnerable.   The spaces of the body
Are suddenly limitless, and riding flesh
Shapes constellations over the golden breast,
Confusion of scents and illuminated touch—
Monster touch, the throat printed with brightness,
Wide outlined gesture where the bodies ride.
Bells, and the spirit flashing.   The religious bells,
Bronze under the sunlight like breasts ringing,
Bronze in the closed air, the memory of walls,
Great sensual shoulders in the web of time.

III—LES TENDRESSES BESTIALES

A procession of caresses alters the ancient sky
Until new constellations are the body shining:
There's the Hand to steer by, there the horizon Breast,
And the Great Stars kindling the fluid hill.
All the rooms open into magical boxes,
Nothing is tilted, everything flickers
Sexual and exquisite.
The panther with its throat along my arm

Turns black and flows away.
Deep in all streets passes a faceless whore
And the checkered men are whispering one word.
The face I know becomes the night-black rose.
The sharp face is now an electric fan
And says one word to me.
The dice and the alcohol and the destruction
Have drunk themselves and cast.
Broken bottle of loss, and the glass
Turned bloody into the face.
Now the scene comes forward, very clear.
Dream-singing, airborne, surrenders the recalled,
The gesture arrives riding over the breast,
Singing, singing, tender atrocity,
The silver derelict wearing fur and claws.
O love, I stood under the apple branch,
I saw the whipped bay and the small dark islands,
And night sailing the river and the foghorn's word.
My life said to you : I want to love you well.
The wheel goes back and I shall live again,
But the wave turns, my birth arrives and spills
Over my breast the world bearing my grave,
And your eyes open in earth.   You touched my life.
My life reaches the skin, moves under your smile,
And your throat and your shoulders and your face and your
     thighs
Flash.
          I am haunted by interrupted acts,
Introspective as a leper, enchanted
By a repulsive clew,
A gross and fugitive movement of the limbs.
Is this the love that shook the lights to flame?
Sheeted avenues thrash in the wind,
Torn streets, the savage parks.
I am plunged deep.   Must find the midnight cave.

IV—BLACK BLOOD

A habit leading to murder, smoky laughter
Hated at first, but necessary later.
Alteration of motives.   To stamp in terror
Around the deserted harbor, down the hill
Until the woman laced into a harp
Screams and screams and the great clock strikes,
Swinging its giant figures past the face.
The Floating Man rides on the ragged sunset
Asking and asking.   Do not say, Which loved?
Which was beloved? Only, Who most enjoyed?
Armored ghost of rage, screaming and powerless.
Only find me and touch my blood again.
Find me.   A girl runs down the street
Singing Take me, yelling Take me Take
Hang me from the clapper of a bell
And you as hangman ring it sweet tonight,
For nothing clean in me is more than cloud
Unless you call it.   —As I ran I heard
A black voice beating among all that blood:
"Try to live as if there were a God."

V—THE BROKEN WORLD

Came to Ajanta cave, the painted space of the breast,
The real world where everything is complete,
There are no shadows, the forms of incompleteness.
The great cloak blows in the light, rider and horse arrive,
The shoulders turn and every gift is made.
No shadows fall.   There is no source of distortion.
In our world, a tree casts the shadow of a woman,
A man the shadow of a phallus, a hand raised
The shadow of a whip.
Here everything is itself,
Here all may stand
On summer earth.
Brightness has overtaken every light,

And every myth netted itself in flesh.
New origins, and peace given entire
And the spirit alive.
In the shadowless cave
The naked arm is raised.
Animals arrive,
Interlaced, and gods
Interlaced, and men
Flame-woven.
I stand and am complete.
Crawls from the door,
Black at my two feet
The shadow of the world.

World, not yet one,
Enters the heart again.
The naked world, and the old noise of tears,
The fear, the expiation and the love,
A world of the shadowed and alone.

The journey, and the struggles of the moon.

❧ THE MEETING ❧

One o'clock in the letter-box
Very black and I will go home early.
Now I have put off my dancing-dress
And over a sheet of distance write my love.
I walk in the city with my pride of theme
While the lean girls at their betrayal smiling
Dance, do their sea-green dance, and laugh in dancing.
And all the stars fade out of my sky.

Early in the morning on a windy ocean.
My sleep opens upon your face to kiss and find

And take diversion of the meeting waters,
The flameless sky of peace, blue-sided white air.
I leave you as the trivial birds careen
In separation, a dream of easy parting.
I see you through a door. The door sails away,
And all the ships move into the real sea.

Let that far day arrive, that evening stain!
Down the alleys of the night I trail a cloak;
Field-dusk and mountain-dusk and final darkness —
Each absence brings me nearer to that night
When I stone-still in desire standing
Shall see the masked body of love enter the garden
To reach the night-burning, the perpetual fountain.
And all the birds fly out of my scene.

❧ DRUNKEN GIRL ❧

Do you know the name of the average animal?
Not the dog,
    Nor the green-beaded frog,
Nor the white ocean monster lying flat —
    Lower than that.
The curling one who comes out in the storm—
The middle one's the worm.

Lift up your face, my love, lift up your mouth,
Kiss me and come to bed
    And do not bow your head
Longer on what is bad or what is good —
    The dead are terribly misunderstood,
And sin and godhead are in the worm's blind eye,
We'll come to averages by and by.

ঙ WHO IN ONE LIFETIME ঙ

Who in one lifetime sees all causes lost,
Herself dismayed and helpless, cities down,
Love made monotonous fear and the sad-faced
Inexorable armies and the falling plane,
Has sickness, sickness. Introspective and whole,
She knows how several madnesses are born,
Seeing the integrated never fighting well,
The flesh too vulnerable, the eyes tear-torn.

She finds a pre-surrender on all sides:
Treaty before the war, ritual impatience turn
The camps of ambush to chambers of imagery.
She holds belief in the world, she stays and hides
Life in her own defeat, stands, though her whole world
     burn,
A childless goddess of fertility.

ঙ LOVE AND ITS
DOORS AND WINDOWS ঙ

History melts my houses,
But they were all one house
Where in the dark beginning
A tall and maniac nurse
Hid tortures behind the door
And afterwards kissed me
Promising all as before.

The second house was music;
The childish hands of fear
Lying on a piano
That was blackness and light,

Opened my life with sound —
Extorting promises
Loud in the ringing air.

After that, broken houses,
The wealthy halls of cloud
Haunted by living parents
And the possessive face.
Power and outrage looking
At the great river
Marvellous filthy and gold.

When love lay in my arms
I all night kissed that mouth,
And the incredible body
Slept warm at my side;
But the walls fell apart
Among my lifetime dream —
O, a voice said crying,
My mother's broken heart.

Nothing was true in the sense
I wanted it to be true.
Victory came late,
Excitement returned too soon.
If my love were for the dead,
Desire would restore
Me to my life again.

My love is for the living;
They point me down to death,
And death I will not take.
My promises have grown,
My kiss was never false,
The faint clear-colored walls
Are not forever down.

❧ LONG PAST MONCADA ❧

Nothing was less than it seemed, my darling:
The danger was greater, the love was greater, the suffering
        Grows daily great—
And the fear we saw gathering into that Spanish valley
Is rank in all countries, a garden of growing death;
Your death, my darling, the threat to our lifetime
        And to all we love.

Whether you fell at Huesca during the lack of guns,
Or later, at Barcelona, as the city fell,
        You reach my days;
Among the heckling of clocks, the incessant failures,
I know how you recognized our war, and ran
To it as a runner to his eager wedding
        Or our immediate love.

If I indeed killed you, my darling, if my cable killed
Arriving the afternoon the city fell,
        No further guilt
Could more irrevocably drive my days
Through the disordered battles and the cities down
In a clash of metal on murder, a stampede of
        Hunger and death.

Other loves, other children, other gifts, as you said,
"Of the revolution," arrive—but, darling, where
        You entered, life
Entered my hours, whether you lie fallen
Among those sunlight fields, or by miracle somewhere stand,
Your words of war and love, death and another promise
        Survive as a lifetime sound.

❧ A GAME OF BALL ❧

On a ground beaten gold by running and
Over the Aztec crest of the sky and
Past the white religious faces of the
Bulls and far beyond, the ball goes flying.

Sun and moon and all the stars of the moon
Are dancing across our eyes like the flight of armies
And the loser dies. Dark player and bright
Play for the twinned stiff god of life and death.
They die and become the law by which they fight.

Walls grow out of this light, branches out of the stone,
And fire running from the farthest winds
Pours broken flame on these fantastic sands
Where, sunlit, stands the goddess of earth and death,
A frightful peasant with work-hardened hands.

But over the field flash all the colors of summer,
The battle flickers in play, a game like sacrifice.
The sun rides over, the moon and all her stars.
Whatever is ready to eat us, we have found
This place where the gods play out the game of the sky
And bandy life and death across a summer ground.

❧ DARKNESS MUSIC ❧

The days grow and the stars cross over
And my wild bed turns slowly among the stars.

&❧ SONG &❧

The world is full of loss;   bring, wind, my love,
    My home is where we make our meeting-place,
    And love whatever I shall touch and read
    Within that face.

Lift, wind, my exile from my eyes;
    Peace to look, life to listen and confess,
    Freedom to find to find to find
    That nakedness.

❧ V.
ELEGIES ❧

For Otto Boch

FIRST ELEGY. ROTTEN LAKE

As I went down to Rotten Lake I remembered
the wrecked season, haunted by plans of salvage,
snow, the closed door, footsteps and resurrections,
    machinery of sorrow.

The warm grass gave to the feet and the stilltide water
was floor of evening and magnetic light and
reflection of wish, the black-haired beast with my eyes
    walking beside me.

The green and yellow lights, the street of water standing
point to the image of that house whose destruction
I weep, when I weep you.   My door (no), poems, rest,
    (don't say it!) untamable need.

*

When you have left the river you are a little way
nearer the lake;   but I leave many times.
Parents parried my past;   the present was poverty,
the future depended on my unfinished spirit.
There were no misgivings because there was no choice,
only regret for waste, and the wild knowledge:
growth and sorrow and discovery.

When you have left the river you proceed alone;
all love is likely to be illicit;   and few
friends to command the souls;   they are too feeble.
Rejecting the subtle and contemplative minds
as being too thin in the bone;   and the gross thighs
and unevocative hands fail also.   But the poet
and his wife, those who say Survive, remain;
and those two who were with me on the ship
leading me to the sum of the years, in Spain.

When you have left the river you will hear the war.
In the mountains, with tourists, in the insanest groves

the sound of kill, the precious face of peace.
And the sad frightened child, continual minor,
returns, nearer whole circle, O and nearer
all that was loved, the lake, the naked river,
what must be crossed and cut out of your heart,
what must be stood beside and straightly seen.

*

As I went down to Rotten Lake I remembered
how the one crime is need.   The man lifting the loaf
with hunger as motive can offer no alibi, is
    always condemned.

These are the lines at the employment bureau
and the tense students at their examinations;
needing makes clumsy and robs them of their wish,
    in one fast gesture

plants on them failure of the imagination;
and lovers who lower their bodies into the chair
gently and sternly as if the flesh had been wounded,
    never can conquer.

Their need is too great, their vulnerable bodies
rigidly joined will snap, turn love away,
fear parts them, they lose their hands and voices, never
    get used to the world.

Walking at night, they are asked Are you your best friend's
best friend? and must say No, not yet, they are
love's vulnerable, and they go down to Rotten Lake
    hoping for wonders.

Dare it arrive, the day when weakness ends?
When the insistence is strong, the wish converted?
I prophesy the meeting by the water
    of these desires.

I know what this is, I have known the waking
when every night ended in one cliff-dream
of faces drowned beneath the porous rock
        brushed by the sea;

suffered the change : deprived erotic dreams
to images of that small house where peace
walked room to room and always with one face
        telling her stories,

and needed that, past loss, past fever, and the
attractive enemy who in my bed
touches all night the body of my sleep,
        improves my summer

with madness, impossible loss, and the dead music
of altered promise, a room torn up by the roots,
the desert that crosses from the door to the wall,
        continual bleeding,

and all the time that will which cancels enmity,
seeks its own Easter, arrives at the water-barrier;
must face it now, biting the lakeside ground;
        looks for its double,

the twin that must be met again, changeling need,
blazing in color somewhere, flying yellow
into the forest with its lucid edict:
        take to the world,

this is the honor of your flesh, the offering
of strangers, the faces of cities, honor of all your wish.
Immortal undoing! I say in my own voice. These prophecies
        may all come true,

out of the beaten season.   I look in Rotten Lake
wait for the flame reflection, seeing only

the free beast flickering black along my side
    animal of my need,

and cry I want! I want! rising among the world
to gain my converted wish, the amazing desire
that keeps me alive, though the face be still, be still,
the slow dilated heart know nothing but lack,
now I begin again the private rising,
the ride to survival of that consuming bird
beating, up from dead lakes, ascents of fire.

ટ SECOND ELEGY. AGE OF MAGICIANS ટ

A baroque night advances in its clouds,
maps strain loose and are lost, the flash-flood breaks,
the lifting moonflare lights this field a moment,
while death as a skier curves along the snows,
death as an acrobat swings year to year,
turns down to us the big face of a nurse.
Roads open black, and the magicians come.

The aim of magicians is inward pleasure.
The prophet lives by faith and not by sight,
Being a visionary, he is divided,
or Cain, forever shaken by his crime.
Magnetic ecstasy, a trance of doom
mean the magician, worshipping a darkness
with gongs and lurid guns, the colors of force.
He is again the unity of light.

The Magician has his symbols, brings up his children by them:
the march-step, the staircase at night, the long cannon.
The children grow in authority and become
Molitor, Dr. Passavant, powerful Dr. Falcon,

bring their professors, and soon may govern
the zone, the zodiac, the king on his throne.
"Because the age holds its own dangers.
"Because snow comes with lightnings, omens with all seasons."
(The Prophet covers his face against the wall,
weeps, fights to think again, to plan to start
the dragon, the ecliptic, and the heart.)

The Magician lifts himself higher than the world.
The Prophets were more casual. They endured,
and in the passive dread of solitude
heard calls, followed veiled, in midnight humility.
They claimed no preference;   they separated
unity from blindness
living from burning
tribute from tribute.

They have gone under, and do they come again?
The index of prophecy is light
and steeped therein
the world with all its signatures visible.

*

Does this life permit its living to wear strength?
Who gives it, protects it.   It is food.
Who refuses it, it eats in time as food.
It is the world and it eats the world.
Who knows this, knows.   This has been said.

This is the vision in the age of magicians:
it stands at immense barriers, before mountains:
'I came to you in the form of a line of men,
and when you threw down the paper, and when you sat at the play,
and when you killed the spider, and when you saw the shadow
of the fast plane skim fast over your lover's face.
And when you saw the table of diplomats,
the newsreel of ministers, the paycut slip,
the crushed child's head, clean steel, factories,

the chessmen on the marble of the floor,
each flag a country, each chessman a live man,
one side advancing southward to the pit,
one side advancing northward to the lake,
and when you saw the tree, half bright half burning.
You never inquired into these meanings.
If you had done this, you would have been restored.'

The word is war.
And there is a prediction that you are the avenger.

They cut the people's hands, and their shoulders were left,
they cut their feet off, and their thighs were whole,
they cut them down to the torse, but the voice shouted,
they cut the head off, but the heart rang out.

And in the residential districts, where nothing ever happens,
armies of magicians filled the streets,
shouting
Need!   Bread!   Blood!   Death!

And all this is because of you.
And all this is avenged by you.
Your index light, your voice the voice,
your tree half green and half burning,
half dead half bright,
your cairns, your beacons, your tree in green and flames,
unbending smoke in the sky, planes' noise, the darkness,
magic to fight.   Much to restore; now know.   Now be
Seer son of Sight, Hearer, of Ear, at last.

‏‮ᕧ‬ THIRD ELEGY. THE FEAR OF FORM ‏‮ᕧ‬

Tyranny of method!   the outrageous smile
seals the museums, pours a mob skidding
up to the formal staircase, stopped, mouths open.
And do they stare?   They do.
At what?   A sunset?

Blackness, obscurity, bravado were the three colors;
wit-play, movement, and wartime the three moments;
formal groups, fire, facility, the three hounds.

This was their art : a wall daubed like a face,
a penis or finger dipped in a red pigment.
The sentimental frown gave them their praise,
prized the wry color, the twisted definition,
and said,   "You are right to copy."

But the car full of Communists put out hands and guns,
blew 1 − 2 − 3 on the horn before the
surrealist house, a spiral in Cataluña.

New combinations : set out materials now,
combine them again!   the existence is the test.
What do you want?   Lincoln blacking his lessons
in charcoal on an Indiana shovel?
or the dilettante, the impressario's beautiful skull
choosing the tulip crimson satin, the yellow satin
as the ballet dances its tenth time to the mirror?
Or the general's nephew, epaulets from birth,
run down the concourse, shouting Planes for Spain?

New methods, the staring circle given again
force, a phoenix of power, another Ancient
sits in his circle, while the plaster model
of an equation slowly rotates beneath him,
and all his golden compass leans.
Create an anti-sentimental : Sing!

"For children's art is not asylum art,
"there are these formal plays in living, for
"the equal triangle does not spell youth,
"the cube nor age, the sphere nor ever soul.
"Asylum art is never children's art.
"They cut the bones down, but the line remained.
"They cut the line for good, and reached the point
"blazing at the bottom of its night."

*

A man is walking, wearing the world, swearing
saying You damn fools come out into the open.
Whose dislocated wish?   Whose terrors whine?
I'll fuse him straight.
The usable present starts by calendar.

Chorus of bootblacks, printers, collectors of shit
Your witwork works, your artwork shatters, die.
Hammer up your abstractions.   Divide, O zoo.
—He's a queer bird, a hero, a kangaroo.
What is he going to do?

He calls Rise out of cities, you memorable ghosts
scraps of an age whose choice is seen
to lie between evils.   Dazzle-paint the rest,
it burns my eyes with its acetylene.
Look through the wounds, mystic and human fly,
you spiritual unicorn, you clew of eyes.

Ghosts to approach the blood in fifteen cities.
Did you walk through the walls of the Comtesse de Noailles?
Was there a horror in Chicago?
Or ocean?   Or ditches at the road.   Or France,
while bearing guarding shadowing painting in Paris,
Picasso like an ass Picasso like a dragon Picasso like a
romantic movement
and immediately after, stations of swastikas

Prague and a thousand boys swing circles clean
girls by the thousand curve their arms together
geometries of wire
the barbed, starred
Heil

Will you have capitals with their tarnished countesses
their varnished cemetery life
vanished Picassos
or clean acceptable Copenhagen
or by God a pure high monument
white yellow and red
up against Minnesota?

Does the sea permit its dead to wear jewels?

Flame, fusion, defiance are your three guards,
the sphere, the circle, the cluster your three guides,
the bare, the blond and the bland are your three goads.

Adam, Godfinger, only these contacts function:
light and the high accompanied design,
contact of points   the fusion say of sex
the atombuster too along these laws.
Put in a sphere, here, at the focal joint,
he said, put it in.   The moment is arrangement.
Currents washed through it, spun, blew white,
fused.   For! the sphere! proving!

This was the nightmare of a room alone,
the posture of grave figure, finger on other head,
he puts the finger of power on him,
optic of grandiose delusion.
All you adjacent and contagious points,
make room for fusion;   fall,
you monuments, snow on your heads,
your power, your pockets, your dead parts.

97 ès

Standing at midnight corners under corner-lamps
we wear the coat and the shadow of the coat.
The mind sailing over a scene lets light arrive
conspicuous sunrise, the knotted smoke rising,
the world with all its signatures visible.
Play of materials in balance,
carrying the strain of a new process.
Of the white root, the nature of the base,
contacts, making an index.
And do they stare?   They do.
Our needs, our violences.
At what?   Contortion of body and spirit.
To fuse it straight.

❧ FOURTH ELEGY. THE REFUGEES ❧

And the child sitting alone planning her hope:
I want to write for my race.   But what race will you speak,
being American?   I want to write for the living.
But the young grow more around us every day.
They show new faces, they come from far, they live
occupied with escape, freeze in the passes, sail
early in the morning.   A few arrive to help.
        Mother, those were not angels, they were knights.

Many are cast out, become artists at rejection.
They saw the chute, the intelligible world
so wild become, it fell, a hairy apparent star
this time with not a public saint in sight
to record miracle.   The age of the masked and the alone begins,
we look for sinister states, a loss shall learning suffer
before the circle of this sun be done,
the palace birds of the new tyrants rise
flying into the wounded sky, sky of catastrophe;

help may be near, but remedy is far,
rain, blood, milk, famine, iron, and epidemic
pour in the sky where a comet drags his tail.
The characters of the spectacles are dead,
nothing is left but ventriloquists and children,
and bodies without souls are not a sacrifice.

It is the children's voyage must be done
before the refugees come home again.
They run like lemmings out
building their suffocated bodies up
to let the full stream pass.
The predatory birds sail over them.
They dash themselves into lighthouses, where the great
     lights hold up,
they laugh at sympathy : "Have you nothing better to do
     in the trenches?"
And at that brink, that bending over doom,
become superior to themselves, in crisis.
There is an addition and fusion of qualities.

They are the children.   They have their games.
They made a circle on a map of time,
skipping they entered it, laughing lifted the agate.
I will get you an orange cat, and a pig called Tangerine.
The gladness-bird beats wings against an opaque glass.
There is a white bird in the top of the tree.
They leave their games, and pass.

Cut.   Frozen and cut.   Off at the ankle.   Off at the hip.
     Off at the knee.   Cut off.
Crossing the mountains many died of cold.

We have spoken of guilt to you too long.
The blame grows on us who carry you the news.
And as the man bringing the story of suicide
lives with the fact, feels murder in himself,
as murderous regents with their gentle kings

know the seductions of crime long before death takes hold,
we bear their—
                    a child crying shrill in a white street
"Aviación!" among the dust of geysers,
the curling rust of Spanish tile.
We bear their smile, we smile under the guilt,
in an access of sickness,   "Let me alone, I'm healthy!"
cry.   And in danger, the sexually witty
speak in short sentences, the unfulfilled.
While definition levels others out.
Wish : the unreality of fulfilled action.
Wish : the reality of fulfilled thought.
Images of luxury.   Image of life.
A phoenix at play among the peonies.
The random torture predicts the random thought.
Over the thought and bird and flowers, the plane.

Coming to strange countries refugee children find
land burned over by winter, a white field and black star
falling like firework where no rockets are
into hell-cities with blank brick and church-bells
(I like this city.   This is a peaceful city)
ringing the bees in the hot garden with their mixing sounds,
ringing the love that falters among these hills,
red-flowering maple and the laugh of peace.
It will take a bell-ringing god tremendous imagined descending
for the healing of hell.

A line of birds, a line of gods.   O bells.
And all the birds have settled on their shadows.
And down the shadowed street a line of children.
You can make out the child ahead of you.
It turns with a gesture that asks for a soft answer.
It sees the smaller child ahead of it.
The child ahead of it turns.   Now, in the close-up
faces throw shadow off.   It is yourself
walks down this street at five-year intervals,
seeing yourself diminishing ahead,

five years younger, and five years younger, and young,
until the farthest infant has a face
ready to grow into any child in the world.

    They take to boats.   The shipwreck of New York.
    To trains whose sets of lines pass along boxes,
    children's constructions.
    Rush to rejection
    foreknowing the steps,
        disfigurement of women, insults of disease,
        negations of power.   They people the earth.
        They are the strong.   They see the enemy.
        They dream the relaxed heart, coming again to power,
        the struggle, the Milk-Tree of Children's Paradise.

They are the real creation of a fictional character.
They fuse a dead world straight.

A line of shadowy children issues, surf issues it,
sickness boiled in their flesh, but they are whole,
insular strength surrounds them, hunger feeds them strong,
the ripened sun finds them, they are the first of the world,
free of the ferryman Nostalgia, who stares at the backward shore.
Growing free of the old in their slow growth of death,
they hold the flaming apples of the spring.
They are exposed to danger.
Ledges of water trick them,
they fall through the raw colors of excavations,
are crushed by monuments, high stone like whale-blow rising,
the backwash of machines can strike them down.
A hill on a map claims them, their procession reaches
a wavy topographical circle where
two gunners lie behind their steelwork margins,
spray shot across the line, do random death.
They fire in a world infected by trenches,
through epidemics of injuries, Madrid, Shanghai,
Vienna, Barcelona, all cities of contagion,
issue survivors from the surf of the age.

Free to be very hungry and very lonely.
And in the countries of the mind, Cut off at the knee.   Cut off
    at the armpit.   Cut off at the throat.
Free to reclaim the world and sow a legend,
to make the adjustments never made,
repair the promises broken and the promise kept.
They blame our lives, lie on our wishes with their eyes our own,
to say and to remember and avenge.   A lullaby for a believing
    child.

ह FIFTH ELEGY. A TURNING WIND ह

Knowing the shape of the country.   Knowing the midway
                travels of
migrant fanatics, living that life, up with the dawn and
moving as long as the light lasts, and when the sun is falling
    to wait, still standing;

and when the black has come, at last lie down, too tired to
turn to each other, feeling only the land's demand under them.
Shape that exists not as permanent quality, but varies with
    even the movement of bone.

Even in skeletons, it depends on the choices of action.
A definite plan is visible.   We are either free-moving or
fixed to some ground.   The shape has no meaning
    outside of the function.

Fixed to Europe, the distant, adjacent, we lived, with the land-
promise of life of our own.   Course down the East—frontiers
meet you at every turn—the headlights find them, the plain's,
    and the solar cities'

recurrent centers.   And at the middle of the great world the
                wind

answers the shape of the country, a turning traveller
follows the hinge-line of coast, the first indefinite
    axis of symmetry

torn off from sympathy with the past and planted,
a primitive streak prefiguring the west, an ideal
which had to be modified for stability,
    to make it work.

Architecture is fixed not only by present needs but
also by ancestors.   The actual structure means a plan determined
by the nature of ancestors;   its details are determined by
    function and interference.

There are these major divisions : for those attached to the sea-
        floor,
a fan at freedom, flexible, wavering, designed to catch food
from all directions.   For the sedentary, for those who crouch
        and look,
    radial symmetry,

spokes to all margins for support.   For those who want move-
        ment,
this is achieved through bilateral symmetry only,
a spine and straight attack, all muscles working,
    up and alive.

*

And there are years of roads, and centuries of need,
of walking along the shadow of a wall, of visiting houses,
hearing the birds trapped in the wall, the framework trembling
    with struggles of birds,

years of nightwalking in stranger cities, relost and unnamed,
recurrent familiar rooms, furnished only with nightmare,
recurrent loves, the glass eye of unreal ambition,
    years of initiation,

of dishallucination on the diamond meadows,
seeing the distances of false capes ahead,
feeling the tide-following and turning wind,
    travelling farther

under abrasive weather, to the bronzy river,
the rust, the brown, the terrible dead swamps,
the hanging moss the color of all the hanged,
    cities whose heels

ring out their news of hell upon all streets,
churches where you betray yourself, pray ended desire,
white wooden houses of village squares.   Always one gesture:
    rejecting of backdrops.

These are the ritual years, whose lore is names of shapes,
Grabtown, Cockade Alley, Skid Row where jobless live,
their emblem a hitch-hiker with lips basted together,
    and marvel rivers,

the flooded James, a double rainbow standing over Richmond,
the remnant sky above the Cape Fear River, blue stain on red
            water,
the Waccamaw with its bone-trees, Piscataqua's rich mouth,
    red Sound and flesh of sand.

—A nation of refugees that will not learn its name;
still shows these mothers enduring, their hidden faces,
the cry of the hurt child at a high night-window,
    hand-to-hand warfare,

the young sitting in libraries at their only rest
or making love in the hallway under an orange bulb,
the boy playing baseball at Hungry Mother State Park,
    bestiaries of cities

and this shape, this meaning that promises seasonal joy.
Whose form is unquietness and yet the seeker of rest,

whose travelling hunger has range enough, its root
    grips through the world.

The austere fire-world of night : Gary or Bethlehem,
in sacred stacks of flame — or stainless morning,
anti-sunlight of lakes' reflection, matchlight on face,
    the thorny light of fireworks

lighting a way for the shape, this country of celebrations
deep in a passage of rebirth.   Adventures of countries,
adventures of travellers, visions, or Christ's adventures
    forever following him

lit by the night-light of history, persevering
into the incredible washed morning air.
The luisarne swamp is our guide and the glare ice,
    the glow of tracklights,

the lights winding themselves into a single beacon,
big whooping riders of night, a wind that whirls
all of our motives into a single stroke,
    shows us a country

of which the birds know mountains that we have not dreamed,
climbing these unsuspected slopes they fade.   Butte and pavil-
            ion
vanish into a larger scape, morning vaults all those hills
    rising on ranges

that stand gigantic on the roots of the world,
where points expand in pleasure of raw sweeping
gestures of joy, whose winds sweep down like stairs,
    and the felled forests

on hurricane ridges show a second growth.   The dances
of turkeys near storm, a pouring light, tornado
umbilical to earth, fountains of rain, a development
    controlled by centers,

until the organs of this anatomy are fleshed away at last
of gross, and determining self, develop a final structure
in isolation.   Masterpieces of happiness arrive,
       alive again in another land,

remembering pain, faces of suffering, but they know growth,
go through the world, hunger and rest desiring life.
Mountains are spines to their conquest, these wrecked houses
       (vines spiral the pillars)

are leaning their splintered sides on tornadoes, lifted careening
in wheels, in whirlwind, in a spool of power
drawing a spiral on the sun, drawing a sign of
       strength on the mountains,

the fusing stars lighting initiated cities.
The thin poor whiteness raining on the ground
forgotten in fickle eclipses, thunderbirds of dream
       following omens,

following charts of the moving constellations.
Charts of the country of all visions, imperishable
stars of our old dream : process, which having neither
       sorrow nor joy

remains as promise, the embryo in the fire.
The tilted cities of America, fields of metal,
the seamless wheatfields, the current of cities running
       below our wings

promise that knowledge of systems which may bless.
May permit knowledge of self, a lover's wish of conversion
until the time when the dead lake rises in light,
the shape is organized in travelling space,
this hope of travel, to find the place again,
rest in the triumph of the reconceived,
lie down again together face to face.

❧ SIXTH ELEGY. RIVER ELEGY ❧

In burning summer I saw a season of betrayal,
the world fell away, and wasteful climbing green
covered the breaking of bodies, covered our hearts.
Unreal in the burning, many-motioned life
lay like a sea, but fevers found my grief,
I turned in that year to retrieve the stainless river,
the lost, the flowing line of escaped music.

Year of judgment!   Century of betrayal!
They built their cities on the banks of war
and all their cities are down, the Floating Man
swims in the smoke of their sky, the Double Woman
smiles up through the water with her distorted mouth.
I stand over reflection as the world darkens in
destruction of countries, all souls downward set,
life narrowing to one color of a choked river
and hell on both its banks.   My city, my city!
They never built cities.   Cities are for the living.
They built for the half-dead and the half-alive.
Their history is a half-history.   And we go down.
They built their villages whose lame towers fell
where error was overgrown until the long
tentacular ruin touches all fields.   My love!
Did I in that country build you villages?
Great joy my love, even there, until they fell
and green betrayal climbed over the wall.

Defeat and raging and a burning river.
Half-faced, half-sexed, the living dead arrive
passing, a lip, a breast, half of a hand.
Gaudy sadistic streets, dishonest avenues
where every face has bargained for its eyes.
And they come down to the river, driven down.
And all the faces fly out of my city.
The rich streets full of empty coats parading
and one adolescent protesting violin,

the slum full of their flayed and faceless bodies,
they shiver, they are working to buy their skin.
They are lost. They come down to look for life in a river,
plunge, turn and plunge, they cannot change their life,
swimming, their head is in another world.

World without form.   Chaos beaten and beaten,
raging and suffering and hoping to take shape.
I saw your summer.   I saw your river flow.
I being wasted everywhere saw waste.
Hell's entropy at work and torment general,
friend against most-known friend, love fighting off love.
They asked for an end to emptiness; their sick throats
      filled with foam,
prayed to be solved, and rose to deal betrayal.
And I falling through hell passed many friends, and love,
and a haunted woman warned me as I fell.
Downward through currents, the horrors with little hands.

The chaos, the web of the heart, this bleeding knot;
raises me swimming now, one moment in the air
and light is on my face, the fans over the river
of wind, of goodness.   Lie gasping on this shore,
there is nothing in the world but an honest word
which the severed away may speak before we die.
Let me tell you what I have held to all along:
when I said that I loved you, when I crossed the frontier,
when I learned the obscurities of a frightened child,
when I shut the door, and felt the sprouting tears,
when I saw the river, when I learned resurrection,
the joy of your hands in a pain that called More Life.
Let me tell you what I have meant all along:
meaning of poetry and personal love,
a world of peace and freedom, man's need recognized,
and all the agonies that will begin that world.

Betrayed, we are betrayed.   The set of the great faces
mean it, the following eyes.   They are the flayed men,

their strength is at the center, love and the time's disease
lie at their skin.   The kiss in the flaring garden
when all the trees closed in.   The knotted terrible lips.
The black blood risen and the animal rage.
The last fierce accident, whose back-thrown drowning head
among the escaping sound of water hears
slows insane music groping for a theme.

My love, reach me again.   The smell of the sea,
wind-flower, sea-flower, the fallen gull-feather.
Clear water and order and an end to dreams:
ether-dreams, surrounded beasts, the aftertoll of fear,
the world reduced to a rising line of water,
the patient deserted by the analyst.
To keep the knowledge that holds my race alive:
spiritual grace of the material world.

I walked under the sky, and the high clouds
hollowed in ribs arched over their living heart:
the world, the corporeal world that will not die.
No, world's no heart—here is yourself walking
in a cage of clouds looking up wanting one face
over you and that look to fill the sky.
Carrying counter-agony into the world,
dream-singing, river-madness, the tragic fugal love
of a theme balancing another theme.

Disorder of suffering, a flight of details, a world
with no shadows at noontime and never at night a light.
Suddenly the flame-blue of a drunken sky
and it is the change, the reds and metals of autumn.
But I curse autumn, for I do not change,
I love, I love, and we are far from peace,
and the great river moves unbearably;
actual gestures of giving, and I may not give.
Water will hold my shadows, the kiss of darkness,
maternal death's tender and delicate promises
seethe at the lips, release and the full sleep.

Even now the bright corporeal hand
might come to redeem the long moment of dying.
Even now if I could rest my life,
my forehead on those knees and the arriving shadows
in rising quiet as the long night arrives.
Terror, war, terror, black blood and wasted love.
The most terrible country, in the heads of men.
This is the war imagination made;
it must be strong enough to make a peace.
My peace is strong enough if it will come
flowing, the color of eyes.   When the world burns away
nothing is left can ever be betrayed.

All broken promises, adulterate release—
cast in the river Death, charred surface of waste,
a downward soulset, never the old heaven
held for a moment as breath held underwater;
but we must rise into a breathing world.
And this dark bellowing century, on its knees—?
If all this must go down, it must.
And all this brilliance go to dust?
Only the meanings can remain alive.
When the cemeteries are military objectives
and love's a downward drawing at the heart
and every letter bears the stamp of death.

There is no solution.   There is no happiness.
Only the range must be taken, a way be found to use
the inmost frenzy and the outer doom.
They are here, they run their riot in the clouds,
fly in our blood and over all our mountains,
corrupt all waters, poison the pride of theme.

Years of judgment!   Century screaming for
the flowing, the life, the intellectual leap
of waters over a world grown old and wild,
a broken crying for seasonal change until
O God my love in time the waste become
the sure magnificent music of the defeated heart.

SEVENTH ELEGY. DREAM-SINGING ELEGY

Darkness, giving us dream's black unity.
Images in procession start to flow
among the river-currents down the years of judgment
and past the cities to another world.

There are flat places.   After the waterfall
arched like the torso of love, after the voices
singing behind the waterfall, after the water
lying like a lover on the heart,
there is defeat.

And moving through our spirit in the night
memories of these places.
Not ritual, not nostalgia, but our cries,
the axe at the heart, continual rebirth,
the crying of our raw desire,
young.   O many-memoried America!

*

In defeat there are no prophets and no magicians,
only the look in the loved and tortured eyes
when every fantasy restores, and day denies.
The act of war debased to the act of treason
in an age of treason.   We were strong at the first.
We resisted.   We did not plan enough.   We killed.
But the enemy came like thunder in the wood,
a storm over the treetops like a horse's head
reared to a great galloping, and war
trampled us down.   We lost our young men in the fighting,
we lost our homeland, our crops went under the frost,
our children under the hunger.   Now we stand
around this fire, our black hills far behind,
black water far before us, a glitter of time on the sea,
glitter of fire on our faces, the still faces—

stillness waiting for dreams
and only the shadows moving,
shadows and revelations.

In the spring of the year, this new fighting broke out.
No, when the fields were blond.   No, the leaves crimson.
When the old fighting was over, we knew what we were
seeing as if for a first time our dark hills masked with green,
our blond fields with the trees flame-shaped and black
in burning darkness on the unconsumed.
Seeing for a first time the body of our love,
our wish and our love for each other.
Then word came from a runner, a stranger:
"They are dancing to bring the dead back, in the mountains."
We danced at an autumn fire, we danced the old hate and change,
the coming again of our leaders.   But they did not come.
Our singers lifted their arms, and a singer cried,
"You must sing like me and believe, or be turned to rock!"

The winter dawned, but the dead did not come back.
News came on the frost, "The dead are on the march!"
We danced in prison to a winter music,
many we loved began to dream of the dead.
They made no promises, we never dreamed a threat.
And the dreams spread.

But there were no armies, and the dead were dead,
there was only ourselves, the strong and symbol self
dreaming among defeat, our torture and our flesh.
We made the most private image and religion,
stripped to the last resistance of the wish,
remembering the fighting and the lava beds,
the ground that opened, the red wounds opening,
remembering the triumph in the night,
the big triumph and the little triumph—
wide singing and the battle-flash—
assassination and whisper.

In the summer, dreaming was common to all of us,
the drumbeat hope, the bursting heart of wish,
music to bind us as the visions streamed
and midnight brightened to belief.
In the morning we told our dreams.
They all were the same dream.

Dreamers wake in the night and sing their songs.
In the flame-brilliant midnight, promises
arrive, singing to each of us with tongues of flame:
"We are hopes, you should have hoped us,
We are dreams, you should have dreamed us."
Calling our name.

When we began to fight, we sang hatred and death.
The new songs say, "Soon all people on earth
will live together."   We resist and bless
and we begin to travel from defeat.
Now, as you sing your dream, you ask the dancers,
in the night, in the still night, in the night,
"Do you believe what I say?"
And all the dancers answer "Yes."

To the farthest west, the sea and the striped country
and deep in the camps among the wounded cities
half-world over, the waking dreams of night
outrange the horrors.   Past fierce and tossing skies
the rare desires shine in constellation.
I hear your cries, you little voices of children
swaying wild, nightlost, in black fields calling.
I hear you as the seething dreams arrive
over the sea and past the flaming mountains.
Now the great human dream as great as birth or death,
only that we are not given to remember birth,
only that we are not given to hand down death,
this we hand down and remember.

Brothers in dream, naked-standing friend
rising over the night, crying aloud,
beaten and beaten and rising from defeat,
crying as we cry : We are the world together.
Here is the place in hope, on time's hillside,
where hope, in one's image, wavers for the last time
and moves out of one's body up the slope.
That place in love, where one's self, as the body of love,
moves out of the old lifetime towards the beloved.
Singing.

Who looks at the many colors of the world
knowing the peace of the spaces and the eyes of love,
who resists beyond suffering, travels beyond dream,
knowing the promise of the night-flowering worlds
sees in a clear day love and child and brother
living, resisting, and the world one world
dreaming together.

✎ EIGHTH ELEGY. CHILDREN'S ELEGY ✎

Yes, I have seen their eyes.   In peaceful gardens
the dark flowers now are always children's eyes,
full-colored, haunted as evening under fires
showered from the sky of a burning country.

Shallow-featured children under trees
look up among green shadows of the leaves.
The angel, flaming, gives — into his hands
all is given and he does not change.
The child changes and takes.
All is given.   He makes and changes.
The angel stands.

A flame over the tree.   Night calling in the cloud.
And shadow among winds.   Where does the darkness lie?
It comes out of the person, says the child.
A shadow tied and alive, trying to be.

In the tremendous child-world, everything is high,
active and fiery, sun-cats run through the walls,
the tree blows overhead like a green joy,
and cloudy leopards go hunting in the sky.

The shadow in us sings, "Stand out of the light!"
But I live, I live, I travel in the sun.

On burning voyages of war they go.
Like starving ghosts they stumble after nuns.
Children of heroes, Defeat the dark companion.
But if they are told they are happy, they will know.

Who kills the father burns up the children's tears.
Some suffering blazes beyond all human touch,
some sounds of suffering cry, far out of reach.
These children bring to us their mother's fears.

Singing, "O make us strong O let us go—"
The new world comes among the old one's harms,
old world carrying new world in her arms.
But if you say they are free, then they will know.

War means to me, sings a small skeleton,
only the separation,
mother no good and gone,
taken away in lines of fire and foam.
The end of war
will bring me, bring me home.

The children of the defeated, sparrow-poor and starved,
create, create, must make their world again.
Dead games and false salutes must be their grace.

One wish must move us, flicker from our lives
to the marred face.

My child, my victim, my wish this moment come!
But the martyr-face cries to us fiercely
"I search to learn the way out of childhood;
I need to fight.   I wish, I wish for home."

This is what they say, who were broken off from love:
However long we were loved, it was not long enough.

We were afraid of the broad big policeman,
of lions and tigers, the dark hall and the moon.

After our father went, nothing was ever the same,
when mother did not come back, we made up a war game.

*My cat was sitting in the doorway when the planes
went over, and my cat saw mother cry;
furry tears, fire fell, wall went down;
did my cat see mother die?*

Mother is gone away, my cat sits here coughing.
I cough and sit.   I am nobody's nothing.

However long they loved us, it was not long enough.
For we have to be strong, to know what they did, and then
our people are saved in time, our houses built again.

You will not know, you have a sister and brother;
my doll is not my child, my doll is my mother.

However strong we are, it is not strong enough.
I want to grow up.   To come back to love.

*

I see it pass before me in parade,
my entire life as a procession of images.
The toy, the golden kernel, the glass lamp.

The present she gave me, the first page I read,
the little animal, the shadowless tall angel.

The angel stands.   The child changes and takes.
He makes a world, stands up among the cousins,
cries to the family, "Ladies and gentlemen—
The world is falling *down!*"   After the smooth hair
darkens, and summer lengthens the smooth cheek,
and the diffuse gestures are no longer weak,
he begins to be the new one, to have what happened,
to do what must be done.

O, when the clouds and the blue horse of childhood
melt away and the golden weapons,
and we remember the first public day's
drums and parades and the first angel
standing in the garden, his dark lips
and silver blood, how he stood,
giving, for all he was was given.

I begin to have what happened to me.

O, when the music of carousels and stars
is known, and the music of the scene
makes a clear meeting, greeting and claim of gods,
we see through the hanging curtain of the year
they change each other with one change of love!
see, in one breath, in a look!
See, in pure midnight a flare of broken color
clears to a constellation.
Peace is asleep, war's lost.   It is love.
I wanted to die.   The masked and the alone
seemed the whole world, and all the gods at war,
and all the people dead and depraved.   Today
the constellation and the music!   Love.

You who seeking yourself arrive at these lines,
look once, and you see the world,
look twice and you see your self.

And all the children moving in their change.

To have what has happened, the pattern and the shock;
and all of them walk out of their childhood,
give to you one blue look.

And all the children bowing in their game,
saying Farewell, Goodbye;   Goodbye, Farewell.

❧ NINTH ELEGY. THE ANTAGONISTS ❧

Pieces of animals, pieces of all my friends
prepare assassinations while I sleep.
They shape my being, a gallery of lives
fighting within me, and all unreconciled.
Before them move my waking dreams, and ways
of the spirit, and simple action.   Among these
I can be well and holy.   Torn by them I am wild,
smile, and revenge myself upon my friends
and find myself among my enemies.
But all these forms of incompleteness pass
out of their broken power to a place
where dream and dream meet and resolve in grace.

The closing of this conflict is the end
of the initiation.   I have known the cliff
and known the cliff-dream of the faces drowned.
Stood in the high sun, a dark girl looking down,
seeing the colors of water swaying beneath me, dense
in the flood-summer, various as my love
and like my hope enchanted.   Drawn to blue
chance and horizons, and back as sea-grasses move
drawn landward slowly by incoming tides—
and then the final cancelling and choice,

not tilted as flowers under wind, but deep
blessing of root and heart, underwater swung,
wrenched, swayed, and given fully to the sea.
Heaven not of rest, but of intensity.

The forms of incompleteness in our land
pass from the eastern and western mountains where
the seas meet the dark islands, where the light
glitters white series on the snowlands, pours its wine
of lenient evening to the center.   Green
on shadows of Indiana, level yellow miles . . .
The prairie emblems and the slopes of the sky
and desert stars enlarging in the frost
redeems us like our love and will not die.
All origins are here, and in this range
the changing spirit can make itself again,
continually love, continually change.

> Out of the myth the mother leaned;
> From out the mother shines the child;
> Man rises, in the mass contained;
> And from this growth creation grows.
> The fire through all the spiral flows:
> Create the creative, many-born!
> And use your love, unreconciled!

*

In wheels, in whirlwind, in a storm of power
alive again and over every land
the thunderbird with lightnings at his wrists.
Eclipses uncloud and show us miracle,
gleaming, our ancestors, all antagonists:
Slave and Conquistador, dead hand-to-hand,
scented fastidious Tory with his whore,
distinguished rebel and woman at the plow.
The fiery embryo umbilical
always to failure, and form developing
American out of conflict.

                              Fierce dissenting ghosts,
the second Adams' fever and eagle voice
and Jackson's muscular democratic sense.
Sprung in one birth John Brown, a mad old man
whose blood in a single broken gesture freed
many beliefs;   and Lincoln's agony
condemning and confirming.   O, they cry,
the oppositions cry, O fight for me!
Fight, you are bound to freedom, and be free!
When Hawthorne saw the fabulous gift, he tore
flesh from his guilt, and found more guilt;   the bells
rang barter of the self, but Melville drowned.
The doubled phantoms bring to our terrible
chaos the order of a meeting-place
where the exchange is made, the agonies
lie down at last together face to face.

In the black night of blood, the forms begin
to glitter alive, fathers of constellations,
the shining and the music moving on.
We are bound by the deepest feuds to unity.
To make the connections and be born again,
create the creative, that will love the world.

                              *

Not glistening Indies, not continents, but the world
opening now, and the greatness of our age
that makes its own antagonists of the wish.
We want to find and will spend our lives in finding:
the landfall of our broken voyages
is still our America of contradictions.
Ancestors of that dream lie coupled in our flesh,
pieces of animals, pieces of all our friends
meet in us and we live.   We do not die.

Magical keen Magellan sought a rose
among the compass and legendary winds.
Green sequels rocked his eyes in water;   he

hung with the scorpion sun on noon's glass wall,
stared down, down into the future as he sailed.
Fanatic travels, recurrent mysteries.
Those who want the far shore spend their lives on the ocean.
The hand of God flowers in coasts for these.

Those who want only home spend their lives in the sky.
Flying over tonight, while thirteen searchlights join
high incandescent asters on black air.
The blinding center fastens on a plane
floating and white, glare-white; he wanting land
and intimate fertile hours, hangs there.   Sails
great scends of danger, or wades through crazy sand.

Those who most long for peace now pour their lives on war.
Our conflicts carry creation and its guilt,
these years' great arms are full of death and flowers.
A world is to be fought for, sung, and built:
Love must imagine the world.
                        The wish for love
moving upon the body of love describes
closing of conflict, repeats the sacred ways
in which the spirit dances and survives.

To that far meeting-place call home the enemies—
they keep their oppositions, for the strong
ironic joy of old intensities
still carries virile music.
                        O, the young
will come up
            after us
                        and make the dream,
the real world of our myth.
                        But now, the song
they will discover is a shadowy theme—

Today we are bound, for freedom binds us—we
live out the conflict of our time, until

Love, finding all the antagonists in the dance,
moved by its moods and given to its grace,
resolves the doom
                        and the deliverance.

ᥱ TENTH ELEGY. ELEGY IN JOY ᥱ

Now green, now burning, I make a way for peace.
After the green and long beyond my lake,
among those fields of people, on these illuminated
hills, gold, burnt gold, spilled gold and shadowed blue,
the light of enormous flame, the flowing light of the sea,
where all the lights and nights are reconciled.
The sea at last, where all the waters lead.
And all the wars to this peace.

For the sea does not lie like the death you imagine;
this sea is the real sea, here it is.
This is the living.   This peace is the face of the world,
a fierce angel who in one lifetime lives
fighting a lifetime, dying as we all die,
becoming forever, the continual god.

Years of our time, this heart!   The binding of the alone,
bells of all loneliness, binding our lands and our music,
branches full of motion each opening its own flower,
lands of all song, each speaking in his own voice.
Praise in every grace
among the old same war.

Years of betrayal, million death breeding its weaknesses
and hope, buried more deep more black than dream.
Every elegy is the present : freedom eating our hearts,
death and explosion, and the world unbegun.

Now burning and unbegun, I sing earth with its war,
and God the future, and the wish of man.

*

Though you die, your war lives : the years fought it,
fusing a dead world straight.

The living will be giving you your meanings,
widening to love because of the love of man.
All the wounds crying
I feare, and hope : I burne, and frese like yse . . .
saying to the beloved
For your sake I love cities,
on your love I love the many,
saying to the people,
for your sake I love the world.
The old wounds crying
I find no peace, and all my warres are done.

> Out of our life the living eyes
> See peace in our own image made,
> Able to give only what we can give:
> Bearing two days like midnight.   "Live,"
> The moment offers;   the night requires
> Promise effort love and praise.

Now there are no maps and no magicians.
No prophets but the young prophet, the sense of the world.
The gift of our time, the world to be discovered.
All the continents giving off their several lights,
the one sea, and the air.   And all things glow.

Move as this sea moves, as water, as force.
Peace shines from its life, its war can become
at any moment the fierce shining of peace,
and all the life-night long many voices are saying
The name of all things is Glowing.

A beginning, a moment of rest that imagines.
And again I go wandering far and alone,
I rise at night, I start up in the silence—
lovely and silver-black the night remembers.
In the cities of America I make my peace;
among the bombs and commands,
the sound that war makes
NO   NO
We see their weeping and their lifetime dreams.

All this, they say to us, because of you.
Much to begin.   Now be your green, your burning,
bear also our joy, come to our meeting-place
and in the triumph of the reconceived
lie down at last together face to face.

*

We tell beginnings : for the flesh and answer,
for the look, the lake in the eye that knows,
for the despair that flows down in widest rivers,
cloud of home;   and also the green tree of grace,
all in the leaf, in the love that gives us ourselves.

The word of nourishment passes through the women,
soldiers and orchards rooted in constellations,
white towers, eyes of children:
saying in time of war What shall we feed?
I cannot say the end.

Nourish beginnings, let us nourish beginnings.
Not all things are blest, but the
seeds of all things are blest.
The blessing is the seed.

This moment, this seed, this wave of the sea, this look, this
        instant of love.
Years over wars and an imagining of peace.   Or the expiation
        journey

toward peace which is many wishes flaming together,
fierce pure life, the many-living home.
Love that gives us ourselves, in the world known to all
new techniques for the healing of a wound,
and the unknown world.   One life, or the faring stars.

VI.
From THE GREEN WAVE ❧

❧ WATER NIGHT ❧

The sky behind the farthest shore
Is darker than I go to sleep.

Blackness of water, the crater at the core,
The many blacknesses begin to gleam.

Rivers of darkness bind me to this land
While overhead the moon goes far to shine,

And now nothing nobody is my own.
The motion of streams glitters before my eyes:

Sources and entrances, they lie no more,
Now darkly keep, now flow now bright

Until all wandering end, a hand
Shine, and the leadings homeward of delight

Seem to begin my deepest sleep
To make a lake of dream.

❧ EYES OF NIGHT-TIME ❧

On the roads at night I saw the glitter of eyes:
my dark around me let shine one ray;   that black
allowed their eyes : spangles in the cat's, air in the moth's
   eye shine,
mosaic of the fly, ruby-eyed beetle, the eyes that never weep,
the horned toad sitting and its tear of blood,
fighters and prisoners in the forest, people
aware in this almost total dark, with the difference,
the one broad fact of light.

Eyes on the road at night, sides of a road like rhyme;
the floor of the illumined shadow sea
and shallows with their assembling flash and show
of sight, root, holdfast, eyes of the brittle stars.
And your eyes in the shadowy red room,
scent of the forest entering, various time
calling and the light of wood along the ceiling
and over us birds calling and their circuit eyes.
And in our bodies the eyes of the dead and the living
giving us gifts at hand, the glitter of all their eyes.

ᓂ SALAMANDER ᓂ

Red leaf.   And beside it, a red leaf alive
flickers, the eyes set wide in the leaf head,
small broad chest, a little taper of flame for tail
moving a little among the leaves like fear.

Flickering red in the wet week of rain
while a bird falls safely through his mile of air.

ᓂ THE MOTIVE OF ALL OF IT ᓂ

The motive of all of it was loneliness,
All the panic encounters and despair
Were bred in fear of the lost night, apart,
Outlined by pain, alone.   Promiscuous
As mercy.   Fear-led and led again to fear
At evening toward the cave where part fire, part
Pity lived in that voluptuousness
To end one and begin another loneliness.

This is the most intolerable motive : this
Must be given back to life again,
Made superhuman, made human, out of pain
Turned to the personal, the pure release:
The rings of Plato and Homer's golden chain
Or Lenin with his cry of Dare We Win.

❧ GREEN LIMITS ❧

My limits crowd around me
like years, like those I loved
whose narrow hope could never
carry themselves.

My limits stand beside me
like those two widowed aunts
who from an empty beach
tore me into the wave.

Green over my low head
the surf threw itself down
tall as my aunts whose hands
locked me past help.

The sand was far behind
and rushing underfoot
water and fear and childhood,
surf of love.

Green limits walled me, water
stood higher than I saw—
glass walls, fall back! let me
dive and be saved.

My limits stand inside me
forever like that wave
on which I ride at last
over and under me.

ଛ MRS. WALPURGA ଛ

In wet green midspring, midnight and the wind
floodladen and ground-wet, and the immense dry moon.
Mrs. Walpurga under neon saw
the fluid airs stream over fluid evening,
ground, memory, give way and rivers run
into her sticky obsessive kiss of branches,
kiss of a real and visionary mouth,
the moon, the mountain, the round breast's sleepless eye.

Shapes of her fantasy in music from the bars,
swarming like juke-box lights the avenues;
no longer parked in the forest, from these cars,
these velvet rooms and wooden tourist camps,
sheetless under the naked white of the moon.
Wet gaze of eye, plum-color shadow and young
streams of these mouths, the streaming surface of earth
flowing alive with water, the egg and its becoming.

Coming in silence.   The shapes of every dread
seducing the isolated will.   They do not care.
They are not tortured, not tired, not alone.
They break to an arm, a leg, half of a mouth,
kissing disintegrate, flow whole, couple again;
she is changed along, she is a stream in a stream.

These are her endless years, woman and child, in dream
molded and wet, a bowl growing on a wheel,

not mud, not bowl, not clay, but this *becoming*,
winter and split of darkness, years of wish.
To want these couples, want these coupling pairs,
emblems of many parents, of the bed,
of love divided by dream, love with his dead wife,
love with her husband dead, love with his living love.

Mrs. Walpurga cries out : "It is not true!"
The light shifts, flowing away.   "It was never like—"
She stops, but nothing stops.   It moves.   It moves.
And not like anything.   And it is true.
The shapes disfigure.   Here is the feature man,
not whole, he is detail, he gleams and goes.
Here is the woman all cloth, black velvet face,
black, head to ground, close black fit to the skin,
slashed at the mouth and eyes, slashed at the breasts,
slashed at the triangle, showing rose everywhere.

Nights are disturbed, here is a crying river
running through years, here is the flight among
all the Objects of Love.   This wish, this gesture
irresisted, immortal seduction!   The young sea
streams over the land of dream, and there
the mountain like a mist-flower, the dark upright peak.
And over the sheet-flood Mrs. Walpurga
in whitened cycles of her changing moon.

The silence and the music change;   this song
rises and sharps, and never quite can scream—
but this is laughter harsher than nakedness
can take — in the shady shady grove the leaves
move over, the men and women move and part,
the river braids and unfolds in mingling song;
and here is the rain of summer from the moon,
relenting, wet, and giving life at last,
and Mrs. Walpurga and we may wake.

ৡ FOGHORN IN HORROR ৡ

I know that behind these walls is the city, over these rooftops is
    the sun.
But I see black clothes only and white clothes with the fog running
    in all their shadows.
Every minute the sound of the harbor
intruding on horror with a bellow of horror:
blu-a!   blu-aa!   Ao. . . .

I try to write to you, but here too I meet failure.
It has a face like mine.
Silence and in me and over the water
only the bellowing,
Niobe howling for her life and her children.
Did you think this sorrow of women was a graceful thing?
Horrible Niobe down on her knees:
Blu-a!   Blu-aa!   Ao. . . .

Thirty years, and my full strength, and all I touch has failed.
I sit and see
the black clothes on the line are beautiful, the sky drifting away.
The white clothes of the fog beyond me, beautiful and the shadows.
Blu-aa!   Blu-aa!   Ao.

ৡ SUMMER, THE SACRAMENTO ৡ

To this bridge the pale river and flickers away in images of blue.
And is gone.   While behind me the stone mountains
stand brown with blue lights;   at my right shoulder standing
Shasta, in summer standing, blue with her white lights
near a twilight summer moon, whiter than snow
where the light of evening changes among these legends.

Under me islands lie green, planted with green feathers,
green growing, shadowy grown, gathering streams of the green
     trees.
A hundred streams full of shadows and your upland source
pulled past sun-islands, green in this light as grace,
risen from your sun-mountains where your voices go
returning to water and music is your face.

Flows to the flower-haunted sea, naming and singing, under my
     eyes
coursing, the day of the world.   And the time of my spirit
     streams
before me, slow autumn colors, the cars of a long train;
earth-red, earth-orange, leaf, rust, twilight of earth
stream past the evening river and over into the dark of north,
stream slow like wishes continuing toward those snows.

❧ EASTER EVE ❧

Wary of time O it seizes the soul tonight
I wait for the great morning of the west
confessing with every breath mortality.
Moon of this wild sky struggles to stay whole
and on the water silvers the ships of war.
I go alone in the black-yellow light
all night waiting for day, while everywhere the sure
death of light, the leaf's sure return to the root
is repeated in million, death of all man to share.
Whatever world I know shines ritual death,
wide under this moon they stand gathering fire,
fighting with flame, stand fighting in their graves.
All shining with life as the leaf, as the wing shines,
the stone deep in the mountain, the drop in the
     green wave.

Lit by their energies, secretly, all things shine.
Nothing can black that glow of life;   although
     each part go crumbling down
     itself shall rise up whole.

Now I say there are new meanings;   now I name
death our black honor and feast of possibility
to celebrate casting of life on life. This earth-long
     day
between blood and resurrection where we wait
remembering sun, seed, fire;   remembering
that fierce Judaean Innocent who risked
every immortal meaning on one life.
Given to our year as sun and spirit are,
as seed we are blessed only in needing freedom.
Now I say that the peace the spirit needs is peace,
not lack of war, but fierce continual flame.
For all men : effort is freedom, effort's peace,
it fights. And along these truths the soul goes home,
     flies in its blazing to a place
     more safe and round than Paradise.

Night of the soul, our dreams in the arms of dreams
dissolving into eyes that look upon us.
Dreams the sources of action, the meeting and the end,
a resting-place among the flight of things.
And love which contains all human spirit, all wish,
the eyes and hands, sex, mouth, hair, the whole woman —
fierce peace I say at last, and the sense of the world.
In the time of conviction of mortality
whatever survive, I remember what I am. —
The nets of this night are on fire with sun and moon
pouring both lights into the open tomb.
Whatever arise, it comes in the shape of peace,
fierce peace which is love, in which move all the stars,
and the breathing of universes, filling, falling away,
and death on earth cast into the human dream.

What fire survive forever
myself is for my time.

&❦ NINE POEMS
FOR THE UNBORN CHILD &❦

I.

The childless years alone without a home
Flashed daily with the world's glimpse, happiness.
Always behind was the dark screen of loss
Hardly moving, like heavy hardly-moving cloud.
"Give me myself," or "Take me," I said aloud;
There was little to give, and always less to take.
Except the promise, except the promise darkness
Makes, night and daylight, miracle to come.

Flying over, I suddenly saw the traces
Of man : where man is, you may read the wind
In shadow and smoke, know how the wind is gone
And know the way of man;   in the fall of the plane
Into its levels, encounter the ancient spaces:
The fall to life, the cliff and strait of bone.

II.

They came to me and said, "There is a child."
Fountains of images broke through my land.
My swords, my fountains spouted past my eyes
And in my flesh at last I saw.   Returned
To when we drove in the high forest, and earth
Turned to glass in the sunset where the wild
Trees struck their roots as deep and visible
As their high branches, the double planted world.

"There is no father," they came and said to me.
—I have known fatherless children, the searching, walk
The world, look at all faces for their father's life.
Their choice is death or the world.   And they do choose.
Earn their brave set of bone, the seeking marvelous look
Of those who lose and use and know their lives.

III.

There is a place.   There is a miracle.
I know the nightmare, the black and bone piano,
The statues in the kitchen, a house dissolving in air.
I know the lilac-turreted cathedral
Taking its roots from willows that changed before my eyes
When all became real, real as the sound of bells.
We earthly are aware of transformation;
Miraculously, life, from the old despair.

The wave of smooth water approaches on the sea-
Surface, a live wave individual
Linking, massing its color.   Moving, is struck by wind,
Ribbed, steepened, until the slope and ridge begin;
Comes nearer, brightens.   Now curls, its vanishing
Hollows darken and disappear;   now high above
Me, the scroll, froth, foam of the overfall.

IV.

Now the ideas all change to animals
Loping and gay, now all the images
Transform to leaves, now all these screens of leaves
Are flowing into rivers, I am in love
With rivers, these changing waters carry voices,
Carry all children;   carry all delight.
The water-soothed winds move warm above these waves.
The child changes and moves among these waves.

The waves are changing, they tremble from waves of waters
To other essentials — they become waves of light

And wander through my sleep and through my waking,
And through my hands and over my lips and over
Me;   brilliant and transformed and clear,
The pure light.   Now I am light and nothing more.

V.

Eating sleep, eating sunlight, eating meat,
Lying in the sun to stare
At deliverance, the rapid cloud,
Gull-wing opposing sun-bright wind,
I see the born who dare
Walk on green, walk against blue,
Move in the nightlong flare
Of love on darkness, traveling
Among the rings of light to simple light,
From nowhere to nowhere.
And in my body feel the seasons grown.
Who is it in the dim room?   Who is there?

VI.

Death's threat!   Today I have known laughter
As if for the first time;   have seen into your eyes,
Death, past the still gaze, and found two I love.
One chose you gladly with a laugh advancing,
His hand full of guns, on the enemy in Spain.
The other living with the choice of life
Turning each day of living to the living day.
The strength, the grossness, spirit and gall of choice.

They came to me and said, "If you must choose,
Is it yourself or the child?"   Laughter I learned
In that moment, laughter and choice of life.
I saw an immense ship trembling on the water
Lift by a gesture of hands.   I saw a child.   I saw
A red room, the eyes, the hands, the hands and eyes.

VII.

You will enter the world where death by fear and explosion
Is waited;   longed for by many;   by all dreamed.
You will enter the world where various poverty
Makes thin the imagination and the bone.
You will enter the world where birth is walled about,
Where years are walled journeys, death a walled-in act.
You will enter the world which eats itself
Naming faith, reason, naming love, truth, fact.

You in your dark lake moving darkly now
Will leave a house that time makes, times to come
Enter the present, where all the deaths and all
The old betrayals have come home again.
World where again Judas, the little child,
May grow and choose.   You will enter the world.

VIII.

Child who within me gives me dreams and sleep,
Your sleep, your dreams;   you hold me in your flesh
Including me where nothing has included
Until I said : I will include, will wish
And in my belly be a birth, will keep
All delicacy, all delight unclouded.

Dreams of an unborn child move through my dreams,
The sun is not alone in making fire and wave
Find meeting-place, for flesh and future meet,
The seal in the green wave like you in me,
Child.   My blood at night full of your dreams,
Sleep coming by day as strong as sun on me,
Coming with sun-dreams where leaves and rivers meet,
And I at last alive sunlight and wave.

IX.

Rider of dream, the body as an image
Alone in crisis.   I have seen the wind

Its tall cloud standing on a pillar of air,
The toe of the whirlwind turning on the ground.
Have known in myself hollow bodiless shade,
The shadow falling from the tree to the ground,
Have lost and lost and now at last am found
For a moment of sleep and waking, striking root.

Praise that the homeless may in their bodies be
A house that time makes, where the future moves
In his dark lake.   Praise that the cities of men,
The fields of men, may at all moments choose.
Lose, use, and live.   And at this daylight, praise
To the grace of the world and time that I may hope
To live, to write, to see my human child.

❧ VII.
From ONE LIFE ❧

❧ ARE YOU BORN?—I ❧

A man riding on the meaning of rivers
Sang to me from the cloud of the world:
Are you born?   Are you born?
My name is gone into the burning heart
That knows the change deep in the form of things.
—I saw from the treeline all our cities shine.

A woman riding on the moon of ocean
Sang to me through the cloud of the world:
Are you born?   Are you born?
The form of growing in leaf and crystal flows,
And in the eyes and rivers of the land.
—From the rock of our sky, I came to recognize.

A voice riding on the morning of air
Sang to me from the cloud of the world:
Are you born?   Are you born?
Bring all the singing home;
There is a word of lightning in the grass.
—I stood alive in the young cloud.

❧ FIELDS WHERE WE SLEPT ❧

Fields where we slept
Lie underwater now
Clay meadows of nightmare
Beneath the shallow wave.

A tremor of speech
On all lips and all mirrors;
Pink sweater and tornado
Announce dawn's littoral.

South lies evocative
On the fine Negro mouth.
Play of silver in streams
Half lake under.

High on the unplowed red
The waterweeds respond,
Where Sheriff Fever
Ordered me to trial.

Where once hatred and fear
Touched me the branch of death,
I may float waves of making
Hung above my lost field.

Remember they say and Incarnatus Est,
The fire-tailed waves, never forget the eyes
Or the distorted jailers or their kindness
Even while they were torturing Mr. Crystal.

Psalms awake and asleep, remember the manmade
Lake where those barren treecrowns rode.
Where air of curses hung, keel of my calm
Rides our created tide.

৯৯ POWER NEVER DOMINION ৯৯

Power never dominion.
Some other power.
Some force flaking in light, avalanches of lilies,
Days and the sun renewed in semen, pure
Among the uncorrupted fires, fire's ancestor,
Forgotten;   worshipped secretly;
Where the vestigial Lucifer regales

Craters of memory; where leans
Some fleshly girl, the shaped stones of desire
Leaping in color at her human cunt.
They will translate this girl.   She will appear
In textbooks as a sacrificed antelope
Guilt running shiny over the short fur.
Ideas of shame did split that throat.
But none of that is true tonight.
The girl was leaning over the crater, I dreamt it,
The shrivelled flowers twisted in her hair,
And jewels budded at her throat.
The girl of choice, remembering the past fires,
Praising the word, the columns in the grove,
Arbor vitae uterinae
Locked by such branches, light in the dense forest,
Praising the world unknown and feeling beat
Among her branches
A human child.
Brambles of sense! and that responding power
Rocking the fulness of time.
Until it shall be, what never was:
River and born and dream.

Canals of music downward serenade
New satin gleams under her haunches;
And, running laterally,
And backwards across ripples,
Passing the lower stairs,
Even above the unforgettable murmur,
The sound of oars.

Body of the splendid, bear me now!
Completed by orbits of unhorséd comets,
The bronze, paternal stars.

PHANERON

Whatever roams the air is travelling
Over these griefs, these wars and this good.
Whatever cries and changes, lives and reaches
Across the threshold of sense;   I know the piercing name;
Among my silence, in cold, the birth-cry came.
Salt of these tears whitens my eyelashes.

Whatever plows the body turns to food:
Before my face, flowers, color which is form.
Cries plow the sea and air and turn to birth
Upon the people-sown, people-flowering earth.
A year turns in its crisis.   In its sleep.
Whatever plows our dreams is ours to keep.

Whatever plows our dreams is ours to give:
The threshold rises and changes.
I give, I perceive;
Here are the gifts of day risen at last;
Blood of desire, the riding of belief
Beyond our fury and our silences.

Phaneron—anything over the threshold of sense; a perception
word first used by Charles S. Pierce.

THE RED BRIDGE, SAN FRANCISCO

A red bridge fastening this city to the forest,
Telling relationship in a stroke of steel;
Cloud-hung among the mist it speaks the real,
In the morning of need asserts the purest
Of our connections : for the opposites
To call direct, to be the word that goes,

Glowing from fires of thought to thought's dense snows,
Growing among the treason and the threats.

Between the summer strung and the young city,
Linking the stonefall to the treefall slope,
Beyond the old namings of body and mind
A red bridge building a new-made identity:
Communion of love opened to cross and find
Self the enemy, this moment and our hope.

❧ "IN YOUR TIME,
THERE HAVE BEEN THOSE" ❧

In your time, there have been those who spoke clearly
For the moment of lightning.
Were we all brave, but at different times?
Even raped open and split, even anonymous,
They spoke.　　They are not forgotten.
But they are.　　In late summer;　　forgot;　　caught at
　　cross-purposes,
Interrupted in an hour of purity,
Their lives careening along in the fierce cities,
Through atrocious poverties and magnificence,
The unforgotten, the early gone forgot.

Late daytime, and nothing left to hide but an eye endowed
With the charred, guilty, gouged by war, the raging splendor;
Despised like you, criminal in intent;　　sunburnt, in love
　　and splendid;
This heart, naked and knocking, going in clouds,
Smoke and a cry of light.
In pain, the voice of pain.　　The shadow of your cry.
And never forget : you are magnificent beyond all colors.

૪ "NO ONE EVER WALKING THIS
OUR ONLY EARTH" ૪

No one ever walking this our only earth, various, very clouded,
    in our forests, in all the valleys of our early dreams,
No one has ever for long seen any thing in full, not live
As any one river or man has run his changes, child
Of the swarms and sowings.   Death nor the woman, seed
Of the born, all growing, going through the grass.
However deep you have looked into the well of the cradle
Or into any dream or open eyes the grave
While the soul, many-leaved and waiting,
Began to assume another exact flower.
Smoke and smell in the wind, a single life!
However true you tell, you never have told.
And even that is not altogether true.   It changes, we say,
    changes, for yes,
Indeed we all know this, any, any of us, there are secrets known
    to all.

Was it indeed shown you in a flash of journey, the flicker along
    change?
In the fine shadow between the curve of lips, shadow of days
    lengthening,
In the flicker of meaning revealed by many windows;
In the form of the eye, the form of words, of the word;   mean-
    ing that formed
These marvelous genitals, nameless as God;
Or in the informing light behind his dream, and he was dreaming
    of you.
Did his own self escape him, now to reach us, reaving the edge
    of cloud?

Has a gift then been given, each other giving our lives?
As air is given to the mouth of all?

⮾ "MURMURS FROM THE EARTH
OF THIS LAND" ⮾

Murmurs from the earth of this land, from the caves and craters,
from the bowl of darkness.   Down watercourses of our
dragon childhood, where we ran barefoot.
We stand as growing women and men.   Murmurs come down
where water has not run for sixty years.
Murmurs from the tulip tree and the catalpa, from the ax of
the stars, from the house on fire, ringing of glass;   from
the abandoned iron-black mill.
Stars with voices crying like mountain lions over forgotten colors.
Blue directions and a horizon, milky around the cities where the
murmurs are deep enough to penetrate deep rock,
Trapping the lightning-bird, trapping the red central roots.
You know the murmurs.   They come from your own throat.
You are the bridges to the city and the blazing food-plant green;
The sun of plants speaks in your voice, and the infinite shells of
accretion
A beach of dream before the smoking mirror.
You are close to that surf, and the leaves heated by noon, and
the star-ax, the miner's glitter walls.   The crests of the sea
Are the same strength you wake with, the darkness is the eyes
of children forming for a blaze of sight and soon, soon,
Everywhere your own silence, who drink from the crater, the
nebula, one another, the changes of the soul.

⮾ ARE YOU BORN?—II ⮾

A child riding the stormy mane of noon
Sang to me past the cloud of the world:
Are you born?   Are you born?
The form of this hope is the law of all things,
Our foaming sun is the toy of that force.

—Touch us alive, developing light!   Today,
Revealed over the mountains, every living eyes.

Child of the possible, who rides the hour
Of dream and process, lit by every fire.
Glittering blood of song, a man who changed
And hardly changed, only flickered, letting pass
A glint of time, showers of human meanings
Flashing upon us all : his story and his song.
The song of a child;   the song of the cloud of the world,
Born, born, born.   Cloud become real,   and change,
The starry form of love.

❧ VIII.
From BODY OF WAKING ❧

HAYING BEFORE STORM

This sky is unmistakable. Not lurid, not low, not black.
Illuminated and bruise-color, limitless, to the noon
Full of its floods to come. Under it, field, wheels, and mountain,
The valley scattered with friends, gathering in
Live-colored harvest, filling their arms; not seeming to hope
Not seeming to dread, doing.
        I stand where I can see
Holding a small pitcher, coming in toward
The doers and the day.
       These images are all
Themselves emerging : they face their moment : love or go
  down.
A blade of the strong hay stands like light before me.
The sky is a torment on our eyes, the sky
Will not wait for this golden, it will not wait for form.
There is hardly a moment to stand before the storm.
There is hardly time to lay hand to the great earth.
Or time to tell again what power shines past storm.

A BIRTH

Lately having escaped three-kinded death
Not by evasion but by coming through
I celebrate what may be true beginning.
But new begun am most without resource
Stupid and stopped. How do the newborn grow?
I am of them. Freshness has taken our hearts;
Pain strips us to the source, infants of further life
Waiting for childhood as we wait for form.

So came I into the world of all the living
The maimed triumphant middle of my way

Where there is giving needing no forgiving.
Saw now the present that is here to say:
Nothing I wrote is what I must see written,
Nothing I did is what I now need done.—
The smile of darkness on my song and my son.

Lately emerged I have seen unfounded houses,
Have seen spirits not opened, surrounded as by sun,
And have, among limitless consensual faces
Watched all things change, an unbuilt house inherit
Materials of desire, that stone and wood and air.
Lit by a birth, I defend dark beginnings,
Waste that is never waste, most-human giving,
Declared and clear as the mortal body of grace.
Beginnings of truth-in-life, the rooms of wilderness
Where truth feeds and the ramifying heart,
Even mine, praising even the past in its pieces,
My tearflesh beckoner who brought me to this place.

𝕯 MOTHER GARDEN'S ROUND 𝕰

The year was river-throated, with the stare of legend,
Then truth the whirlwind and Mother Garden.   Death.
And now these stars, antlers, the masks of speech,
And the one ghost a glove in the middle of the floor.
            Garden my green may grow.

If you were here tonight, my heart would rest,
Would rest on a support, happy thereon.
Something is dancing on leafdrift, dancing across the graves:
A child is watching while the world breaks open.
            Garden my green may grow.

Speed of a red fox running along this street.
Everyone could have seen it, no one is now awake.

Separations all year and the seeking of roots.
It was a lie, Mother Garden, they do not wish for death.
                    Garden my green may grow.

They wish only to live again.   No more the whirlwind.
One colored pebble now, one look, the singular
Opening of the lips;   a leaf happens to speak.
I remember in love you walked to me straight across the room.
                    Garden my green may grow.

The suffering of your absence flies around me now,
No house can keep out this flying of small birds.
Feathers, bird-feathers, settle upon my waking.
The agonies are open.   Faces, dead within them; and on these faces
And filling the clefts and on my hands and eyes
The little fresh pain flutters.   Whitening the grass,
Snowing through the windows.   Drifting over the floor.
Touching my face when, almost, touch means kindness.
My dear dream, Mother Garden.   We wish to be born again.
                    Death death may my green grow.

ॐ AFTER THEIR QUARREL ॐ

After the quarrel in the house I walked the grasses of the field
Until the hissing of breakers and the hissing on the sand
Lowered, and I could see the seed heads and the sky.

A pod of the milkweed burst;   it was speaking to me:
Never mind, never mind.   All splits open.   There is new inside,
We witness.   Downwind, the softened asters let me see

A lengthened sky in its mixed oranges of sunset
Gone east and west, glazing the first bare branches.
The branches said : We know you. I remembered a tiger

The winter I was five not leaping in my dream but fusing
All my wishes to run, with his endless glowing look telling:
I recognize you. Kill them if they deny;   or wake them. Now wake!

Autumn announcing birds, the flights calling from sunset.
One bird crying : I see you down there, bird! The quick furry
    ground
Moves with me in small animals whispering:
You are like us, too.   And the stars.   —I my own evidence

That even the half-eaten and accursed can be a season.
Search yourself, said all the field, understand growth.
When lack consents to leave its seed, waste opens, you will see
Even there, the husband of the spring, who knows his time.

୫ NIGHT FEEDING ୫

Deeper than sleep but not so deep as death
I lay there dreaming and my magic head
remembered and forgot.   On first cry I
remembered and forgot and did believe.
I knew love and I knew evil:
woke to the burning song and the tree burning blind,
despair of our days and the calm milk-giver who
knows sleep, knows growth, the sex of fire and grass,
renewal of all waters and the time of the stars
and the black snake with gold bones.

Black sleeps, gold burns;   on second cry I woke
fully and gave to feed and fed on feeding.
Gold seed, green pain, my wizards in the earth
walked through the house, black in the morning dark.
Shadows grew in my veins, my bright belief,
my head of dreams deeper than night and sleep.

Voices of all black animals crying to drink,
cries of all birth arise, simple as we,
found in the leaves, in clouds and dark, in dream,
deep as this hour, ready again to sleep.

❧ THE WATCHERS ❧

for Carson and Reeves
She said to me, He lay there sleeping
Upon my bed cast down
With all the bitterness dissolved at last,
An innocent peace within a sleeping head;
He could not find his infant war, nor turn
To that particular zoo, his family of the dead.
I saw her smile of power against his deep
Heart, his waking heart,
Her enmity, her sexual dread.

He said to me, She slept and dreaming
Brought round her face
Closer to me in silence than in fire,
But smiled, but smiled, entering her dark life
Whose hours I never knew, wherein she smiles.
Wherein she dim descending breathes upon
My daylight and the color of waking goes.
Deep in his face, the wanderer
Bringing the gifts of legend and the wars,
Conspiracy of opposing images.

In the long room of dream I saw them sleep,
Turned to each other, clear,
With an obliterated look—
Love, god of foreheads, touching then
Their bending foreheads while the voice of sleep

Wept and sang and sang again
In a chanting of fountains,
A chattering of watches,
Love, sang my sleep, the wavelight on the stone.
I weep to go beyond this throne and the waterlight,
To kiss their eyelids for the last time and pass
From the delicate confidence of their sly throats,
The conversation of their flesh of dreams.
And though I weep in my dream,
When I wake I will not weep.

੩❧ F. O. M. ੩❧

the death of Matthiessen
It was much stronger than they said.   Noisier.
Everything in it more colored.   Wilder.
More at the center calm.
Everything was more violent than ever they said,
Who tried to guard us from suicide and life.
We in our wars were more than they had told us.
Now that descent figures stand about the horizon,
I have begun to see the living faces,
The storm, the morning, all more than they ever said.
Of the new dead, that friend who died today,
Angel of suicides, gather him in now.
Defend us from doing what he had to do
Who threw himself away.

❧ THE SIXTH NIGHT : WAKING ❧

That first green night of their dreaming, asleep beneath the Tree,
God said, "Let meanings move," and there was poetry.

❧ THE BIRTH OF VENUS ❧

Risen in a
welter of waters.

Not as he saw her
standing upon a frayed and lovely surf
clean-riding the graceful leafy breezes
clean-poised and easy.   Not yet.

But born in a
tidal wave of the father's overthrow,
the old rule killed and its mutilated sex.

The testicles of the father-god, father of fathers,
sickled off by his son, the next god Time.
Sickled off.   Hurled into the ocean.
In all that blood and foam,
among raving and generation,
of semen and the sea born, the
great goddess rises.

                However, possibly,
on the long worldward voyage flowing,
horror gone down in birth, the curse, being changed,
being used, is translated far at the margin into
our rose and saving image, curling toward a shore
early and April, with certainly shells, certainly blossoms.

And the girl, the wellborn goddess, human love—
young-known, new-knowing, mouth flickering, sure eyes—
rides shoreward, from death to us as we are at this moment, on
the crisp delightful Botticellian wave.

ঙ SUITE FOR LORD TIMOTHY DEXTER ঙ

I.

They face us in sea-noon sun, just as he saw them waiting,
Bolted down, fastened together by their nailhead proverbs.
The sun still pouring all male all female through their blood
And away through the salt marsh and the white salt sand
Sea-blaze over their shoulders, fantasy
A blue invisible mountain up whose side
Laughter and sharp clouds race as he saw them ride
In whiteness when he as a boy walked down
With morning for a sign.
Smelling of acid, like his trade.
Ready to throw their lifeday down their throats like wine,
Death-rotten proverbs and the jokes all made,
Himself the wine-bottle burning in the sun.

More here than power over proverbs. But that power pours here.
And the sure sun of story, on top the live gold mast.
What's strong, what's lost? What boy walked salty in the light?
A raging worshipping fantastic man,
Tasting money and words, live-breasted women,
The tanner's boy streaked with truth. In the young States
He saw young morning. Wild he was.
And most
A clap of mockery clean in the sea-brightness,
A legend of this coast.

II. How to Impress Massachusetts

A name's a name but
Nothing's the same,
Now King-No-More knows
Lady-No-More;
There may be shame but
He's Mr. Guilt, and
Hell is Mr. War.
The wooden golden eagle
Announces from the rooftree:
Miss Equal, Mr. E.,
Dr. and Mrs. Eden, and
I am Miss Liberty.
But we see Timothy,
No more the colonized,
Look around after labor.
Not a single neighbor
Gives him his due acclaim.
Timothy's surprised:
A harsh laugh, a short knife,
Started his prodigious life.
But he took hold of fate,
Invested in the State, with
Money not worth a damn.
"I," he said, "am what I am,
What's to be done will be done,
The capital will be Washington.
Mr. Hamilton keeps his word,
This country's bond's as sound as me,
Timothy.
What 'dyou say?
'Sound as I'—?
Very well; me is I,
I the tree
Flourishing."
Mr. Hamilton truly meant
An almost infinite per cent

The tanner's boy, after we become the United States, invests in our currency, which is generally regarded as worthless;

Would accrue
Quickly to
The trustful and the nourishing.
The newborn Federal bank has stirred.   becomes rich,
Timothy is a sword.
A sword without blessing,
A sword without fame,
A sword bearing no signal name.
If Newburyport
Will be blind,
Will seem boréd,
Never mind.   and acquires
New Hampshire's kind, and   his new
Calls him "Lord."   first name.
Apprentice then, on the road
Next day wore his freedom suit,
Brided widow and won his house,
Ground their proverbs underfoot.
A poor boy made and found
And funding came to his own tune.
"Lord" is the center of that sound,
And all the songs proclaim
He is the bright blue morning rhyme,
A great name rides before his name.
Turn, burn, and overturn!
Among the squarest houses, he
Is more than Timothy,
And more than merry.
Can forever now retort
Very much Newbury-
Port:
The voice of the people and I can't help it,
But all's easy and no bones broken,
All is well, all in Love.
The first Lord of the age has spoken.
Now all the torment Massachusetts bore
Triumphs in a blaze of love.
Love, love, fantasy,

For
Out of shame and poverty,
From oppression, commerce, war,
Rose a new sovereignty:
The states are free and trade is free
And Dexter's Lord Timothy.

III. Three Nights I Dreamed

Sharp clouds and a sea-moon sang to me
Where were you born my young my dear
I said nowhere vary your singing

He makes his
fortune as
a merchant:

Now where was your mother shaded, they sang,
Nowhere I answered the ring the rung
Dark bells rang and I was young —
O on the water then, wine on the sea —
Nowhere they cried and they sang to me —
Nowhere my dear my darling,
My dearly darling beware.

Where and nowhere and then the singing changed
Past hills of prophecy the words went ranging,
The colors of the words to images
Went formed.   And all I saw was warming-pans,
Three nights of warming-pans until I woke

selling warming-
pans in the
West Indies,

And a great ship's bare spars sailing my window,
Up to my tall room window a ship's spars,
And I remembered all the nights and wars,
Sang in my waking of poverty and dream:
My dearly darling beware.

The sun all male and female through me poured,
Awake I bought a cargo all of dream,
Warming-pans for the South, to all the roaring

where they are
snapped up for
molasses-ladles;

Nothing, to those who mock at my song.
I have entrusted south my folly cargo,
A full hold coming home now showers gold.

My warming-pans sailed gently to Jamaica —
Rum, rum, my darling beware.

Gold I am, lord of the cats of gold,
Mittens and kittens and coals of gold,
Malta, the Baltic, the Caribbee,
And Britain commend their money to me
As I go funding among the dreamers,
Among their golden nightmares ringing
Among their proverbs a wine-gold bell,
Sounding a folly my dear my darling
My dearly darling dream well.

And then, to spite
their business
sayings, cats to
Malta; mittens
north; and
finally, coals
to Newcastle.

IV. Kings and Contemporaries

How can I speak to them today? What can I know,
What can I show so that we see ourselves?
Voices of stinted singing in the towns,
Voices of wildness and fear of wilderness.
The rhythm, the root.   Gathering in
Sources of music and the wild sea-rose.

Sea-music and the sea building its waters,
The weathervane beast.   My song.

Whenever I say what I mean
They mock and call me mad.
They slip my meaning —
When I mock at them, I
always make money —
How can this go on?
Harum scarum, merchant marum,
My house is built, and my wall of pillars,
A noted house to the Isles of Shoals.
My kings, my presidents, stand round:
I speak in images so they may know
My gold spread-eagle on the cupalow.

*   *   *

Dr. Franklin, Mr. Hamilton, John Hancock, Rufus King,
John Jay, two grenadiers.
Four lions, and here the roof runs so,
That a lamb can lie down with one of the lions,
And an eagle on the cupalow.

He sets up,
around his
house, the
figures of
those he
most admires.

One unicorn, one dog, one horse,
And in the Garden Adam and Eve —
I will if I please have Adam and Eve.
If no man murders me summer or snow
I'll carry this to its fair concluding
With an eagle on the cupalow.

Three of the apostles, viz.
St. Paul St. Peter and St. John.
Venus, Hiram, and Solomon —
The President's platform and columns grow —
I meant marble, but wood it is,
And an eagle on the cupalow.

The Royal Arch,
with lifesize
painted figures
carved by Joseph
Wilson, the
figurehead
sculptor.

George Third, L'Ouverture,
Lord Nelson Baron of the Nile.
Constantinople's Grand Signior,
All heroes, each one in his style—
The Chief Cornplanter with his bow,
His moccasins, arrows, and tomahawk,
And an eagle on the cupalow.

*   *   *

Black rum and silver gin,
Drink for this company.

For the resident poet, Jonathan Plummer,
With a wheelbarrow full of broadsides and haddock —
Malaga wine for Madam Hooper,
Timothy Dexter's fortune-teller;

And for brandy-breasted Lucy, Lucy Lancaster,
Daughter of Princes in Africa,
Feathers and majesty — what for her?
Black rum and silver gin
And a coach with cream-color horses.

Filisy, folosy, silver gin,
Stingalum, stangalum, wine for day,
Ram pan, muski dan,
And wine for night on the sound blind sea.
Stingalum, stangalum, buck.

Rum, whalerbone, whackerbone,
Waterfront, turnpike, Merrimack bridge,
Sea-berry, sea-gold, pine-forest edge;
Wire, briar, limber lock,
Timothy's a red red rock
Surrounded by waves of whisky and wine,
Loving waves called Jonathan,
Lucy Lancaster, Madam Hooper,
And a coach with cream-color horses.

V. The Pickle; The Temple

THE PICKLE

I will say what I mean here;   in a book;
I wants to make
My Enemies grin
Like a cat over
A hot puddin.

If you can bear the truth   From *A Pickle For*
Then I will tell the truth: *the Knowing Ones,*
Man's the best animal,   Timothy Dexter's book.
And the worst —
All men, I say, are more or
Less the Devil's.

Odds make the difference
And there's a sight of odds.
Some half, some quarters.
Odds make the difference.
I see in all places God, the God
Of nature in all things.
We live and move in God,
We live in God.

*   *   *

When great powers ruled,
I was born.
In a snowstorm, the signs
In the seventh house.
Mars came forward
Holding the candle —
Jupiter stood by.
I was to be
One great man.
(I think I am a Quaker
But have so little sense
I can't deceive.)
The bubble is the soul . . .
Man is the giant toad . . .
I have thoughts about clocks
Nobody will believe.
Ask me and I will tell.

*Of his birth
and becoming.*

*   *   *

Now turn the system of knowledge
Into light —
Parents and masters begin, begin schoolmasters
At Cadameys and Collegeys,
Begin ministers,
Leave off, scarecrows in courage,
Brave good apelets —
One thing masters must teach:
Have good manners

To parents and people in streets,
And don't be too nosey.
I recommend a school
Of languages,
Scholars to go to
Far parts to trade —
Go supercargo
To learn navigation
And character.
There will in time take
Many brave men,
Advantage to merchants
And funding to country —
Wise men pos-pos on this.
Goodbye — Timothy Dexter.

A plan for
the young:

*   *   *

I command peace and the
Gratest brotherly love
And Not fade, be linked
Together with that best of troue Love
So as to govern all nasions
On the fass of the gloub
Not to
Tiranize over them
But to
Put them to order . . .
A Congress of nasions
To be allways in france
All Despouts is
To be there settled
And this way be Dun
This will balless power
And then all was Dun
A Way — there-for I have the Lam
To Lay Dow with the Lion
Now this may be dun

A Congress of Nations;

If the powers would
A geray to Lay whats called
Devel to one side.

*　　*　　*

I being a man without learning
Please to give me Light.

His appeal.

*　　*　　*

The knowing ones complain
Of my book
The first edition
Had no stops
I put in a Nuf here
And they may peper
And solt it as they plese

,,,,,,,,, ,,,,,,,,,
,,,,,,,,, ,,,,,,,,,
....
,,,,,,,,,,,,,,,,,,,,
......!!!!!!!!!!......
.......!!!!!!!.......
.........!!!.........
..........!..........
,,,,,,,,,,,,,,,,,,,,,,,
....??????????....

THE TEMPLE

Then with a touch of the gout, and being
A little sober in the morning
I raised in the garden a Temple of Reason
For my own funeral,
Furnished with pipes and tobacco, a speaking trumpet
And fireworks in the tomb,
A Bible to read, and some good songs.
I sent out invitations.
Now it was time to begin.

He holds his
own funeral,

It was a fine clear day,
I had fine pallbearers
Lord East Lord West Lord North and Lord South
Lord Megul and Lord Shambow.
The minister made his prayer —
Doctor Strong, he was —
And the flimsy sextons were there
And very much crying.
About 3000 came,
Oh, half the town, I'd say.
The procession wound
Under my window
Across the garden to my
Temple of Reason.
My coffin was long ready,
Painted in my house.
White lead inside
And outside touched with green.
Noble trimmings, eight handles
And an uncommon lock.
Now it was put into the
Temple of Reason.
Out in the kitchen I was
Beating my wife;
The ghostly lady
Had hardly mourned at all.

Very few people
Should attend funerals.
Many catch cold, and we
Want to settle Ohio;
We can't spare these beauties
To die so soon.

VI. The Kind of Woman

Ghostly in my house
A woman I married —

and watches from
an upper window.

Ghostly up the stairs,
Like snow in the hall.
At midnight in her bed
The ghostly-breasted;
I cannot have her ghost
Walking my palace.
They say she is alive.
I say she will ever be
Mrs. Dexter that was.
The attacks of the ghost
Will not let me sleep. —
Now to save my life.

He is haunted by his living wife.

I will sell the house,
Horses, the cream-color horses
And the coach.
If not I will let it.
Wait.   I can sweep my house
And get all anew
And go out of hell.
I will advertise.

"I must have a Companion four good by all."

"A very colding wife
Is poison to me.
I wish to be still
And master of my cash;
And therefore I wish for
One very good housekeeper.
Them that know me know
The kind of woman.
Now I will say
What kind of a person,
From thirty to forty
And a good jade
That will trot pace and gallop—
Not to heave one off
But, rather of the two,
Heave on. —I mean right well.

Now stop, I got off the path;
Now I am honest : I wish for
A middling woman for size,
Sensible honest and comely,
Knowing when to speak
And when to be silent,
With a nose like mine."

VII. Guessing Time

A feat of laughter and a coastwise dance
Among the ills of ocean, in pauper light
Imagining truth, at dawn turning from madness
Into the unknown world, up blue invisible
Mountains of fantasy climbing
To the sea.
Where he as a boy walked down, salty, in brightness
Raging and worshipping.
Their faces turn again the nailhead stare
Of proverbs glaring at the intuitive.
My old head has
Worn out three bodies.
Amen.   Clean truth.
Pay the whole debt, it will make nations tremble.
Keep up to what we set out to be, honest republicans,
No king, but you won't go it long without being honest;
If dishonest, you must have a king.
Keep Judas out of your councils.
Watch day and night, for mankind is mankind.
Jockey-handed priests, deacons, grunters, whiners —
(And I will show you one more private torture:
Abraham Bishop my son-in-law from whom
I live in hell on earth;   pity me, fellow mortals,
A.B. mad with learning, as poor as a snake,
As proud as Lucifer.   A.B. is a beast,
A Connecticut bull, short neck, thick curly hair.
When I see my father, the great good man,
Father Thomas Jefferson, he'll shed great tears with grief.)

A sortment, a sortment is good in a shop.

How many nicknames three things have:
Sex and glory and the grave.

Now I suppose I may guess
As it is guessing time:
I guess the world is all one
Very large living creature;
Mankind is the master beast,
As in the sea the whale
Is head fish — master over the
Whole of beasts and fish,
But still we're all one creature.
Man is the masterly beast,
And also the worst of the whole,
Knowing the most and acting the worst
According to what we know.

I think when the candle goes out
Men and women are done at one blow,
We will lie then as dirt of rocks
Until the great gun go —
9,000,000,000 tons
Of the best good powder.
That will shake and bring all the
Bones together,
Then the world will be to an end.
All kinds of music then,
And funding laid aside,
The melody will be very great, —
Now why won't you believe me?

It is true as apple-seed,
The sea and sea-music.
True as the voices that through me burn —
As true as we died and we are born,
Apple-seed and apple-thorn

Calling root and calling hand,
Saying Amen, mockery, Amen, fantasy,
Sea-music and the sea.

ᚙ VOICES OF WAKING ᚙ

for the eightieth birthday of Frances G. Wickes
Whenever you wake, you will find journeying —
Even in deep night, dreams surrounding your dreams —
The song of waking begun, prepared in silence,
Planted in silence as her life is planted
Among the constellations and the days.

Whenever you wake, you will hear entering
The song of meanings, a melody of green;
The image of a legendary woman
Dancing among her mercies, in essence emerging
Female to leap into the dragon-thronging sea.

Voices of nourishing, lifting the newborn up,
Away, —they lift away, newborn to all,
To the nourisher, to self born, to new life.
Voices of waking that journey in our lives
As renaissance and rain of images.

All of the people of the play are here,
In a storm of light;   birthday;   at any moment.
Full in their powers, and the voice of waking
Sings for beginnings;   she sings, wherever waking is.
Wherever the deep moon stands, the song arrives.
Nevertheless the moon goes voyages.

Nevertheless, the journeying is time:
Makes birthdays, makes this birthday a resonance

And the remote boundaries of imagining
Acknowledge the voices, her daily human voice,
Blessing this birthday moment her monument.

Deep in the waking, her life builds in light
The vision of the body of the soul.

❧ BODY OF WAKING ❧

Fire-thread in the valley.   Bird-voice in darkness.
Before the opening of the world.   In our own time.
Days we then heard the cities in their singing,
Armies standing in their graves imagining certain mornings,
Hours a naked man in the stream high on the mountain
Imagined this, too, among the cold water,
Looking up at the forming sky.

Century of absence in the valley of confusion.

When you wake, even startled awake, even in shadowless night,
      even alone, the song
Will be growing.   The song begun will be growing in fiery
      night;   in blackness, voices
Pouring over the unseen cities, and the mountains wake,
Riverlands unseen, immediacy of song.

*

Century of absence.   It could be like a time
When the soul that has slept leaps from its priests,
Spring when the old idea is at last available to all children,
And God in the world is on the lips of love.
Hot out of the dried blood of the separate churches,
The nations, separate wards in the same hospital.
Revenge which spikes the cross and splits the star

Withers the crescent.   The world circles among
The solitude of Spain, the solitude of Stalingrad,
Solitude in the hills of loess and the caves of Africa,
And now your solitude, New York, who raised yourself above.

Now the buried questions flicker on all faces.
Does the fat belly know its heart is broken?
Do you drag yourself through the wilderness saying
Never mind how we got here;   that will come later?
Much later, after you speak of the weapon birds
And the spies in your milk and the little split children
Bleeding models of cars;   you told their fortunes
According to a harvest of slot-machines;
According to the obscene pattern of bombers.
Much later, after you glare for eight days, silent,
After you howl for a century and a half,
You look at the clock and see it has not moved.
What do you do then?   Weep for the generations?
You change your life.   No.   You begin again
Going on from the moment in which you stand today.
Will there be suffering?   Perhaps not as much as now.
But will there be suffering, in the healing?   Yes.
Only with a difference.   You will know it then.
Walking down Basin Street, will be aware.
And that, my darling, my dear dear, is what Mother prays for,
Beside the cradle, lighting the candles of the days,
In retreat, in the kitchen, watching by living bodies
And waiting endlessly by the unmoving face
While the door is still not, not really, not yet, opened.
My darling, my baby, my people, my own self.

The words rising from the sleep of America:
I had all my children, and they locked themselves in,
My babies are sick to death, and the doctor is not well.
Ruddy we are, strong we are, and insane.
They built doors around themselves, and then they locked the
        doors.
Some believe they are doctors.   Some believe they are patients,
Some think they are statisticians.   Some are ambassadors.

178 &

We eat very well.   We keep the pictures on.
Sometimes the clocks jump fifty minutes.   Some days they do
    not move.
Some play they are parents.   Some always are the children.
We are careful to flush the toilet.   We sleep well.
Of course it's a toilet.   Of course it's a swimming pool.

The force that split the spirit could found a city,
That held the split could shine the lights of science.
This rigid energy could still break and run dancing
Over the rockies and smokies of all lives.
How many moons circle our dreams?   America,
Did you think only of wars and luxury?
Can you remember your early dreaming?

Who of us fully living
Among these inward murders,
Among the ritual
Of domination?

I remember the structure of towers
Torches over New York
I remember the structure of crystals
A single sheet of flow
I know an immortal journey
And we all walk hypnotized by a cliff
Speed and explosion.

Voices of process, river of human meanings.
Put your hand in, come into the dance,
Turn around fine, take out your hand,
Dance yourself once.
You know this music.
You were born among these songs.

Now we tell, sing, and relate.
The buried life and the body of waking.

*

Bird-voice in darkness.   Tremor of night moving.
The rocks accept blackness.   Now I remember trees.
Across the crystals of time forming I suddenly feel
The flow of a cold breeze following a bird-voice
The river remade, the invitation of water
Moving in praise of process.
In time the river turns, in time turn the wakers
Among their colored dreams,
In time our frightful processions
May turn toward morning and turn toward form.

Now the praise of the moving into light,
The melody of this walking, the broken breathing even of us
Who moved to discover the children in the forest,
The children of our own dreams who would save us.
Even among our broken failing years
And the acts to bind us, the look between two faces,
Ways and grace,
The melody of praise and the whisper of green
Before the opening of the world,
In our own time.
That was long before we knew what was required,
Before we began ever to hear the questions.

But the young, talking together of growth and form,
Arrived once more at the terms.   In praise of process,
Our songs were, of the seed;   we took the joy
Of the eye dancing unborn, its precise fore-lighting
Moving in unborn dark toward the achieved gaze,
Seeking continually developing light.
Seeking as we began to grow, and resting without distrust,
We moved toward a requirement still unknown.

We spoke of the heroes, the generous ones, who gave their mean-
      ings,
Knowing again meaning as music,
Meaning in all its moving, as process, as song,
As the enlightened seed transformed in dark and light.

Color transformed us.   We knew the dance of selves,
Growing, meaning giving us our green.
And toward a future the music goes.

Flashing of meaning as the light we breathe,
And through the whole night moving, coming as music.
Music that grows in silence, along dark a single voice
On its long stair of sound going up darkness
Moving toward form, moving becoming meaning
That makes our sleeping.
                              Silent
Until the river under the voice discovers
Its own currents, a flowing in a stream.
While air follows its own music.

Throat of song.   The air-achieving bird
Sings in the blackness.
Hours past midnight and a throat of music,
The dark night offering.
Fleet of voices in a single turning
Stair of calling and the flying pauses
Go as darkness and grow as constellations.
Voices of all music going toward its form
In human meanings and in silences.
Arriving again as the weather of our days
Over born water, on waking faces.
Growing to feed each other, lover, mother of gesture
To turn against fear and withholden reach,
The movement at the center of all things
Making a stillness never a refusal.
Dream and creation and sea,
Violent precise act,
Movement to match our lives,
Wish at the center of growth
We feel as peace.
Peace the love of the process of our lives
For the movement at the center of all things.

Voice diving deep.
Deep in the lights of silence.
When night no longer imagines sunlight,
And we going darker come to all music,
Deep in the clearoscure, where we alone
And all alone go through the texture of time
To the flowing present that becomes all things,
The energy of myth and star and bone.

Now the heroes of process
Not leaders but lives
Is even the lost girl walking the length of the forest
Even the child whose January wrists
Stuck out below his blowing sleeves.   Weeping, he was,
Along the avenue.   And the man who faced the spies
At the Segre River.   Long ago.   In Spain.

Another image of the born, the next woman,
Another image of the next power of man
Finds itself dreaming in the world of form.
Entering, long before we enter,
The new requirement, the world of morning.

*

Here's day beginning, the blessed, the unbegun, the song, the
    given.
For that the human wish to grow acts through his giving
The living will be giving you your doors and apples.
Self torn from its old lies, walking and eating,
Becoming music and bone,
All incomplete without the rest
And peaceful over time
No longer cruel in partial truth,
Knowledge of giving and taking
Enters now and lets us live.
Lets us arrive at the present when the world
Has the choice of each of us, to make life or suicide,
To give or die.

*

They have eluded us.   They are not here.
Statues turning to cloud among the music
Float overhead, promising rain and seasons
In the black, the day in midnight.
Dayray before the way.
Rides on a flickering breath, the changes of darkness,
Exchange of murders.   Bodies exchanging life.
Where the belief flows somewhere
Uncorrupt, hidden, under violence,
Making its own and dawn-announcing act,
River of daybreak, where the waking is,
Still to be sung among the deaths and days.

These meanings become the light we breathe,
The breathing of a theme;   in our own time.

℘ IX.
WATERLILY FIRE ℘

THE SPEAKING TREE

for Robert Payne

Great Alexander sailing was from his true course turned
By a young wind from a cloud in Asia moving
Like a most recognizable most silvery woman;
Tall Alexander to the island came.
The small breeze blew behind his turning head.
He walked the foam of ripples into this scene.

The trunk of the speaking tree looks like a tree-trunk
Until you look again.   Then people and animals
Are ripening on the branches;   the broad leaves
Are leaves;   pale horses, sharp fine foxes
Blossom;   the red rabbit falls
Ready and running.   The trunk coils, turns,
Snakes, fishes.   Now the ripe people fall and run,
Three of them in their shore-dance, flames that stand
Where reeds are creatures and the foam is flame.

Stiff Alexander stands.   He cannot turn.
But he is free to turn : this is the speaking tree,
It calls your name.   It tells us what we mean.

TO ENTER THAT RHYTHM
WHERE THE SELF IS LOST

To enter that rhythm where the self is lost,
where breathing : heartbeat : and the subtle music
of their relation make our dance, and hasten
us to the moment when all things become
magic, another possibility.
That blind moment, midnight, when all sight
begins, and the dance itself is all our breath,
and we ourselves the moment of life and death.

187

Blinded;   but given now another saving,
the self as vision, at all times perceiving,
all arts all senses being languages,
delivered of will, being transformed in truth —
for life's sake surrendering moment and images,
writing the poem;   in love making;   bringing to birth.

❧ THE WAY OUT, *from* "AKIBA" ❧

The night is covered with signs.   The body and face of man,
    with signs, and his journeys.   Where the rock is split
    and speaks to the water;   the flame speaks to the cloud;
    the red splatter, abstraction, on the door
    speaks to the angel and the constellations.
The grains of sand on the sea-floor speak at last to the noon.
And the loud hammering of the land behind
    speaks ringing up the bones of our thighs, the hoofs,
    we hear the hoofs over the seethe of the sea.

All night down the centuries, have heard, music of passage.

Music of one child carried into the desert;
    firstborn forbidden by law of the pyramid.
Drawn through the water with the water-drawn people
    led by the water-drawn man to the smoke mountain.
The voice of the world speaking, the world covered by signs,
    the burning, the loving, the speaking, the opening.
Strong throat of sound from the smoking mountain.
Still flame, the spoken singing of a young child.
The meaning beginning to move, which is the song.

Music of those who have walked out of slavery.

Into that journey where all things speak to all things,
    refusing to accept the curse, and taking

for signs, the signs of all things, the world, the body
which is part of the soul, and speaks to the world,
all creation being created in one image, creation.
This is not the past walking into the future,
the walk is painful, into the present, the dance
not visible as dance until much later.
These dancers are discoverers of God.

We knew we had all crossed over when we heard the song.

Out of a life of building lack on lack:
the slaves refusing slavery, escaping into faith:
an army who came to the ocean : the walkers
who walked through the opposites, from I to opened Thou,
city and cleave of the sea.   Those at flaming Nauvoo,
the ice on the great river : the escaping Negroes,
swamp and wild city;   the shivering children of Paris
and the glass black hearses;   those on the Long March:
all those who together are the frontier, forehead of man.

Where the wilderness enters, the world, the song of the world.

Akiba rescued, secretly, in death-windings
by his disciples carried from Jerusalem
to whatever he was loving with his life.
The wilderness journey through which we move
under the whirlwind truth into the new,
the only accurate.   A cluster of lights at night:
faces before the pillar of fire.   A child watching
while the sea breaks open.   This night.   The way in.

Barbarian music, a new song.

Acknowledging opened water, possibility:
open like a woman to this meaning.
In a time of building statues of the stars
valuing certain partial ferocious skills
while past us the chill and immense wilderness

spreads its one-color wings until we know
rock, water, flame, cloud, or the floor of the sea,
the world is a sign, a way of speaking.   To find.
What shall we find?   Energies, rhythms, a journey.

Ways to discover.   The song of the way in.

෴ FOR A MEXICAN PAINTER ෴

Carlos, your art is embryos,
These eyes are shaping in the dark;
There is a fate map in this red
Line and that bright red line,
The earliest map of all.

These eyes are shaping in the dark
Toward the requirement of light
And all will grow as they have grown;
Even transplanted will perform
Selfwise, themselves, this one, that one.

Deep in the hieratic blood
Toward sleep toward dream the process goes,
Toward waking move the sex, the heart,
The self as woman man and rose.
Carlos, your art is embryos.

❧ A SONG OF ANOTHER TRIBE ❧

Guilt   said the bony man
Do you feel guilt
At your desires?
No   I said   my guilt comes when
My desires find no way.
Country of sand and claws;
I wait for my rescuer.
No one will venture there.

Out of long silences
Come I to wordless song
O let my singing bring me
To that place
Where live waters
Rise and go.
There may the living arrive,
Go and return.
Find me, and I find,
And go finding.
A beating sound, I hear
A sound of riding.
Speed after silence
And at last music,
Words of another tribe:

My riding is on swift mares,
My love is by the green water-springs;
For a short moment I will sit there,
I will look upon her wandering face,
I will put an end to the black delay.

❧ SONG ❧

A voice flew out of the river as morning flew
    out of the body of night, a voice sending
    out from the night of the sleeping
Morning : a voice in its own voice, naked, made
    of the whole body and the whole life
But without anything
Breath
Breath of the fire love
Smoke of the poems voices

❧ WATERLILY FIRE ❧

for Richard Griffith

I. The Burning

Girl grown woman   fire   mother of fire
I go the stone street turning to fire.   Voices
Go screaming   Fire   to the green glass wall.
And there where my youth flies blazing into fire
The   dance   of sane and insane images, noon
Of seasons and days.   Noontime of my one hour.

Saw down the bright noon street the crooked faces
Among the tall daylight in the city of change.
The scene has walls   stone   glass   all my gone life
One wall a web through which the moment walks
And I am open, and the opened hour
The world as water-garden   lying behind it.
In a city of stone, necessity of fountains,
Forced water fallen on glass, men with their axes.

An arm of flame reaches from water-green glass,
Behind the wall I know waterlilies
Drinking their light, transforming light and our eyes
Skythrown under water, clouds under those flowers,
Walls standing on all things stand in a city noon
Who will not believe a waterlily fire.
Whatever can happen in a city of stone,
Whatever can come to a wall can come to this wall.

I walk in the river of crisis toward the real,
I pass guards, finding the center of my fear
And you, Dick, endlessly my friend during storm.

The arm of flame striking through the wall of form.

II. The Island

Born of this river and this rock island, I relate
The changes : I born when the whirling snow
Rained past the general's grave and the amiable child
White past the windows of the house of Gyp the Blood.
General, gangster, child.　　I know in myself the island.

I was the island without bridges, the child down
　　　　　　　　　　　　　whose blazing
Eye the men of plumes and bone raced their canoes and fire
Among the building of my young childhood, houses;
I was those changes, the live darknesses
Of wood, the pale grain of a grove in the fields
Over the river fronting red cliffs across —
And always surrounding her the river, birdcries, the wild
Father building his sand, the mother in panic her parks —
Bridges were thrown across, the girl arose
From sleeping streams of change in the change city.
The violent forgetting, the naked sides of darkness.
Fountain of a city in growth, an island of light and water.
Snow striking up past the graves, the yellow cry of spring.

Whatever can come to a city can come to this city.

Under the tall compulsion
                    of the past
I see the city
              change like a man changing
I love this man
            with my lifelong body of love
I know you
          among your changes
                              wherever I go
Hearing the sounds of building
                        the syllables of wrecking
A young girl watching
                    the man throwing red hot rivets
Coals in a bucket of change
How can you love a city that will not stay?
I love you
          like a man of life in change.

Leaves like yesterday shed, the yellow of green spring
Like today accepted and become one's self
I go, I am a city with bridges and tunnels,
Rock, cloud, ships, voices.   To the man where the river met
The tracks, now buried deep along the Drive
Where blossoms like sex pink, dense pink, rose, pink, red.

Towers falling.   A dream of towers.
Necessity of fountains.   And my poor,
Stirring among our dreams,
Poor of my own spirit, and tribes, hope of towers
And lives, looking out through my eyes.
The city the growing body of our hate and love,
The root of the soul, and war in its black doorways.
A male sustained cry interrupting nightmare.
Male flower heading upstream.

Among a city of light, the stone that grows.
Stigma of dead stone, inert water, the tattered
Monuments rivetted against flesh.

194 ঌ

Blue noon where the wall made big agonized men
Stand like sailors pinned howling on their lines, and I
See stopped in time a crime behind green glass,
Lilies of all my life on fire.
Flash faith in a city building its fantasies.

I walk past the guards into my city of change.

III. Journey Changes

Many of us   Each in his own life waiting
Waiting to move   Beginning to move   Walking
And early on the road of the hill of the world
Come to my landscapes emerging on the grass

The stages of the theatre of the journey

I see the time of willingness between plays
Waiting and walking and the play of the body
Silver body with its bosses and places
One by one touched awakened into into

Touched and turned one by one into   flame

The theatre of the advancing goddess   Blossoming
Smiles as she stands intensely being in stillness
Slowness in her blue dress advancing standing I go
And far across a field over the jewel grass

The play of the family stroke by stroke acted out

Gestures of deep acknowledging on the journey stages
Of the playings the play of the goddess and the god
A supple god of searching and reaching
Who weaves his strength   Who dances her more alive

The theatre of all animals, my snakes, my great horses

Always the journey   long   patient   many haltings
Many waitings for choice and again easy breathing
When the decision to go on is made
Along the long slopes of choice and again the world

The play of poetry approaching in its solving

Solvings of relations in poems and silences
For we were born to express   born for a journey
Caves, theatres, the companioned solitary way
And then I came to the place of mournful labor

A turn in the road and the long sight from the cliff

Over the scene of the land dug away to nothing and many
Seen to a stripped horizon carrying barrows of earth
A hod of earth taken and emptied and thrown away
Repeated farther than sight.   The voice saying slowly

But it is hell.   I heard my own voice in the words
Or it could be a foundation   And after the words
My chance came.   To enter.   The theatres of the world.

IV. Fragile

I think of the image brought into my room
Of the sage and the thin young man who flickers and asks.
He is asking about the moment when the Buddha
Offers the lotus, a flower held out as declaration.
"Isn't that fragile?" he asks.   The sage answers:
"I speak to you.   You speak to me.   Is that fragile?"

V. The Long Body

This journey is exploring us. Where the child stood
An island in a river of crisis, now
The bridges bind us in symbol, the sea
Is a bond, the sky reaches into our bodies.
We pray : we dive into each other's eyes.

Whatever can come to a woman can come to me.

This is the long body : into life from the beginning,
Big-headed infant unfolding into child, who stretches and finds
And then flowing the young one going tall, sunward,
And now full-grown, held, tense, setting feet to the ground,
Going as we go in the changes of the body,
As it is changes, in the long strip of our many
Shapes, as we range shifting through time.
The long body : a procession of images.

This moment in a city, in its dream of war.
                          We chose to be,
Becoming the only ones under the trees
                                    when the harsh sound
Of the machine sirens spoke. There were these two men,
And the bearded one, the boys, the Negro mother feeding
Her baby. And threats, the ambulances with open doors.
Now silence. Everyone else within the walls. We sang.
              We are the living island,
We the flesh of this island, being lived,
Whoever knows us is part of us today.

Whatever can happen to anyone can happen to me.

Fire striking its word among us, waterlilies
Reaching from darkness upward to a sun
Of rebirth, the implacable.   And in our myth
The Changing Woman who is still and who offers.

Eyes drinking light, transforming light, this day
That struggles with itself, brings itself to birth.
In ways of being, through silence, sources of light
Arriving behind my eye, a dialogue of light.

And everything a witness of the buried life.
This moment flowing across the sun, this force
Of flowers and voices body in body through space.
The city of endless cycles of the sun.

I speak to you   You speak to me

❧ NOTES ❧

LIVES. This group of poems will include *Gibbs, Ryder, Chapman, Ann Burlak, Ives, Timothy Dexter, Akiba, Kathe Kollwitz, Bessie Smith,* and *Boas.*

I wish to acknowledge my debt to Horace Gregory and Dr. Theodore Shedlovsky, who first told me about Gibbs; to Marsden Hartley, for his talk about Ryder; to Ives' "Essays Before a Sonata"; to the staff of the Portsmouth Public Library, and to Richardson Wright's and John P. Marquand's books about Timothy Dexter; to Louis Finkelstein's biography, and my mother's story that we were descended from Akiba. *Akiba* has not yet been published in book form; the last three of the *Lives* are not yet published.

ELEGIES. "When the elegy appears, in surviving Greek literature, we find it dedicated, not to death, but to war and love."
—*The Encyclopædia Britannica,* 11th ed.

In the second elegy, there are quotations from *The Sixth Book of Moses,* and from "Peredur" in *The Mabinogion.* The references in the third elegy are to the war in Spain; I went into Catalonia on a quite different errand on the first day, when none of us in England knew there would be war. The "sphere at the joint" was a recommendation made by the artist Charles Biederman, when he saw the first cyclotron at Chicago. The recommendation worked. The seventh elegy uses a paper by Philleo Nash on Revivalism among the Klamath Indians in 1870. It quotes from *Peer Gynt,* and from material from the concentration camps; and the ninth elegy uses Anna Freud's reports. The quotation in the tenth elegy is from Wyatt.

MRS. WALPURGA. Dr. René Dubos saying to me, "Pasteur said, 'La vie, c'est l'œuf et son devenir.'"

WATERLILY FIRE. The time of this poem is the period in New York City from April, 1958, when I witnessed the destruction of Monet's *Waterlilies* by fire at the Museum of Modern Art, to the present moment.

The two spans of time assumed are the history of Manhattan Island and my lifetime on the island. I was born in an apartment house that had as another of its tenants the notorious gangster Gyp the Blood. Nearby was Grant's Tomb and the grave of the Amiable Child. This child died very young when this part of New York was open country. The place with its memory of amiability has been protected among all the rest. My father, in the building business, made us part of the building, tearing down, and rebuilding of the city, with all that that implies. Part II is based on that time, when building still meant the throwing of red-hot rivets, and only partly the pouring of concrete of the later episodes.

Part IV deals with an actual television interview with Suzuki, the Zen teacher, in which he answered a question about a most important moment in the teachings of Buddha.

The long body of Part V is an idea from India of one's lifetime body as a ribbon of images, all our changes seen in process.

The "island of people" was the group who stayed out in the open in City Hall Park in April of 1961, while the rest of the city took shelter at the warning sound of the sirens. The protest against this nuclear-war practice drill was, in essence, a protest against war itself and an attempt to ask for some other way to deal with the emotions that make people make war.

Before the Museum of Modern Art was built, I worked for a while in the house that then occupied that place. On the day of the fire, I arrived to see it as a place in the air. I was coming to keep an appointment with my friend the Curator of the Museum's Film Library, Richard Griffith, to whom this poem is dedicated.

M. R.

811   Rukeyser, Muriel
R   Waterlily fire.

Wilmington Public Library
Wilmington, N. C.

RULES

1. ~~Books marked 7 days may be kept one week.~~ ~~Books marked 14 days, two weeks. The latter~~ ~~may be renewed, if more than 6 months old.~~

2. ~~A fine of two cents a day will be charged~~ ~~on each book which is not returned according to~~ ~~these rules.~~ No book will be issued to any person having a fine of 25 cents or over.

3. A charge of ten cents will be made for mutilated plastic jackets. All injuries to books beyond reasonable wear and all losses shall be made good to the satisfaction of the Librarian.

4. Each borrower is held responsible for all books drawn on his card and for all fines accruing on the same.

Author's Note

All royalties from this book are being paid directly to the Seton Foundation for Learning, Inc., on Staten Island, which provides special education within Catholic schools for children with serious learning disabilities, regardless of their faith tradition.

Acknowledgments

Many thanks are owed to many people. Foremost and first my gratitude goes to John Cardinal O'Connor, who from the moment I decided to write this book has been immensely helpful and encouraging. Very special thanks are due to my editor, Angela Iadavaia Cox, whose help in planning and rewriting it has been invaluable. Ethel Slattery spent endless hours typing the original version. Anne Ridge has retyped it so many times that she knows it by heart. Peggy Peet, our Secretary at St. Thomas More Parish, never tired of helping and encouraging me with it. And Eva Grace has lived with Maurice and Thérèse almost as long as I have. To Eric Major, Trace Murphy, Andrew Corbin, and Megan Downing at Doubleday, I shall always be grateful for believing in the book and for their help in bringing it to birth. There are others to whom gratitude is certainly due, but they are too many to name. They know how very grateful I am.